CYCLE TOURING IN IRELAND

About the Author

After some years of bashing out stories and editing copy for newspapers in both England and Australia, Tom Cooper decided to turn his hand to writing a book. His inspiration? It was Ireland itself – happy scene of many teenage and adult holidays alike. When Tom decided to explore even further by bike he couldn't find a guidebook he liked, so decided to write one that he hoped would help, and inspire, cyclists to enjoy touring in Ireland as much as he does.

Photo: The author at the Coomakesta Pass, Co Kerry (Route 8, Stage 6)

CYCLE TOURING IN IRELAND

by Tom Cooper

2 POLICE SQUARE, MILNTHORPE, CUMBRIA LA7 7PY
www.cicerone.co.uk

© Tom Cooper 2010
First edition 2010
ISBN: 978 1 85284 562 9

Printed by KHL Printing, Singapore

A catalogue record for this book is available from the British Library.
All photographs are by the author unless otherwise stated.

Acknowledgements

Thanks to my parents for their encouragement and support and to Charlotte for her help with the text and enthusiasm for the project.

Advice to Readers

Readers are advised that, while every effort is made by our authors to ensure the accuracy of guidebooks as they go to print, changes can occur during the lifetime of an edition. Please check the Cicerone website (www.cicerone.co.uk) for any updates before planning your trip. It is also advisable to check information on such things as transport, accommodation and shops locally. Even rights of way can be altered over time. We are always grateful for information about any discrepancies between a guidebook and the facts on the ground, sent by email to info@cicerone.co.uk or by post to Cicerone, 2 Police Square, Milnthorpe LA7 7PY.

Front cover: Author crossing the Ox Mountains above Foxford

CONTENTS

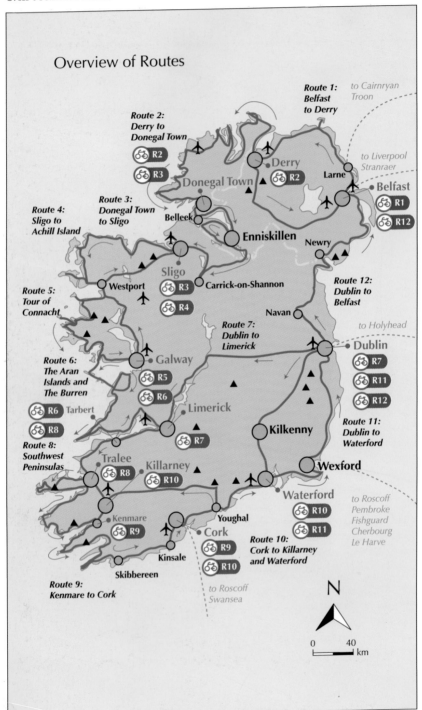

Overview of Routes

Route 1:
Belfast
to Derry
to Cairnryan
Troon

Route 2:
Derry to
Donegal Town

🚲 R2

🚲 R3

Derry

🚲 R2

to Liverpool
Stranraer

Donegal Town

Larne

Belfast

🚲 R1

🚲 R12

Route 4:
Sligo to
Achill Island

Route 3:
Donegal Town
to Sligo

Belleek

Enniskillen

Newry

Sligo

Westport

🚲 R3

Carrick-on-Shannon

🚲 R4

Route 5:
Tour of
Connacht

Route 12:
Dublin to
Belfast

Navan

to Holyhead

Route 7:
Dublin to
Limerick

Dublin

🚲 R7

Route 6:
The Aran
Islands and
The Burren

Galway

🚲 R5

🚲 R11

🚲 R6

🚲 R12

🚲 R6

Tarbert

Limerick

Kilkenny

Route 11:
Dublin to
Waterford

🚲 R8

🚲 R7

Route 8:
Southwest
Peninsulas

Tralee

Killarney

Wexford

🚲 R8

🚲 R10

Waterford

to Roscoff
Pembroke
Fishguard
Cherbourg
Le Harve

Kenmare

Youghal

🚲 R10

🚲 R9

🚲 R11

🚲 R9

Cork

Route 10:
Cork to Killarney
and Waterford

🚲 R10

Kinsale

Skibbereen

Route 9:
Kenmare to Cork

to Roscoff
Swansea

N

0   40
⊢———⊣ km

Map Key

🚲 R1	Route start and finish
🚲 R1	Route start
🚲 R1	Route finish
Sligo ●—	Stage start/finish (Route start/finish on overview map)
1	Stage number
N59	Major road
R297	Intermediate road
	Minor road
————	Route
··········	Alternative route
- - - - -	Ferry
↰	Direction

◯	Major town		
○	Small town/village	✈	Airport
▲	Hill or mountain	⋀	Camp site
)(	Pass	⬆	Hostel
✳	Viewpoint	⸸	Church/cathedral
✦	Point of interest	♜	Castle

Muiredach's High Cross at Monasterboice is Ireland's finest (Route 12, Stage 2)

INTRODUCTION

The forces that have shaped Ireland over the centuries have left their marks – on the rocks, the soil and also the people who cling to this place at the far northwest corner of Europe – marks which can still be seen today.

Ireland's history is not an uncommon one for a small country: the ebb and flow of peoples, the rise and fall of influence from powerful neighbours, the development of a cultural and national identity. But what makes Ireland unique is just how much of that history remains vividly present today. There are valleys here where it seems that the ice melted only yesterday and, after all, conflict and loss leave scars on a nation's soul even longer-lasting than the scourings of glaciers on rock. In this curious land, the 13th-century Norman castle at Carrickfergus seems as much a part of living history as the Nationalist murals in Derry's Bogside, while the music in a County Clare pub links back to the same traditions as the carved Celtic High Cross at Monasterboice.

Cycle touring in Ireland is not about passing through the country, but about becoming part of it.

Three of Ireland's biggest tourist attractions highlight the variety of landscape that has emerged from the island's complex geology. The hexagonally jointed basalt columns of the Giant's Causeway were formed 60 million years ago by the cooling of volcanic lava. Along the Clare Coast the 200m Cliffs of Mohr are made up of Namurian slates and sandstones about 320 million years old, while it is only a short way to the rock pavements of the Aran Islands, and the neighbouring Burren shaped from slightly older Carboniferous limestone.

Other parts of Ireland too owe their beauty to their geological origins. The bays and peninsulas of Kerry and Cork were shaped into their east–west alignment by movements some 270 million years ago (known as Armorican folding), while in the north and west the mountains follow the northwest–southeast alignment of the far earlier Caledonian stage of mountain building, some 500 million years ago.

On the east coast, Ireland's highest mountains outside County Kerry – the Mountains of Mourne and the Wicklow Mountains – are

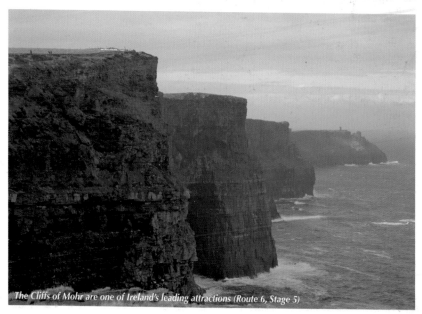

The Cliffs of Mohr are one of Ireland's leading attractions (Route 6, Stage 5)

both granite intrusions, but they date from completely different periods. The Mourne Mountains overlooking Newcastle, like the Antrim Plateau to the north, are the result of igneous activity from the opening up of the North Atlantic, while the Caledonian trend of the rocks of the Wicklows, on Dublin's doorstep, have much older origins.

During the last ice age much of what is now Ireland was covered by ice, and the landscape retains some of the finest glacial scenery in Europe. Doo Lough Glen in County Mayo and the Poisoned Glen in County Donegal are glacial valleys of the highest order. Equally impressive are the features deposited by the ice, and two glacial landforms, the esker and the drumlin, take their English names from Irish words. Drumlins are low, whale-backed hills deposited under the ice, while eskers are long sinuous ridges believed to result from water flowing under the ice. Both these landforms have had an impact on the geography of modern Ireland.

The boundaries of the kingdom of Ulster are marked by a once-impenetrable drumlin belt some 50km wide stretching from Strangford Lough to Donegal Bay. In the heart of Ireland, with its bogs and floods, the Esker Road (Esker Riada) at one time offered the only passable east–west route from Dublin to Galway. The monastic settlement of Clonmacnoise is situated where the road crossed the Shannon, and the N6 main road still closely follows this ancient route to the west.

WILDLIFE AND FLOWERS

The development boom of the 'Celtic Tiger' economy has increased the pressures on Ireland's wild places, but as any trip around the island by bike will show, Ireland remains predominantly rural. The human population has, after all, still has not recovered to its level before the Great Famine of 1845–49.

Ireland's plant and animal populations are typical for a northwest European country. The main points of interest are some absences – Ireland has a slightly impoverished flora and fauna compared to mainland Europe and Britain – and a handful of unexpected species. Of the absences on the animal side, most notable are the snakes which, according to legend, St Patrick banished from Ireland in the fifth century. The less romantic explanation for this, and the slightly diminished species counts, is that, as the glaciers retreated at the end of the last ice age, some plants and animals did not have time to re-colonise Ireland before sea

Burren wildflowers (Route 6, Stage 4)

Clonmacnoise Castle, by the Shannon, is Norman (Route 7, Stage 2)

levels rose and cut off land bridges to Britain and Europe.

The few unexpected residents mostly fall into the category of Lusitanian species – which are more commonly found in northern Spain and Portugal and are absent from Britain. There is no conclusive explanation for these disjunct populations. The most visible Lusitanian species to the casual observer is the strawberry tree (*Arbutus unedo*) of West Cork, Kerry and Sligo, which produces spiky bright-red fruits from September to December. A similar curiosity in the animal kingdom is the spotted Kerry slug, which is found in only three sites in Ireland – including the Killarney National Park – although it also occurs on the Iberian peninsula.

The importance of Ireland as a bird habitat can not be overstated. The long coastline and position at the northwest corner of the Eurasian land mass attract countless seabirds. Rathlin Island is Northern Ireland's largest seabird colony, with puffins, razorbills, guillemots, kittiwakes and fulmars on view. The birdlife of Little Skellig Island off the Kerry coast is similarly impressive. Away from the coasts, traditional farming practices survived longer than in many other parts of Europe, leaving Ireland as one of the few places in Europe where the rasping call of the corncrake (*Crex crex*) can still be heard (the Shannon Callows and Inishbofin have populations).

Three areas deserve special mention for their combination of stunning landscapes and biological importance. On an island where much of the attention goes to the coastal mountains, it is right that the Shannon Callows get first mention. This section of Ireland's longest river, between Lough Ree and Lough Derg, is one of the last largely unmodified flood plains in Europe. Each winter, and in some summers, the river rises to form an inland sea of up to 100,000 hectares. With the natural fertiliser of silt and wading birds, the meadows of the callows have been spared the touch of agricultural chemicals. To look down on the shining Shannon from the sixth-century abbey of Clonmacnoise is to witness a scene that has changed little since the monks' day.

The second area worthy of special attention is the limestone pavement of the Burren and the nearby Aran Islands. While aficionados of wildflowers will rave about the rare, calcium-loving species found here, the overall appeal is as much sensual as scientific. Just sitting, or better still lying down, among the sweet grasses of the Burren and watching the white, yellow and blue flowers dance in the Atlantic wind as they peep from fissures in the limestone is a pleasure all to itself.

Third on this short list are the woodlands and lakes of Killarney. These are by far the largest native woodlands in Ireland, covering some 12,000 hectares of lakeside and valley. The oak

11

and yew woodlands here are of international importance, while the juxtaposition of glacial valley, lakes and woods produces a landscape unique in Ireland. Wild red deer still live on the mountain slopes, and can be seen feeding by the lakes. The area is also, for Ireland, very accessible, being the site of Ireland's first national park (established 1932), with a good cycleway through some of the prettiest parts.

HISTORY

Ireland has a turbulent history that has continued into the recent past. For many centuries the island was ruled by England, later Great Britain, and much of Ireland's more recent history has been consumed by tensions relating to that colonial past.

The island of Ireland is currently divided into two political units. The statelet of Northern Ireland, part of the United Kingdom of Great Britain and Northern Ireland, has some degree of political autonomy through its assembly, which sits at the Parliament Buildings at Stormont, near Belfast. Northern Ireland consists of six Irish counties – Fermanagh, Antrim, Tyrone, Down, Armagh and Derry. The remaining 26 counties of Ireland form the sovereign country of Ireland (the term Republic of Ireland is sometimes used to distinguish this state from the geographical island, also called Ireland).

The Anglo-Norman invasion of Ireland began in 1169, while partial independence from Britain came with the Anglo-Irish Treaty of 1921. Any attempt to summarise in this guidebook the events in between, or since, would be doomed to failure, but some key dates are given below and there are suggestions for further reading in Appendix 4.

Key Dates	Event
8000BC	First people arrive in Ireland.
3000BC	Arrival of Neolithic peoples who built Newgrange passage tomb.
300–100BC	Arrival of Celtic peoples.
AD432	Arrival of St Patrick to convert the Gaelic kings to Christianity (traditional date).
AD550	Monasticism spreads in Ireland (approximate).

Key Dates	Event
AD563	Columba founds monastery on Iona, Scotland.
AD600–800	Golden Age – *Book of Kells* written.
AD795	Viking raids begin – Iona, Rathlin, Inishmurray and Inishbofin attacked.
AD837–42	Large Viking fleets overwinter in Ireland.
AD914	Second wave of Viking raids begins.
1002–14	Brian Boru – King of Ireland.
1014	Brian Boru dies in Battle of Clontarf – traditionally ridding Ireland of the Vikings.
1169	Arrival of the Anglo-Normans.
1175	Irish kings submit to Henry II under Treaty of Windsor.
1297	Irish parliament meets in Dublin.
1557	First 'plantation' settlers from England displace Irish in Offaly and Laois.
1558	Accession of Elizabeth I in England – strong state support for the Reformation is unpopular in Ireland.

Foxford's William Brown is a hero in Argentina (Route 4, Stage 5)

Charles Stewart Parnell looks out on Rathdrum (Route 11, Stage 6)

Key Dates	Event
1594	Start of Nine Years War against English; Hugh O'Neill – the Earl of Tyrone – joins open rebellion in following year.
1601	Defeat for Irish and Spanish at Battle of Kinsale.
1603	Treaty of Mellifont ends Nine Years War.
1607	Flight of the Earls: O'Neill and other Ulster chieftains flee Ireland.
1610	Plantation of Derry/Londonderry (see What's in a Name, below) begins.
1641	Catholic/Gaelic rebellion for return of lands.
1649	Oliver Cromwell subdues Ireland in a bloody campaign.
1652	More than a quarter of Ireland handed to Cromwell's supporters.
1688	Siege of Derry.
1690	James II (deposed Catholic King of England) defeated by William of Orange at the Battle of the Boyne.
1704	Restrictions on Catholics in landholding and public office introduced.
1728	Catholics disenfranchised.

Key Dates	Event
1798	Rebellion by United Irishmen defeated, despite support from French forces landing at Killala. Wolf Tone captured at sea, off the mouth of Lough Swilly, from French ship the *Hoche*, and dies in gaol before sentence of hanging carried out.
1800	Act of Union – Irish Parliament dissolved and the island is now governed from Westminster.
1803	Rebellion led by Robert Emmet is defeated.
1823	Catholic Association formed by Daniel 'the Liberator' O'Connell.
1828	O'Connell elected to Parliament, but as a Catholic cannot take his seat.
1829	Limited voting rights for Catholics who can also now sit as MPs.
1845–9	The Great Famine.
1858	Pro-independence Irish Republican Brotherhood and Fenian Brotherhood founded.
1877	Charles Stewart Parnell leads Home Rule Party – later the Irish Parliamentary Party.

Statue of Annie Moore and her two brothers at Cobh. Annie was the first emigrant to be processed on Ellis Island, New York, when it opened in 1892 (Route 10, Stage 1)

Tom Crean – Antarctic hero (Route 8, Stage 4)

Key Dates	Event
1879	Land League formed to push for fair conditions for tenants.
1881	Gladstone's Land Act – some improvements for tenantry.
1892	Home Rule for Ireland is blocked by House of Lords.
1907	Nationalist Sinn Fein party founded.
1912	Home Rule Bill passed by House of Commons; prospect of forcing the Bill through the Lords galvanises Unionists in the North, and both Nationalists and Unionists soon start to gather arms.
1914	Home Rule Act receives Royal Assent, but suspended until after the war.
1916	Easter Rising put down by British forces. Subsequent executions increase public support for Nationalist cause.
1918	Sinn Fein win majority of Irish seats in general election; Sinn Fein deputies declare Ireland independent and form first Dail Eireann (Irish Assembly), which convenes in the following year.

Key Dates	Event
1919–21	War of Independence.
1921	Anglo-Irish Treaty ends war and establishes the Irish Free State, but excludes six northern counties of Ulster, with a Border Commission to rule on the border.
1922–3	Irish Civil War between pro- and anti-treaty forces. Pro-treaty forces win.
1937	New Irish constitution claims sovereignty of the whole of the island.
1949	Ireland leaves the Commonwealth.
1967	Northern Ireland Civil Rights Association formed.
1968	First civil rights marches in Northern Ireland.
1969	Sectarian riots in Belfast and Derry – British troops deployed in Northern Ireland.
1971	First British soldier killed by IRA in Belfast.
1972	'Bloody Sunday' in Derry as civilians shot by British Paratroopers.
1972–94	Bombings, killings and sectarian violence continue until cease-fire declared by IRA and Loyalist groups in 1994.
1996–7	Cease-fire breaks down, then resumes with first all-party talks in Belfast.
1998	Belfast Agreement (Good Friday Agreement) ratified by all sides. Elections held for Northern Ireland Assembly.
2002	Northern Ireland Assembly suspended amidst claim and counter-claim about IRA disarmament.
2007	Northern Ireland Assembly Elections and resumption of devolved government.

WHAT'S IN A NAME?

In Ireland, a 'Nationalist' is an Irish Nationalist who supports the idea of the whole of Ireland being governed as one independent nation. A Unionist, on the other hand, wants Northern Ireland to remain part of the United Kingdom.

Names can be a point of tension in Ireland – even the word 'Ireland' can be problematic. Ireland refers to the whole island of Ireland, and also to the sovereign country of Ireland that governs 26 of the island's counties. The other six counties form Northern Ireland, which is a region of the United Kingdom of Great Britain and Northern Ireland. 'Northern Ireland' is in itself a problem term – Nationalists rarely use it, preferring 'the north of Ireland', which does not imply an acceptance of the political division of the island.

'Ulster' is sometimes erroneously used interchangeably with 'Northern Ireland'. Ulster is in fact one of the four provinces of the island of Ireland (along with Munster, Leinster and Connacht), and not coterminus with Northern Ireland, as the province of Ulster includes counties Cavan, Donegal and Monaghan, which are part of the Republic of Ireland. Ulster is nevertheless quite a useful geographic name (not least because it includes all of Routes 1 and 2 and much of Route 3), so it is often used in this guidebook when discussing these parts of the island (no political implications are intended).

Practically speaking, however, it is generally helpful to know which part of the island you are travelling in (not least because the currency is different), so this book adopts a pragmatic approach and uses the term Northern Ireland to distinguish the six northern counties and, where necessary, Republic of Ireland, Irish Republic or the Republic to identify the country of Ireland.

A similarly practical approach is used for place names. Arguments over whether Ulster's second largest city is Derry or Londonderry have gone as far as the High Court of Northern Ireland, leaving the incongruous situation whereby the city council is officially Derry City Council, but the city is Londonderry – its name having been established in the 17th century by royal charter. For consistency and brevity, this book uses Derry. Broadly speaking, Unionists prefer the name Londonderry, but again, no political connotation is intended here.

Most places in Ireland have both Irish and Anglicised names. Most visitors to Ireland find the Anglicised names easier to cope with – not least in terms of coming up with something that sounds about right when asking directions – so the book tends to use these. Again this is a purely pragmatic decision and not intended as a slight on the Irish language.

Brantry Lough (Route 1, Stage 7)

Poulnabrone Dolmen is one of the Burren's many megalithic sites (Route 6, Stage 4)

ARCHITECTURE

Starting with the island's oldest buildings, Ireland has megalithic structures and other prehistoric remains of the highest order. The star attractions are the Neolithic Newgrange passage tomb in County Meath and the Iron Age ring fort of Dun Aengus on the Aran Islands, but there are countless other interesting and well-preserved sites.

Ireland is also blessed with some fine early Christian architecture. The High Crosses have already been mentioned while the Skellig Michael monastery is one of the best preserved early Christian sites in Europe. Also of interest are the round towers that are unique to Ireland. Usually part of a monastic settlement, these thin stone towers, usually 25–30m high, typically with a conical roof, served a variety of purposes, including acting as a bell tower, a place of storage and a lookout, and the entrance was often a few metres off the ground. The towers may have also been a temporary refuge from the Viking raids that began in the late eight century – the towers themselves date from the ninth to 12th centuries. There are particularly fine examples at Glendalough in County Wicklow and Clonmacnoise, County Offaly.

The slightly later Christian architecture of Ireland is also impressive. The enthusiasm for the destruction of monasteries that prevailed in Britain during the Reformation was somewhat tempered in Ireland, and while the

monastic communities were dispersed, many of the buildings remain more complete than in Britain. Jerpoint Abbey, County Kilkenny, Muckross Abbey, County Kerry and Ross Errilly Friary, County Galway, remain as particularly fine ruins.

Fast-forwarding to the 18th century, Ireland has more than its fair share of grand houses. Neoclassical Palladian design is to the fore in this period, with Castle Coole in County Fermanagh and Powerscourt near Enniskerry in County Wicklow being out of the very top drawer. There is also some fine 19th-century Gothic Revival architecture in Ireland. Ruined Duckett's Grove in County Carlow and Puxley's Mansion in County Kerry are fine examples. The major cities – Belfast, Dublin, Cork, Galway and Limerick – all have grand public buildings that reflect their wealth and growth during the 18th and 19th centuries.

The castles cannot be separated from the grand houses, literally in some cases, as early tower-house castles are sometimes incorporated into later grand Georgian and Victorian homes. This reflected an increasing confidence amongst the aristocracy through the 18th and 19th centuries, as home comforts and public demonstration of wealth became more important considerations than defence. From the earlier period, however, some fine defensive fortifications remain, including the Norman castles at Carrickfergus and Limerick, and countless tower-house castles dating from the 15th century onwards.

A fortification to look for from an earlier period is the crannog. These lake island fortifications date from the Iron Age through to medieval times. In some cases the island may be entirely artificial, having been defined by an oak palisade driven into the lake floor. Today they typically appear as circular lake islands some 10 to 30m in diameter. There are particularly good examples at Kiltooris Lough (Route 2, Stage 8) and approaching Ballyconnell (Route 3, Stage 4) and on Achill Island (Route 3, Stage 4).

At a more down-to-earth level, the traditional whitewashed thatched Irish cottage is slowly succumbing to modernisation, but there are some fine examples still around, particularly in Donegal.

The large-scale settlement of English and Scottish immigrants in Ireland during the 16th and 17th centuries was largely achieved through a series of 'plantations' on land granted by the British Crown after its confiscation from the Gaelic clans or old Norman dynasties. The plantations of Ulster and Munster were the most significant of these enterprises. The legacy of this period, in terms of the built environment, is some very fine examples of colonial towns, particularly in Ulster. The most characteristic feature of plantation towns is a large central square or diamond where two main roads meet. This diamond and a geometric street pattern have often survived even where colonial-era architecture has not lasted as well as Derry's complete defensive walls.

Malin (Route 2, Stage 2), Donegal Town (Route 2, Stage 9) and Coleraine (Route 1, Stage 4) are fine examples of this form of settlement, but there are many more. Finding towns in Ireland that strongly resemble those in, say, British Colonial Canada (for example Lunenburg in Nova Scotia), emphasises the point that the settlement of Ireland was a colonial enterprise of similar scale and intent to that undertaken in the New World.

CULTURE

Literature

The Irish contribution to literature in English is immense. The island has produced four Nobel Laureates for literature: William Butler Yeats, George Bernard Shaw, Samuel Beckett and Seamus Heaney. Yeats has strong ties with the Sligo area and Heaney was born and educated in Northern Ireland, but now lives in Dublin. In such illustrious company there is also Dublin-born James Joyce, whose novel *Ulysses*, published in 1922, was one of the high watermarks of English language literary modernism.

On any cycling trip there is a fair amount of time when you will not be on a bike. Reading a novel or some poetry, especially where it has a connection with the area you are riding

Duckett's Grove is one of Ireland's finest ruins (Route 11, Stage 2)

through, can add considerably to your experience of Ireland.

Gaelic Sports

Gaelic football and hurling are the two most popular sports in Ireland. Both are fast and skilful games where endurance also counts. Gaelic football is a little like a cross between rugby and soccer, played on a pitch with H-shaped goals. Hurling is a stick-and-ball game played on the same pitch. The hurling stick is axe-shaped and the game far more aerial and physical than games like hockey. Over the summer the counties compete for Ulster, Munster, Leinster and Connacht championships, and the season culminates with the All Ireland Finals, in both

Cushendall, County Antrim (Route 1, Stage 2 alternative)

sports, in September. Women play a variant of hurling called camogie. The most obvious sign of the excitement generated by these sports is the county flags that festoon houses, gardens, cars, lampposts – and pretty much everywhere else – as the season nears its climax. Games are played on Sundays and often televised.

Irish Music

For visitors, the most common place to hear Irish traditional music is the pub. In fact some areas, such as Doolin in County Clare, seem to be building a tourist industry based almost entirely on pub music. To purists, some of the offerings aimed at visitors are not of the highest quality, but the fare is invariably entertaining. It pays to ask locally for advice about the best venues.

GETTING THERE

By Air

The major international airports are Belfast, Shannon (near Limerick) and Dublin, and if you are arriving from the US or the southern hemisphere you will most likely touch down at one of these. The budget airlines have piled into the Irish market in recent years and there is a bewildering array of flights into Irish regional airports from Britain and the rest of Europe. Of these smaller airports, Cork is handy for the southwest, Derry for Donegal, and Galway for the west. Belfast City airport is only a few kilometres from the city centre and more convenient than the International Airport at Aldergrove some 30km to the west.

Flying with a bike throws up no difficulties peculiar to Ireland. Most of the budget airlines will charge a special baggage fee for a bike, which will usually have to be paid at the time of booking. While this will bump up the fare a little, at least the bike is 'booked', and there is usually some guidance about packing. There is often a caveat such as 'subject to space', but this is rarely invoked. It is also worth knowing whether the bike counts as part of your total baggage allowance, and also check the weight of your panniers – excess baggage charges can easily mount up to more than the basic ticket price. Some airlines have moved towards charging luggage 'per piece', so front and rear panniers count as four pieces – in which case a light

Ready to fly – George Best Airport, Belfast

kit bag or holdall can pay for itself. Sometimes these are sold as protective bags for rucksacks. If you are camping, remember that there can be no gas or fuel in your luggage (quite sensibly), which can mean some shopping on arrival.

As far as packing the bike itself is concerned, getting a straight answer from airlines about what is actually required can be frustrating. An added complication is that baggage handling requirements vary from airport to airport, and it is not unheard of to be told your bike is not adequately packed when checking in for a homeward flight, when you had sailed through the same airport, outbound, with the same packing.

Having said that, the trials and tribulations of taking a bike by air are often exaggerated. The bare minimum to pack a bike for flying is to take off or reverse the pedals, turn the handlebars sideways, let down the tyres, and lower the seat and handlebar stem. The bike will have to be packed, at the very least, in something to protect other baggage from the oily parts of the machinery – such as an all-enclosing plastic bag. Further action that might be required is to take off the front and possibly the rear wheels, which should be taped against the frame. A bike-sized cardboard box (these are freely given away at most bike shops) can be used for better protection, but make sure you do a trial pack first – a considerable amount of disassembly is needed to fit some bikes into boxes.

With either the bag or the box method, plenty of tape and some pieces of bubble wrap should be used around delicate parts. Parcel tape with 'FRAGILE' written all over it might help get a point across. If the wheels are off, you should probably put a spacer between the drop-outs (where the wheels slot in). It's easy to make something up from nuts and some long bolts/threaded studs. Special bags are available for bikes, but there will have to be a plan about what to do with them on arrival. The best general advice is to arrive early, be relaxed and friendly with the check-in staff, whatever happens, and – just in case the worst happens – be insured.

On arrival something has to be done with all that packing. If you can get it from the airport to your accommodation, it can be left there for the return trip – this works well for plastic bags. Cardboard boxes can be broken up and left in bins (usually in the airport car park), and another one found for the return trip. If the bike bag is light and packable it can be carried around Ireland, where it might come in handy for bus or train transit.

By Sea

Ferry connections are shown below. The Swansea–Cork service is due to resume in March 2010, after a four-year break. For the latest information on this useful route, see www.bringbacktheswanseacorkferry.com. Flying is so common now that many people neglect this traditional route to Ireland, but ferries can be a practical and economical

way of getting to the Emerald Isle. They can be cheaper than flying – especially if baggage charges are taken into account – and arriving by sea can also be more convenient (no bike assembly and disassembly) and less stressful (no airport check-in).

Any choice is going to be influenced by how you get to the departure ferry port, but from London, for example, it is possible to take an evening train from Euston, an overnight ferry from Holyhead to Dublin Port, and be on the road that morning. Very cheap combined rail and ferry tickets are available from the ferry companies, and also from www.sailrail.co.uk (0845 0755755), and you can book your cycle on the UK end of the train journey. It is also possible to include Irish rail travel on the same ticket – but see the section on trains first.

Of the Irish-side ports, Rosslare is the least convenient for onward itineraries. It is a long way to the west from there, and at the time of writing cycles are not taken on any of the connecting rail services. Dublin Port is only a few minutes from the city centre, and Dun Laoghaire is a little further, but half-an-hour away at most. Belfast Docks are also convenient for the city centre.

Visas

Citizens of EU countries and most Western countries do not require a visa to enter Ireland

Ferry Operators and Routes			
Route	Route frequency	Length of crossing	Operator
From England			
Liverpool Birkenhead–Dublin	12 per week	7h	Norfolkline Irish Sea
Liverpool–Dublin	12 per week	8h	P&O Irish Sea
Liverpool Birkenhead–Belfast	13 per week	8h	Norfolkline Irish Sea
Fleetwood–Larne	9 per day	7h30m	Stena Line
From Wales			
Holyhead–Dublin	3 per day	2h	Irish Ferries
Pembroke–Rosslare	14 per week	3h45m	Irish Ferries
Holyhead–Dublin	4 per day	3h15m	Stena Line
Holyhead–Dun Laoghaire	7 per week	1h59m	Stena Line
Fishguard–Rosslare	4 per day	2h	Stena Line
From Scotland			
Troon–Larne	14 per week	1h50m	P&O Irish Sea
Cairnryan–Larne	4 per day	1h	P&O Irish Sea
Stranraer–Belfast	5 per day	2h	Stena Line

Ferry Operators and Routes			
Route	Route frequency	Length of crossing	Operator
From France			
Roscoff–Cork	1 per week	16h30	Brittany Ferries
Cherbourg–Rosslare	3 per week	18h	Celtic Link Ferries
Cherbourg–Rosslare	3 per week	18h30	Irish Ferries
Roscoff–Rosslare	2 per week	17h30hrs	Irish Ferries
Cherbourg–Rosslare	6 per week	17h	LD Lines
Note: LD Lines Le Havre–Rosslare has been stopped and moved to Cherbourg.			

Ferry Company Contacts				
Company	Web	UK	Ireland	France
Brittany Ferries	www.brittany-ferries.com	0871 2440744	021 427 7801	0825 828828
Celtic Link Ferries	www.celticlinkferries.com	0844 5768834		
Irish Ferries	www.irishferries.com	0870 5171717	0818 300 400	01 70720326
LD Lines	www.ldlines.co.uk	0844 5768836/ 0825 304304		
Norfolkline	www.norfolkline.com	0844 4990007		01 819 2999
P&O Irish Sea	www.poirishsea.com	0871 6644999		01 407 3434
Stena Line	www.stenaline.co.uk	0870 5707070		01 204 7777

or Northern Ireland. Non-UK or non-Irish nationals do require a passport or national identity card. Technically speaking, UK citizens do not need a passport to enter the Republic of Ireland (Northern Ireland is part of the UK in any case), but most carriers (air and sea) insist on valid photographic ID for security reasons. Currently (2009) a UK driving licence is accepted, but some carriers may have their own rules and require passports – so it is best to check when you book.

Also, the 2009 Borders Citizens and Immigration Bill, which was going through Parliament at the the time of writing, may affect the operation of what is effectively a passport-free travel zone (for citizens) encompassing Ireland, Great Britain, the Channel Islands and the Isle of Man – so check the current situation before travelling. The best place to get a jargon-free update is the Discover Ireland website (www.discoverireland.com). Either search for 'visa', or follow the 'facts for the visitor' links from the 'planning your visit' option.

The Northern Ireland–Republic of Ireland border is an open one and is generally not even signed. Sometimes however there are checks on cross-border public transport. The Bill includes plans for routine border controls on air and sea travel between Britain and Ireland as well as, according to the Home Office, some 'intelligence-led' checks on the land border. What this will mean in practice, only time will tell, but if you are in the unfortunate position of needing a visa for either or both countries, and are planning on crossing the land border, it is only sensible to have the correct documentation for both the UK and Ireland, and not just rely on not being checked.

Contacts
- Northern Ireland Visa Information: www.ukvisas.gov.uk
- Republic of Ireland Visa Information: www.dfa.ie (follow 'services to the public' link)

GETTING AROUND

Trains
Trains are only of limited use to cyclists in Ireland. Northern Ireland Railways has a very positive attitude to cyclists, which goes right down to station and train staff, but

unfortunately the network north of the border is limited to a Belfast to Derry service, a handful of services around Belfast, and a cross-border route to Dublin.

The Republic has a more comprehensive network, but very few trains take cycles. The current situation is that cycles can only be taken on the Dublin–Galway and Dublin–Cork lines (and not necessarily on all trains). At the time of writing, Irish Rail is in the middle of a fleet refurbishment, so the situation is highly changeable – check www.irishrail.ie for the latest information, and if possible always confirm, in person, at the station the day before that you can still travel. There is an extra charge for cycles of up to €8, depending on distance, and there are no reservations – it is first-come-first-served for the limited cycle space. Cycles that are packed to resemble normal luggage can be carried onto trains.

In Northern Ireland public transport comes under the Translink banner. On trains cycles are carried free on all services after 9.30am, including the cross-border service to Dublin. Up to four will be taken on any one train, subject to space in the designated area – again it is first-come-first-served. Tandems are not permitted.

Contacts
- Irish Rail: www.irishrail.ie
- Translink: www.translink.co.uk 028 9066 6630 or (for cross-border tickets) 028 9089 9409

Buses
Bus services are operated by different organisations, north and south, but the accommodation of cycles in the Republic is, thankfully, much better than on trains. Here Bus Eireann will carry cycles in the bus luggage compartment if there is space. When things are busy – Fridays and at weekends – luggage space is at a premiun and you may well miss out. If leaving from with a bus station, buy a ticket before boarding, and a separate ticket is needed for the bike – currently €11.5 regardless of distance. Also be aware that if you have to change buses, there is no guarantee there will be space for a bike on the second one. Bikes can travel unpacked, but if they can be packed into reasonably compact bags, they may be treated as normal luggage. If all that sounds a bit gloomy

– don't be put off. In rural areas, during the day and during the week, many services are nearly empty. If there is just one or two of you, a bus hop is a practical way of extending your range, and the network is surprisingly comprehensive.

In Northern Ireland, buses also come under the Translink umbrella. Up to two cycles can be carried in the luggage bay of express services (called Goldline Express) after 9.30am, but again this is subject to space and there are no reservations.

Contacts
- Translink (Northern Ireland): www.translink.co.uk 028 9066 6630
- Bus Eireann: www.buseireann.ie – contact local bus station

WHEN TO GO

The best months for cycling in Ireland are May, June and September. Experience and the statistics suggest that May and June, especially in the north, are as dry, if not drier than, the rest of the summer, while September is a golden month in which to watch the harvest home and notice the first colours of autumn in the trees. The early summer months can also be particularly beautiful, with the gorse in flower on the hillsides and the hedgerows thick with blossom and birdsong.

The Irish tourist season effectively runs from Easter to the end of September, and that is the practical limit for the cycle touring season too. Outside these months the weather is too cold and unreliable, the days too short, and campsites and some other types of accommodation close up. Depending on when Easter falls, some campsites will close again after Easter week and reopen at the beginning of May.

Statistics show a marked peak in tourist numbers in general and cyclists in particular during the months of July and August. At other times all but the most popular areas in the southwest can be very quiet. Travelling at peak times is not a problem – it just pays to plan ahead a little more, as accommodation can book up.

The Ulster marching season peaks in the 12 July fortnight, when parades celebrate the victory of William of Orange at the Battle of the Boyne. In the past these events were occasionally flashpoints for sectarian violence, but things have quietened down in recent years. The Orange Order is even keen on transforming the major marches into tourism events. This fortnight also marks a surge in Northern Ireland residents heading to the coast and hills. The distinctive Northern Ireland accent becomes common in resorts in the north and west, for example Sligo and Achill Island, and these places become noticeably busier.

ACCOMMODATION

Hostels

Official youth hostels are run by Hostelling International in Northern Ireland, and in the Republic by An Óige. These hostels are of a high standard and a membership card is not required, although a card from an affiliated youth hostel association usually secures a small discount. A number of youth hostels have closed in recent years, and there are gaps in the network, but independent hostels have stepped into the breach in Ireland, and these are generally excellent. The standard isn't quite as consistent as the 'official' hostels, and in bigger cities especially the official hostel (unless you have a personal recommendation for somewhere else) is often the best option.

There are two associations of independent hostels in Ireland. These are the Independent Holiday Hostels (IHH) and the Independent Hostel Owners (IHO). Both these groups and An Óige publish a convenient map of all their hostels, and if you are a make-it-up-as-you-go traveller, these are the three most useful bits of paper you can get hold of. The IHO and IHH cover all of Ireland, and the An Óige map includes the Northern Irish HINI hostels. Pick them up at the first hostel you stay at, or from a tourist office. At the time of writing, dormitory beds cost on average about €17–18 (or £11–12 in Northern Ireland), with twins/doubles typically about €25 per person (or £15).

Some of the hostels allow camping, which saves a bit of money (this varies), but still let you use the hostel's self-catering kitchen and bathroom facilities.

Contacts

- IHH: www.hostels-ireland.com
- IHO: www.independenthostelsireland.com
- An Óige: www.anoige.ie 01 830 4555
- Hostelling International Northern Ireland: www.hini.org.uk

Camping

Ireland has a good scattering of official campsites. Generally, sites are more plentiful as you

Dunlewey Church with Errigal Mountain behind (Route 2, Stage 6)

Camping on the Grand Canal (Route 7, Stage 1)

head south, and while there are some counties with no sites at all, it is certainly possible to camp and hostel your way around most of the country. The best source of information is the Irish Camping and Caravan Council. Most touring sites are members, in both parts of Ireland, and are listed on council website and in their annual *Caravan and Camping Guide*, which is available from tourist offices. Supplementing this list is a handful of local authority-run sites and forest parks.

Sites usually charge per person, not per tent, and cyclists are usually charged €8–10 each (or £5–8) in Northern Ireland. Sometimes there is a €1 charge for a token for a hot shower.

There is no right to wild camp anywhere on the island, and in most places this is not a practical proposition. Seeking permission is not always easy, as in remote areas it is hard to find someone to ask. Increasing concerns about legal liability have also made farmers more reluctant to allow access to their land in recent years. Having said that, in some of the quieter corners of Ireland where there are no official sites, such as Donegal and perhaps Connemara, wild camping on or near the beach or in the high country is possible, and can be a wonderful experience. Ordnance Survey maps (1:50 000) are good for ferreting out potential places. Setting up as it gets

dark and leaving early are both a good idea, but bear in mind this might mean as late as 10pm in summer with sunrise before 5am! Be exceptionally clean, well behaved, and if you see anyone – polite. 'No Camping' signs are getting more common, so don't ruin the few wild sites remaining.

Contacts
- Irish Caravan and Camping Council: www.campingireland.ie
- Forest Service (Northern Ireland): www.forestserviceni.gov.uk (look under activities) 028 9052 4480
- Coillte (forests in the RoI): www.coillte.ie

Bed and Breakfast
Ireland has many fine bed and breakfasts. On anything other than a short trip, however, the cost can soon mount up, especially if you are travelling alone, as you will be paying a premium for a single room. In most places you will also have to go out for an evening meal, which further increases the cost.

Nevertheless, bed and breakfasts are useful for filling accommodation gaps in routes, or when you feel like the odd night of luxury. If there is an open tourist office in town, they will often book you a bed and breakfast, for a fee (about €4), but it is best to be prepared with at least a few numbers to call yourself. The annual *Definitive Irish Bed and Breakfast and Self Catering Guide*, produced by the Town and Country Homes Association, is fairly comprehensive, north and south, and not too bulky to carry around.

Expect to pay €35–40 per person sharing, and €50–60 for a single. Some pubs also offer bed and breakfast accommodation – look for the signs.

Contacts
• Town and Country Homes Association:
www.townandcountry.ie
071 98 22222 (Republic of Ireland)

HEALTH AND SAFETY

Crime
The police in the Republic of Ireland are the Gardaí (pronounced 'gardee'), or, in the singular, Garda – but if you ask for the police, people will usually know what you mean. For non-emergency police matters, contact the nearest Garda station, or in Northern Ireland, police station. The Police Service Northern Ireland (PSNI) also has a non-emergency contact number – 0845 600 8000 – or see www. psni.police.uk. In the Republic, the nationwide free Irish Tourist Assistance Service aims to help with the practical and emotional aftermath of crime (www.itas.ie, 01 6668109).

When travelling in Ireland it is sensible to take reasonable precautions against crime, without being paranoid. This generally means keeping valuables out of sight, and for personal

EMERGENCIES

Dialling 112 or 999 will put you through to the emergency services – fire, police, ambulance or mountain rescue.

safety, avoiding deserted urban areas late at night. Good hostels have lockers or will keep your valuables safe for you. Sometimes you will need a small padlock, which you can buy at the hostel or in a hardware store. Anecdotal evidence suggests pilfering is a bigger problem in city hostels than in country areas, but being careful does no harm anywhere. Tents are, obviously, not secure.

Health
Ireland and Northern Ireland are modern European countries. Products such as sanitary towels or tampons, condoms, sunscreens, painkillers and first aid goods such as antiseptics and plasters, are widely available in shops and supermarkets. Pharmacist, or chemists, stock a greater range of medications, some of which are available without prescription, and the pharmacist will also be able to advise you on some medical problems. In the Republic, look for a green cross, in Northern Ireland, look for a 'pharmacy' or 'chemist' sign.

Both countries have public healthcare systems, but access to free treatment is by no means guaranteed for visitors. Since costs such as property loss or damage, legal expenses, repatriation costs and alternative travel

Ballymoran Bay and Strangford Lough (Route 12, Stage 5)

arrangements may also be incurred, visitors to Ireland should take out travel insurance. The one possible exception is UK residents visiting Northern Ireland, who will be entitled to the same level of healthcare as they would receive at home – these visitors might prefer to self-insure for other costs.

Some insurers do not include cycle touring in their basic level of cover, so check this. Also be aware of exactly what theft cover is provided. For example, thefts from tents or hostel dorms are rarely covered, and it is important that insurance does not give a false sense of security. Transit damage to a bike, or its theft, is another area to check.

Most insurers will expect you to access public healthcare where possible. European Union residents should obtain a European Health Insurance Card (EHIC) before travelling. Technically, UK citizens only need proof of UK residence to access the Irish health system, but get a card anyway – they are free. The EHIC will give access to the public system for treatment that becomes necessary during your stay. In both Northern Ireland and Ireland this is a good level of free treatment, although you may have to pay prescription charges. Do expect to pay for dental treatment, and remember that any free emergency treatment is likely to be limited to pain relief and maybe temporary fixes. Some other countries have bi-lateral arrangements with Ireland and the UK, which may give access to either free or below cost healthcare. Without an EHIC or access to these bilateral schemes, expect to pay the full cost of any treatment.

Pharmacists are a good first point of contact for non-emergency problems. As well as being able to supply some medications without a prescription, the pharmacist can advise and point the way to a doctor or hospital if necessary. Most accommodation providers will have contact details for doctors – called general practitioners or GPs – as well. To access free care in the Republic, it is important to see a GP contracted under the Primary Care Reimbursement Services (PCRS) scheme. If you can't find one, the local Health Service Office (www.hse.ie) will have numbers. In Northern Ireland there are fewer doctors working privately, but in all cases it is worthwhile mentioning you want to be treated under the EHIC arrangements.

When appropriate you can go to the accident and emergency (A&E) department of a public hospital, and this is probably where an ambulance will bring you in the event of an accident. EHIC holder or otherwise, if you end up in this situation, the most important thing is to get better, not be worrying about charges, so be insured, keep the details on your person, and get a friend to contact the insurer's helpline for advice.

Take:
- EHIC
- Copy of insurance policy and contact card
- Copy of prescriptions
- Reasonable supply of regular medication
- Spare spectacles/contact lenses and optical prescription

FOOD AND DRINK

Food

Maintaining a healthy diet with a fairly high calorific intake should be a priority on any extended tour.

If the plan is to eat out more often than not, you will find that prices and quality vary considerably, and are not necessarily related. The bigger centres generally have a choice of restaurants where a three-course meal will set you back a minimum of €30. Pubs offer cheaper food, although the quality is sometimes poor, and especially in rural areas some pubs only serve food on certain days, or don't serve food at all. Pubs specialising in good food are more common in Dublin than elsewhere, and they haven't really caught on in many rural areas. At cafés and pubs you can usually pick up a meal for under €10.

In terms of specialities, the seafood is worth a go on the west coast, while in the north you might feel up to taking on an Ulster Fry – bacon, eggs, sausages, fried soda bread, potato bread and tomatoes. Bed and breakfasts usually offer a 'full Irish' breakfast. The core ingredients are bacon, eggs and toast, while the inclusion of sausages, beans, potato cakes, black and white puddings and other fare varies from place to place. Ireland is far from a paradise for vegetarians – count on having to look

Ireland has many interesting pubs – the Beach Bar at Aughris Head started as a shebeen (illegal drinking shack) in the 18th century (Route 4, Stage 1)

around when eating out, and there may only be limited options on the menu.

Most small towns have a takeaway. These again vary considerably, but if you stick to the busy ones you won't go far wrong. Some of the international franchises such as McDonald's have made it to most of the larger towns. Ireland even has its own version – Supermacs – where a burger, chips and soft drink will set you back €4–5 and the quality is consistent.

For food on the road there is no reason to not eat plenty of fresh fruit, breads and cheeses – these are available everywhere. Small-town bakeries are always worth investigating, as there is usually a great choice of scones and small cakes, as well as traditional Irish soda bread – made with baking powder instead of yeast. Similarly, when self-catering, fresh vegetables are widely available, and together with staples such as pasta and rice, a big nutritious evening meal can be made for as little as €5.

Eating-out prices are marginally cheaper in Northern Ireland than the Republic. The J D Wetherspoon's pub chain is worth checking out for combined drink and meal promotions – you can get a meal and a drink for around the £5 mark. Food prices in Northern Ireland retailers are substantially lower than in the rest of Ireland. In 2008 surveys showed grocery prices were up to 40 per cent cheaper north of

the border, and this is another good reason to spend at least some part of your holiday here.

Wherever you are, discount supermarkets such as Aldi and Lidl are the cheapest for groceries, although small and portable quantities are not always available.

Drink

Ireland's national drink is Guinness, but there are other similar dark stout beers available – Beamish and Murphy's are two alternatives. Ireland is also known for its whiskeys. The only working distillery you can still visit is also the world's oldest licensed one – at Bushmills in County Antrim (see Route 1).

LANGUAGE

The revival of Gaelic sports in the late 19th century through the Gaelic Athletic Association (1884) went hand in hand with a revival in the Irish language and culture through the Gaelic League (founded 1893). This cultural revival played a significant part in the country's political development in the 20th century. Irish, which was banned by the English until 1871, is the first official language of the Republic of Ireland, where, according to the 2006 census, 42 per cent of the population can speak it. This figure is considerably higher in the 'Gaeltacht' areas, where Irish is recognised as the predominant language, and it is common to hear it spoken in streets, shops and pubs.

If you don't speak the language, there's no need to be concerned – everyone can speak English too – but hearing Irish spoken and having a go yourself adds to the enjoyment of Ireland. In the Gaeltach the Irish language traffic signs might throw you a little – for example An Daingean for Dingle – but they really are easy to work out, and at least on a bike you have plenty of time to think about them.

In other areas, both the Irish and Anglicised names are usually signed. Most maps have both versions of the name, and as the Anglicised name is usually a transliteration of the Irish one, it is usually possible to work out what is going on. In Northern Ireland, Irish has undergone a revival since the 1998 Belfast Agreement, and some Irish language signs are now starting to appear. The other language you might come across here is Ulster-Scots, or Ullans, which is officially recognised as a minority language.

Visitors for whom English is not a first language find the Irish accent difficult to begin with – but this passes quite quickly. Similarly, speakers of English as spoken in England, the US and elsewhere, might initially have to make an effort to speak clearly to be well understood.

MONEY

Paying

Cash

As part of the United Kingdom, the Northern Ireland currency is the pound sterling (£), while the rest of the island uses the euro. In border areas many businesses will take notes in either currency, but you will tend to get change in the home denomination. Northern Ireland does have its own banknotes, which although issued by local banks (such as Bank of Ireland) are backed by the Bank of England. These notes are sometimes only reluctantly accepted in other parts of the UK, so if you are returning there, do not to take too many home. English and Scottish notes are accepted in Northern Ireland.

Cash is still the most convenient way to pay for small transactions in both countries. Hostels and campsites generally appreciate cash payments, which keep their costs down. Paying cash will also keep down foreign currency transaction charges – if your card-issuer levies them.

ATMs are still rare enough in rural areas to make running out of cash a real possibility. Carrying enough money for at least the

Ardglass is one of the many small ports on the County Down coast (Route 12, Stage 4)

next four or five days is advisable, and will save having to waste time hunting for an ATM. As well as at banks, service stations and shops often have ATMs, but some of the non-bank ATMs in Northern Ireland charge a fee. The Plus/Visa and Cirrus/Mastercard-linked ATMs are the widespread ones, and UK travellers generally have no problems accessing cash from their home accounts through debit cards.

Whatever card you have, check the charges your bank will levy, and at the same time, check your card will be accepted in ATMs. If travelling both sides of the border, it is worth emphasising when you enquire that you need the card to work in both the UK and Ireland.

Break down big denomination notes – €50 and €100 especially – when you shop in bigger stores, in town. Sometimes smaller shops in rural areas run low on change.

Credit and Debit Cards

Visa and Mastercard credit and debit cards are widely accepted in shops. Hostels almost always take cards, and sometimes ask for a card number to secure a booking. Bed and breakfasts and campsites are more likely only to accept cash, so if relying on a card, check when calling ahead. For overseas visitors, cash is still the cheapest and most convenient way to pay (for you and for the supplier). Know how much the bank will charge for transactions and save the debit/credit card for larger purchases.

Budgets

Being extremely frugal, it is just possible to tour the Republic of Ireland for €20 a day if camping or €30 a day in hostels, or in Northern Ireland, £15 (camping) or £20 hostelling. This is an absolute minimum, and assumes you self-cater and stay away from fast food. Since bed and breakfasts will cost from €35, or £25, (per person sharing), and you will also have to buy an evening meal and food during the day, €60–70 or £40 is a more realistic absolute minimum daily budget for bed and breakfast travellers.

At 2009 exchange rates, Northern Ireland is considerably cheaper than the rest of the island for everyday items. If you are concerned about keeping spending down, basing your holiday in Northern Ireland makes a big difference.

Post

Finding a post office in Ireland is generally not a problem – on most days you will pass through at least one small town with one. The Republic has many tiny post offices, some of which are open only part-time, but the future of this network is uncertain. In Northern Ireland look for a red sign with 'Post Office' written in yellow (usually). In the rest of Ireland, look for 'Post' on a green background.

Overseas postcards cost a similar amount from both countries (€0.82 or 50p–81p depending on zone in 2009). If sending items home from either country (for example used maps), keeping the total dimensions below 900mm (longest side under 600mm) ensures it is a packet rather than a parcel – which is sometimes less than half the price for the same weight. For postal rates see www.anpost.ie or www.royalmail.com.

Phones

- Ireland: international code +353
- Northern Ireland: international code +44
- International prefix (north and south) 00

The Irish phone system is complicated by the fact you are dealing with two countries with two international codes. The numbers in the text assume you are calling from within the country in question – for example Northern Ireland from Northern Ireland (or UK). When dialling from the Republic of Ireland to a fixed line in the North, the 028 code is replaced with 048. This does not work calling mobiles. When calling from Northern Ireland to the Republic, dial the full international prefix and code, although these calls are not charged at international rates.

Calling Northern Ireland Numbers

For example, the Belfast Welcome Centre, Northern Ireland number is 028 90246609, so:

- from Northern Ireland or elsewhere in UK dial 028 90246609
- from Republic of Ireland dial 048 90246609
- from overseas dial local international prefix +44 28 902466099.

Phone box, Fenagh, County Leitrim (Route 3, Stage 5)

Calling Republic of Ireland Numbers

The Dublin Tourist Office number is
01 6057799, so:

- from Northern Ireland or elsewhere in UK dial 00 353 1 6057799
- from the Republic of Ireland dial 01 6057799
- from overseas dial local international prefix + 353 1 6057799.

A mobile phone is the most convenient and often the cheapest way to stay in touch when in Ireland. A GSM 900/1800 phone will give the best access to networks. In Northern Ireland the operators are O2, Vodafone, Orange and T-Mobile, while in the Republic there are Meteor, O2, Three and Vodafone. Coverage is almost universal. There are a few blank spots on hill-bound coasts, but coverage usually resumes around the next headland.

Roaming charges within the EU are now at a sensible enough level to make short calls – for example to book accommodation – as cheap as using phone boxes. Text messages are also charged at rates not too far from the costs back at home. Receiving calls can still cost money, so for long calls home, finding a call box, texting the number home and getting people to call back is the cheapest option. If you are a pay-as-you-go customer, top up before leaving, as it isn't easy from Ireland (apart from UK customers in Northern Ireland). If you are a UK or Irish phone customer in border country, make sure your phone hasn't accidentally roamed onto a network on the 'wrong' side of the border. Signals penetrate a long way and this can result in unexpected bills.

For a long trip you might consider getting hold of an Irish or 'international' SIM card for your GSM phone. The main advantage of these is that incoming calls will be free to you – but someone will be paying at the other end. Make sure your phone has been unlocked (to allow it to work with any SIM card) if you are considering this option. Getting your phone unlocked before you travel also gives you the option of buying a SIM card in Ireland. Check out the prices and do the sums, but for most UK travellers their existing phone will be the best options.

The phone box network is shrinking rapidly in Ireland. It's holding on slightly better in Northern Ireland. But in rural areas, you cannot rely on there being a working telephone box near where you are camping. Hostels usually have some sort of pay phone or a call box nearby. Rates from private pay phones are usually higher than the public boxes, however, and they don't always take incoming calls. Public boxes have a minimum charge of €1 (40p in Northern Ireland), making it cheaper to use

Valentia Harbour (Route 8, Stage 5)

a roaming mobile for quick bookings. Phone cards for public boxes are available from An Post – stay away from these, the phones often cannot read the cards.

Don't forget mobile charger and plug adaptor if you need it – all of Ireland has UK-style plug sockets.

Internet

Away from the big towns, treat internet access as a luxury rather than a service to rely on to make, for example, forward travel arrangements. On the plus side, many hostels now have free or cheap internet access, and some have WiFi hubs. In the bigger towns, for example Sligo, there is usually a choice of internet cafés, although these businesses often have a short life span. Getting online in a small town or village is less certain. The best option is to enquire at a tourist office or just in the street.

CYCLING IN IRELAND

Traffic and Driving

Road conditions and regulations are similar in Ireland and Northern Ireland. Ireland has speed limits and distance signs in kilometres, while Northern Ireland uses miles. The signage scheme is different in the two countries, but similar enough to not cause any confusion.

In both countries, motorways have an M prefix and cycles are not allowed on these roads.

In the Republic there are national 'N' roads (100km/h limit), regional 'R' roads (80km/h) and local roads (also 80km/h). There is a general limit of 50km/h in built-up areas and other limits are signed. Speed limits are widely ignored unless there is a chance of getting caught. N roads are divided into primary and secondary routes, with a figure higher than 50 indicating a secondary route.

Cycling on N roads can be quick, but there is generally too much fast, heavy traffic to make this a comfortable experience. Some of the R roads are just as bad. One of the problems with the major roads in the Republic of Ireland is that while some sections have been improved, and the wide shoulders and smooth surface make for easy riding, other stretches are narrow and fast. The good stretches speed up the traffic, which barely slows for the poorer sections. If riding busy roads the idea is to be assertive and ride out far enough in the carriageway to make traffic manoeuvre around you – otherwise vehicles will try and pass you

Author riding the Grand Canal near Macartney Aqueduct (Route 7, Stage 2)

'Give Way' – in Gaeltach areas (where Irish is recognised as the predominant language) road signs are in Irish, but it is usually clear what they mean

without crossing the centre-line of the road – but sometimes it's just too scary, and hugging the kerb at the risk of being buffeted into the ditch is the safer choice. The few N road sections in this book are either in quiet areas, or are short, unavoidable stretches.

In Northern Ireland, after the motorways there are A roads, B roads and minor roads. Some of the A roads – for example the A2 Antrim Coast Road – are very fine riding indeed, while some of the busier main routes are unrideable. The A routes included in this book have all been found to be enjoyable and safe riding. The B roads have no real equivalent elsewhere in Ireland. Often they are wide, well graded and maintained, and carry little traffic.

The routes in this book are built, where possible, around minor and B roads in Northern Ireland and local roads in the rest of Ireland. Typically these are not quite wide enough for two cars to pass without slowing down. They are sealed (tarmac) roads. The quality of the surface varies considerably. Irish roads often break up or suffer subsidence on their edges, making hugging the side of the road a bumpy proposition. Always keep an eye out for potholes, especially on steep descents – these can actually throw you off the bike. Road surfaces are more consistently good in Northern Ireland than elsewhere. The worst local roads are in Donegal and the border counties of Monaghan and Cavan, but all areas have their moments. Roads in built-up areas in the Republic are

often appalling, as a result of continuous patching for pipe-laying and so on during the recent construction boom.

Smaller roads all over Ireland are generally not well graded (that is, they have many short and steep climbs). In some areas, particularly the drumlin belt from Strangford Lough to Donegal Bay, this can make for rollercoaster roads, and very slow progress for little or no overall gain in altitude.

Cycleways are most often encountered leading into towns and cities. Again, the situation is slightly better in the north, where the cycleways are more likely to be off-road and continuous. Both Dublin and Belfast are easy to get out of on cycleways.

Cycleways are generally marked with a cycle symbol painted on the road or pavement surface or, less commonly, with a round blue sign with a white cycle symbol. In the Republic, if there is a cycleway you are legally obliged to use it, although the Irish government's national cycle policy says this rule will be revoked. Using the cycleways is optional in Northern Ireland, but here beware of a circular sign with a red border and a black bike symbol – it means *no cycling*, and is sometimes confused with the blue cycleway sign.

Key Points
- Cycling and driving is on the left
- Stay away from N roads – but the ones in this book are OK
- Cycling is not allowed on motorways (eg M50)
- Distances and limits in km in Ireland, miles in Northern Ireland
- This book uses kms throughout

Hazards
Beware of sheep and pedestrians – both are equally likely to run into the road without warning. Expect the occasional spirited chase from a dog, although most of the ones left alive are well secured. A loud shout usually sends them packing. Thorn hedges are common in Ireland, particularly in the northern parts. Puncture resistant tyres are essential – see below. On narrow roads watch out for stray undergrowth catching your legs, arms or, more seriously, your face and eyes. In summer the odd stinging insect might lodge in your

clothing, but generally Ireland is pretty low risk for things that bite.

Safety Points

- Helmets are not compulsory, but may be a good idea.
- Bright colours are a good idea, but being fluorescent is a fashion choice.
- Keep left-ish, but staying 1–2m in from the edge of the road will give you a safer road surface and encourage cars to manoeuvre around you.
- Cycling at night is not usually necessary, but lights must be used and plenty of reflective gear is a good idea.
- Be sensible about where you ride two abreast.
- Pedestrians stepping into the road, or even walking down the middle of it, are a constant hazard – they will just not hear you coming, but be friendly about it (you are on holiday).
- Sunburn can get you even on seemingly dull days – wear sunscreen and consider long sleeves. Ears are particularly vulnerable to burning.
- Carry food, water and a basic first aid kit.
- Be prepared for changes in the weather – don't get cold or wet through.

Security

The following are specific crime points for cyclists.

- Bike theft is is a real risk in cities and towns. A shackle lock, or at least one you are confident cannot be cut quickly is a minimum requirement.
- Lock your bike every time you leave it – theft is unlikely (apart from in the cities), but bikes occasionally get ridden home from the pub (by someone else) and, in any case, losing your cycle will be a complete holiday disaster.
- If you have quick release wheels, make sure your lock secures these too.
- Luggage does get stolen from bikes. This is a tricky one, and if you are travelling alone there are going to be times you have to leave the bike with luggage attached. Some pannier systems will lock to the carrier, but realistically someone can still empty the bag. Best option is to have your valuables in an easily removable bar bag with a shoulder strap and carry it with you. In town – especially Dublin and Belfast – book into your accommodation and secure your bags before exploring around town.

Bikes should always be locked – this includes the wheels

Inisheer's green lanes are very rideable (Route 6, Stage 3)

WHAT TO TAKE

Bike

The best bike for touring is, well, a touring bike. Bikes sold as tourers generally have a relaxed frame geometry, good clearances for mudguards and tyres, mounting points for carriers, and low gear ratios (these days, 24-speed and up). Wheels are a critical part of the package, and a set of hand-built touring wheels is a good investment, especially for Ireland where the roads are bumpy. Drop handlebars are not for everyone, but they do give a choice of hand positions, and if the bike is set up so you are comfortable riding on the 'drops', they can be a godsend in headwinds. Mountain bikes or mountain–road hybrids are also popular for touring, but since most of this book is on sealed roads, make sure suitable road tyres are fitted.

For Irish conditions, 32mm (width) tyres are a good compromise between speed and comfort. A puncture resistant Kevlar band is pretty much essential in the north, because of thorns, and a good idea elsewhere. Schwalbe Marathons (www.schwalbe.com) work well in Ireland. The basic Marathon is the best choice – the more extreme versions such as the 'Plus'

Good wheels and rubber are essential in Ireland – even steel sculptures get flat tyres, as this sculpture, 'The Time of Day' (1986) by Cillian Rogers, in Easkey, shows (Route 4, Stage 1)

are harder to fit and do not offer anything extra that is vital for the conditions you will encounter. Use the manufacturer's recommended pressures unless experience tells you otherwise.

Simple is generally best on tour, and in Ireland, if you have the absolute latest in gear, spares can be hard to get hold of, even in Dublin and Belfast. Older bikes, maybe upgraded with new wheels and gears, have plenty going for them, especially as they are less attractive to thieves, and you are going to worry less about throwing them onto planes, trains and buses. Sticking to 26-inch or 700c wheel sizes will give you the best choice of spares, if you happen to need them.

If you are already used to clipless pedals, systems with small cleats such as the Shimano SPD are efficient touring platforms, and with the right shoes (see below) the cleats are recessed and you can walk normally. Get used to the pedal system before going on tour – some riders have a few gentle mishaps while getting used to clipless pedals, and a loaded touring bike is not ideal for experimenting.

Fit two water-bottle holders – if your frame does not have the right fixings, brackets are available.

The most important factors with any bike are that it is the right size for you and you are positioned comfortably. Once you get the set-up right, mark the seat tube and stem (if you have one) so that you can re-position correctly after the bike is disassembled for flying.

Spares and Repairs

The starting point is to get the bike in good condition before you leave. Anything tired, worn or loose (such as chains) should be sorted out. Cables are often neglected, and replacing these can give new life to brakes and gears. After that, be sensible about the tools and spares you take. Being self-sufficient is great in principle but heavy in practice, and more weight means more strain for you and the bike. Match the spares and tools you take to your mechanical ability, and remember that Ireland is not a wilderness, and if the worst comes to the worst, you can get the bus to the nearest big town for repairs. Consider taking a spare chain and a spare folding tyre – just because without these you cannot get anywhere. A spoke spanner is handy for adjusting wheels, but don't tinker unless you know what you are doing. The same goes for a headset spanner. A Leatherman-style tool with pliers is handy for small fix-it jobs off and on the bike.

Check round the bike for loose fasteners every few days or more often. Paying heed to any odd sounds or movements can help nip problems in the bud. A liquid chain lubricant suited for wet riding, such as Finish Line Cross Country Wet, is best for Ireland. Dry lubricants are cleaner, but tend to wash off in wet conditions.

If you are going past the minimum lists below, you probably already know enough to make your own sensible choices about what to take.

Luggage

The traditional full touring set-up is front and rear panniers, bar bag for valuables and day use, and possibly a saddlebag. If you are camping this is a realistic arrangement. For hostelling or bed and breakfast tours it is possible to travel extremely light and still be civilised. The only reason, in this case, to have front and rear panniers is to balance out the load on the wheels, or to separate wet and dry gear. Fewer and smaller bags force you to travel light!

Camping or otherwise, a waterproof bar bag with a quick release and shoulder strap means you can keep valuables with you. Ortlieb (www.ortlieb.com) does one that has an optional map case on top, and also takes a padded insert to convert into a camera bag. A bar bag is not perfect for cameras because of the vibration, but it is convenient. A small saddle bag can keep tools, spares, sunscreen, and possibly your lunch, away from the rest of the gear – but don't take one if it encourages you to take too much stuff.

A pair of waterproof rear panniers (15–20 litres each) is more than enough for hostelling or bed and breakfast. The ones made of a vinyl material with roll-top closures do the job – Ortlieb make these too, although there are alternatives.

For camping, put small waterproof panniers on the front and fit rear panniers made of cotton canvas. This material is close to waterproof, but still breathes enough so that wet camping gear doesn't sweat inside and soak everything else. Dry clothing, maps, books, notes and so on can be stowed in the front panniers, and the messy stuff in the back. Wherever you carry your sleeping bag, a waterproof stuff sack is a sensible belt-and-braces precaution.

Quick-release fasteners are good for unloading, especially where you have to take off bags to get on trains and buses or to negotiate gates (see Route 7). On good brands they will still be sturdy, but a broken fastener can be a nightmare.

Do not skimp on luggage racks, especially if you are camping. The steel ones made by Tubus (www.tubus.com) are almost indestructible. Not all luggage fits well on all brands of rack, or all racks on all frames, so ask plenty of

The fairy-tale turrets of Lismore Castle (Route 10, Stage 2)

questions and, if possible, at least marry everything up together at the shop before committing to buy. The ideal load distribution is 60 per cent rear, 40 per cent front, although side-to-side balance is far more important – check this every day to avoid having to wrestle your bike along.

Key Points

- Some luggage must be completely waterproof
- Take an easily removable bar bag for valuables
- 'Essential' is negotiable and smaller bags mean lighter loads
- Think about how you will pack wet and dirty gear
- Buy good racks
- Side-to-side balance is important
- Make sure your lights are visible

Bike checklist

Spares

- front and rear lights
- three spare inner tubes
- puncture repair outfit
- cable ties (really useful!)
- PVC insulating tape (ditto)
- inner cables
- chain lubricant

- couple of rags
- handful of spare nuts and fasteners as appropriate to your bike
- few pairs of disposable latex gloves (keep hands clean)
- brake blocks (on a long tour)
- spare folding tyre (optional)
- spare chain (optional)

Tools

- pump
- tyre levers
- multi-tool including Allen keys to fit your bike
- chain tool – may be part of the multi-tool
- pedal spanner (especially if you are flying)
- wheel nut spanner (if your bike has nuts)
- spanners for everything else
- spoke key (optional)
- Leatherman or similar tool with pliers (optional)

Clothing

General

Ireland's summer climate is warm and at times wet. Atlantic weather systems tend to move through quickly, and it is common for a wet morning to turn into a sunny afternoon (and vice versa), so clothing needs to be adaptable

A pub is the perfect place to plan the next day's riding; John Huston used Moby Dick's in Youghal for the 1954 film of Herman Melville's classic tale (Route 10, Stage 2)

and easily layered. If you are hostelling or using bed and breakfasts, clothing is going to be a significant part of your total load, while on camping trips it is the weight of clothes that can push the load towards being unpleasantly heavy. One set of clothes for the evening and something light to sleep in will always have to be kept dry and quite clean.

As for on-bike gear, the choice is almost limitless. For touring, however, consider not wearing specialist cycling clothes when riding. For example, walking/trekking shorts with zip-off legs, short or long-sleeved T-shirt or base layer and a light jacket or fleece if it's cold. Padded undershorts make ordinary shorts as comfortable as Lycra cycling shorts, and you will feel more human walking around shops and stately homes. Bright colours make sense for safety, but carrying a florescent tabard for busy or gloomy conditions means all your gear does not have to be in high-visibility tones.

If all your gear looks presentable off and on the bike, you will need fewer clothes, and they will be easier to organise and keep clean. Merino wool base layers and socks are particularly handy, as they can be worn several days in a row and are machine washable. Fingerless cycling gloves stop painful sunburn on the back of the hands and reduce palm soreness.

Waterproofs
Be prepared for wet weather – keeping your top half dry goes a fair way to avoid getting too miserable. Whatever coat you have, a peaked cap, preferably a bit waterproof, can be worn under a helmet and stops rain running down your face and into the jacket. The main problems with all waterproofs are controlling temperature and dispersing perspiration. This is something that varies tremendously between cyclists, and it will probably take a few tours to work out the best system for you. In Ireland it is more likely to be cool and wet than hot and wet, so overheating is not too much of a problem. And in any case, if you are really warm, getting a little damp doesn't feel too bad. A lightweight breathable jacket and a long-sleeved base layer will be adequate on most wet days, maybe with a switch to a lighter shirt when it's hot. Another layer might be necessary when you stop, especially if it is windy.

Gore-Tex and other similar fabrics are a good choice, but my touring preference in recent years has been a Paramo Velez smock (www.paramo.co.uk). This is warmer than traditional cycling shells, and works best for me with a really light base layer. When you do warm up, it shifts sweat quickly and the ventilation zips are versatile. It also doubles up as a sweater on cold days/evenings, and doesn't look too hard core in the pub.

Waterproof trousers are a personal choice, but wet legs are not really uncomfortable, and a pair of Lycra leg warmers will keep out the cold. Waterproof gloves and, depending on footwear, neoprene overshoes complete the wet-weather set-up.

Shoes
Few things affect the comfort of cycling as much as shoes, and some cyclists have a cupboard full of failed quests to find the Shangri-la of the perfect shoe. Having cycling shoes that are good walking shoes saves carrying extra footwear. Something different to wear in the evenings, however, is important, to give your shoes an airing and your feet a break. One option that works well is mountain bike shoes with recessed cleats (if you use clipless pedals). Gore-Tex lined shoes keep the wind and showers off, but you will still need overshoes in absolute downpours. A pair of light sandals will make a refreshing change in the evening, and you can always wear socks if it's cold.

Cycling sandals (with or without cleats) work well for summer tours. Add socks if it's cold or you want to protect from sunburn; add neoprene overshoes in the wet – they are warm, just like little wet-suits. Wet feet in sandals are less of a problem than cold and wet feet inside wet shoes and socks. It is also possible to get away with only taking sandals and no other footwear, as they do not need drying out.

Camping
The four essentials are tent, sleeping bag, mat and stove, and it is worth spending a little money to get these right.

Tent
Sooner or later there is going to be a downpour, so buy a top-quality lightweight hiking tent. A double-skin tent (with a separate fly-sheet)

works well in Ireland, as ventilation is generally good and there is usually a vestibule area for wet gear. The inner tent should be insect-screened, as biting midges are occasionally a problem. If you are buying, go to a specialist retailer and explain where you are going. Some lightweight summer tents are just not up to Irish weather, and it's not unusual to see some very wet campers around a site after a night's rain. Macpac tents (www.macpac.co.nz) are made for wet New Zealand conditions and so perform well in Ireland.

Sleeping Bag

No need to go over the top – even in April and September night temperatures rarely drop below 5°C. A reasonable-quality medium-weight bag is fine. Down bags perform better if you are confident of keeping them completely dry. A silk liner keeps the bag clean, makes it warmer, and doubles up as a hostel sheet bag if you need one.

Mat

It is worth spending a little extra on a good mat, as tired muscles and an uncomfortable night's sleep are a bad combination. Thermarest (www.thermarest.com) are the original light-weight inflating mats, but try out a few in the shop to see what suits.

Stoves

Gas canisters for camping stoves are hard to come by in Ireland, apart from at specialist camping retailers and some campsites. Methylated spirits (alcohol) fuelled stoves are not quite as convenient to use as gas, but they are simple, hot, and you can buy the fuel at hardware stores, agricultural suppliers and even paint shops. Trangia (www.trangia.se) are the original brand, but there are alternatives.

Other Accessories

You will need plenty more to make a comfortable camp – including cooking and eating utensils. If you are new to cycle camping, a test run close to home is a good idea.

MAPS

The directions in the book will get you around, but having maps is sensible for impromptu changes of route, getting 'unlost', exploring further, and generally improving your knowledge of the area you are in.

The best cycling maps for Ireland are 1:50 000 Ordnance Survey maps. In Northern Ireland these are produced by the Ordnance Survey of Northern Ireland (OSNI) as the Discoverer Series. In the Republic the same scale maps are published as the Discovery Series by the

The Shay Elliott memorial remembers Ireland's first Tour de France yellow jersey holder
(Route 11, Stage 8)

Ordnance Survey Ireland (OSI). There are minor style differences between the two series, and some small overlaps along the border, but together they are a comprehensive mapping of the island. The series use the same grid, and there is a 10m contour interval throughout.

The only problem with maps at this scale is that you are likely to need a few, and keeping the current section in view will mean plenty of folding and unfolding. A more compact alternative is the four-map Holiday Series, jointly produced by OSI and OSNI at 1:250 000 scale, which covers the whole of Ireland in four sheets (North, South, East and West). They show all roads except the very tiny, and include colour-coded topography above 120m. Some of the tourist information is a little out of date (hostels, campsites and so on) and there are a few new roads not yet included, but on the whole they are comprehensive and accurate.

If cycling in Northern Ireland there is a growing network of signed cycle routes. The Northern Ireland Pack from cycling charity Sustrans (www.sustransshop.co.uk) includes maps of these as well as other cycling information for the province.

USING THIS GUIDE

This guidebook describes 12 cycling routes, each subdivided into manageable stages. Five of the routes are circular and seven linear, and they are intended to link together to create longer itineraries, right up to a grand tour of Ireland – see below and Appendix 2. Ways of making links are included throughout.

The book is focused on cycle touring, and the assumption is that you are going to be carrying some luggage, so the routes try to balance interest and scenery with a cycle tourist's desire to cover some distance and get somewhere.

The route cards provide the route description in detail (see below, and page 43 for an example), and some readers may want to follow them to the letter, while for others the route information might be just for inspiration, or a source of general background about what to expect in an area.

Each route begins with a map, and a route information box summarising its stages, with the distance for each and a brief description of the terrain you will encounter. This is followed by an introduction to the area covered by the route, options along it, advice on getting to the start and when to go, accommodation choices, maps needed, and suggestions for links with other routes.

Each stage within the route begins with distance and terrain, a description of the landscape and points of interest on that stage, followed by a summary of facilities along the way (shops, ATMs and so on), accommodation choices, and options at the end of the stage for continuing along an alternative to the route described in the book.

The routes vary from just over 250km to just over 540km. Overall, the stages average out at just over 63km, and should take, again on average, four to five hours of riding. There are a few longer stages in the book which have generally been necessary because of the unavailability of budget accommodation or, for the sake of completeness, to include some far-flung corners of the island – in which case sensible short-cuts have been suggested in the text. So if riding 100km or more in a day is not your idea of fun, don't be put off by any particular route, take a look at the route descriptions first. For example the longest stage in the book, Route 6, Stage 5 Doolin to Kilrush, takes in Loop Head at the mouth of the Shannon, but there are short-cut options to cut the total distance to 61km or 73km.

The two routes with longer-than-average stages are Route 4 Sligo to Achill Island and Route 10 Cork to Killarney and Waterford. The former includes a day tour of Achill Island, where the panniers can be left behind to keep the overall effort down. Route 10, on the other hand, is relatively short, with only four stages, where the average is brought up by a long stage from Fermoy to Killarney in an area in which there are few stand-out intermediate places for an overnight stop. With these two exceptions, if you can ride an average distance of 60–70km a day, the routes in this book can be covered using the stages described. Remember, however, that this is a guide, not a benchmark – the intention is to help you enjoy and explore Ireland by bike, not to commit you to distances which are, for you, unrealistically long, or short.

Experienced tourers will have a fair idea of their capabilities. Newcomers or comparative newcomers should go for a relaxed itinerary rather than trying to cram the longest possible tour into the number of days available – it is much better to have a 'free' day or two to go to the beach, explore a town or just do nothing rather than be faced with having to double-up on stages with only the prospect of a last-minute dash to the airport to look forward too. A realistic average speed for a loaded tourer on Irish rural roads is in the range of 12–15 km/h.

Experienced rider, or otherwise, do not fall into the trap of underestimating the terrain in Ireland. Ireland's highest road is only 510m above sea level, at Sally Gap in County Wicklow – this compares to several Alpine passes at over 2700m. But Irish rural roads are generally not well graded and characteristically there are many small rises and falls which, while barely showing up on a map with 10m contours, can still sap the energy and slow you down. Added to that, in more remote areas the road surfaces can be badly potholed and uneven, which also militates against fast riding.

Paradoxically, most of the few 'big' climbs, such as to Sally Gap (Route 11, Stage 7) or the Coomakesta Pass in Kerry (Route 8 Stage 6), are faster than some of the roads in supposedly flat areas, say for example drumlin-infested Route 3, Stage 4 in the Fermanagh lakelands. This is simply because the mountain roads tend to have steady gradients and are usually well surfaced.

The other big variable is the wind. The prevailing wind in Ireland is from the southwest – but strong northerlies and easterlies are not unusual, and when the wind swirls around headlands and mountains it can seem to be coming from all directions at once. In some of the exposed coastal areas an unfriendly wind can halve your rate of progress and considerably sap your energy for the days to come. County Donegal suffers from both poor roads and high winds, making Route 2 Derry to Donegal by far the most difficult (as well as the longest) route in the book.

Of the shorter tours, Routes 1 Belfast to Derry (and return), 3 Donegal Town to Sligo, 4 Sligo to Achill Island, 5 Tour of Connacht, 6 The Aran Islands and the Burren, 9 Kenmare to Cork, and 11 Dublin to Waterford (and return) can each be fitted into a week (including two weekends), especially bearing in mind

that Routes 1, 3 and 6 all have one stage that can be skipped (to offshore islands and so on) while Route 5 has two stages that can be left out if time is tight.

Routes 2 Derry to Donegal Town and 8 the Southwest Peninsulas are best fitted into ten days or a fortnight. The former is slow going because of the conditions, while on the latter there are many places to stop and linger along the way.

The two shortest routes in the book, Routes 7 Dublin to Limerick (via the Grand Canal) and 10 Cork to Killarney and Waterford, include some of the best cycling in Ireland. Both also combine well with other routes into some of the longer itineraries, or 'grand tours', summarised in Appendix 2.

Route Cards

To follow the route cards (see example opposite) you will need a cycle computer set up to read kilometres. Set the trip counter at the start point of the stage indicated. Every attempt was made to ensure accurate and consistent calibration, but in practice there are bound to be some minor discrepancies. For this reason, and because you may well make your own small or large detours to explore around the route, a cycle computer which lets you adjust the trip counter will make things easier. This is sometimes known as a 'navigator' or 'navigation' function.

The first entry of each route card indicates the details of the starting point and which direction to head in. 0 in the first column is a reminder to reset your cycle computer. From hereon, a solid black arrow indicates a change of direction, or a confirmation to continue in the same direction (included where roads are badly marked or there is likely to be confusion, for example if the traffic priority is changed at a crossroads), and the figure in the LH column is your cumulative distance in kilometres from the start of the stage. (Where the distance column is left blank, this means that features listed are less than 0.1km further on.)

For all directions, a road sign or signed road name is indicated where possible, with the exact wording as it appears on the sign in single quotation marks, for example, 'Belfast' or 'George Street'. If there are no signs, or sometimes just to ensure that you find the correct

Sample Route Card and Key

←   change of direction/confirmation of direction

O   roundabout

⇐   direction of side-trip, short-cut or to point of interest, accommodation or shop close to route

WC   public toilet

ATM   cashpoint

▲   accommodation

♦   shop, or, rarely, a café where supplies can be bought

☆   point of interest – a beach, building or architectural interest, or view

△(50)   summits (altitude in metres)

		Stage 3 Tour of the Dingle Peninsula
stage no and route name		
← direction to take	0.0	←	From car park exit on Dingle quay, next to tourist informa-tion, turn left
←O roundabout	1.0	←O	'Slea Head Drive'. Rainbow Hostel, straight on in a few hundred metres
▲⇑ accommodation direction		▲⇑	
ATM♦ cashpoint, shop	1.3	ATM ♦	Good shop in service station
⇐☆ side-trip, point of interest	7.4	⇐ ☆	Ventry Strand 100m
WC public toilet		WC	
	10.1	♦	Small shop
	11.2	☆	Celtic and prehistoric museum
△(50) summit (altitude in metres)	12.2	△(50)	Steady climb, don't forget to look back
	13.0	☆	Dunbeg Fort
point of interest		☆	Famine cottages

Ownahincha Strand (Route 9, Stage 4))

road, a further description is included. These descriptions do not have quotation marks. Junctions that have no signs and no distinguishing features are marked as unsigned. At these turns, take special care with distances and keep an eye out for landmarks and other features coming up on the route card to make sure you are on the right road. To help clarify the route, additional information such as 'at T-junction' or 'at crossroads' is included where necessary.

A circle and an arrow together indicates a roundabout. An outline arrow indicates a turn to a place not directly on the route. An up and a down arrow side by side mean that you need to turn around. This may be a side-trip, a short-cut or a point of interest, accommodation or a shop close to the route. It may be accompanied by another symbol, and the text in the third column will explain further. Some of the side-trips are expanded upon in the main text. Other symbols indicate a public toilet, cashpoint, accommodation, shops, points of interest and summits (with spot height).

Note that spellings and punctuation of Irish place names vary widely. If a place is quote in inverted commas on the route card, this is the spelling that you will find on the road sign, which may not match the spelling that this guide has chosen in the route description and elsewhere.

ROUTE 1

BELFAST TO DERRY –
THE CAUSEWAY COAST AND THE SPERRIN MOUNTAINS

Stage		Terrain	Distance (km)	Summit (distance from start/height)
1	Belfast to Carnlough	Mainly flat coastal route	62.4	27km/170m
2	Carnlough to Ballycastle	Some long climbs	70.7	42km/390m
2a	Alternative via Torr Head	Severe gradients	(48.1)	32km/250m
3	Tour of Rathlin Island	Coastal; short steep climbs	25.8	17km/110m
4	Ballycastle to Portrush	Undulating coastal ride	36.5	8km/140m
5	Portrush to Derry	Stiff climb over hills	79.8	35km/330m
6	Derry to Omagh	Steady climb over Sperrins	56.3	45km/250m
7	Omagh to Armagh	Undulating farmland	64.0	22km/51m
8	Armagh to Belfast	Undulating farmland; towpaths	80.9	51km/100m
		Total	**476.4**	

The coastline between Belfast and Derry is one of the most beautiful stretches in Ireland. The Giant's Causeway – a coastal formation of hexagonally jointed basalt columns – is the highlight of the route, but if this is a scenic high watermark, the rest of the coast barely suffers by comparison. After Derry the turn inland through the Sperrin Mountains and onwards to the fertile plains of counties Tyrone and Armagh offers a change of pace. The quiet rolling farmland between Omagh and Armagh is some of Ireland's most idyllic. Armagh, with its two St Patrick's cathedrals, is the ecclesiastical capital of all Ireland, while nearby Emain Macha is an Iron Age site of European significance. Continuing towards Belfast the route passes through the apple orchards of County Armagh, and then Georgian Hillsborough, before slipping back into Belfast by the traffic-free backdoor of the Lagan Navigation towpath.

The route does such a good job getting in and out of Belfast, it is possible to almost completely ignore the city, but if there is time, take a look around the Botanic Gardens, and the town centre, including the Baroque Revival city hall.

Options

The Torr Head road from Cushendall to Ballycastle – an alternative Stage 2 – is the toughest road in Ireland, with gradients steeper than 20 per cent.

In fine weather the trip to cliff-bound Rathlin Island (Stage 3) is a memorable one, but as the weather along this coast is changeable, wait until close to Ballycastle before committing to a night on the island. There are morning and evening ferries – see Stage 3 for details.

The Derry–Belfast railway is an alternative to the inland section of the route (Stages 5 to 7).

Also worth considering is flying into Belfast and out of Derry. With a relaxed itinerary and including a trip to Rathlin Island, and possibly the ancient hill fort of the Grianan of Aileach from Derry (Route 2, Stage 1), a week's cycling could include time for exploring the two cities bookending the route.

The Glens of Antrim (Stage 2) and the Sperrin Mountains (Stage 6) are worthy

Route 1: Belfast to Derry (to Belfast)
Route 2: Derry to Donegal Town

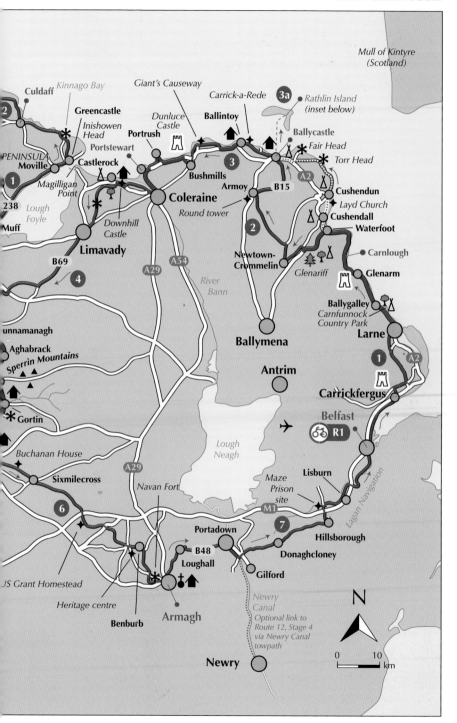

Mull of Kintyre
(Scotland)

Culdaff
Kinnago Bay
Giant's Causeway
Carrick-a-Rede
3a
Rathlin Island
(inset below)
2
Greencastle
Inishowen
Head
Dunluce
Castle
Ballintoy
Ballycastle
Portrush
Fair Head
PENINSULA
Portstewart
Torr Head
Moville
Castlerock
Bushmills
Armoy
B15
A2
Cushendun
1
Magilligan
Point
Coleraine
Laydd Church
238
Lough
Foyle
Round tower
3
Cushendall
Muff
Downhill
Castle
Waterfoot
Limavady
2
Newtown-
Crommelin
Carnlough
B69
A54
A29
Glenariff
Glenarm
4
River
Bann
Ballygalley
Carnfunnock
Country Park
unnamanagh
Larne
Aghabrack
Ballymena
Sperrin Mountains
1
A2
Antrim
Gortin
Carrickfergus
Belfast
Buchanan House
R1
Lough
Neagh
A29
Sixmilecross
Navan Fort
Maze
Prison
site
Lisburn
6
Lagan Navigation
M1
7
Portadown
Hillsborough
B48
Donaghcloney
US Grant Homestead
Loughall
Gilford
Heritage centre
Newry
Canal
Optional link to
Route 12, Stage 4
via Newry Canal
towpath
Benburb
Armagh
N
Newry
0   10
km

47

The Palm House Botanic Gardens, Belfast

cycling destinations in themselves, with many possible itineraries.

If you are heading on around the Donegal coast (Route 2), you could skip Derry and instead cross straight to Greencastle on the Lough Foyle ferry from Magilligan Point (Stage 4), saving yourself the rather tedious 30km or so north of the city.

On Stage 8, an alternative return can be made from Portadown to Belfast via Newry. Follow the canal towpath from Portadown to Newry and then join Route 12 to pass along Strangford Lough (see Route 12, Stage 3).

Getting to the Start

See the introduction for general information and contact details for transport services to and from Ireland. Below are the options to consider for this route.

By Air

If you are arriving at Belfast International Airport, some 25km west of the city, you can cut across country to Larne to join Stage 1, avoiding Belfast itself.

By Sea

Ferries from Scotland and Fleetwood dock at Larne – Stage 1 passes within a few hundred metres of the ferry terminal. Belfast also has ferry connections (see table on page 20).

By Rail/Bus

Belfast has rail connections to Dublin and Derry.

When to Go

Summer and bank holiday weekends can be very busy along the coast road. In spring or early summer (late April to mid-June) the yellow gorse flowers and the hedgerows fill with blossom and birdsong. The apple blossom in County Armagh usually comes out in early May.

Accommodation

Budget accommodation is limited on the first stage of this route. The first hostel is near Cushendall – well into Stage 2. The camping situation on the route is not wonderful either, with a number of sites all along the coast having changed into static caravan sites in recent years. Cushendall has a small campsite, and north of here the camping and hostelling options do improve. On the inland section, the Sperrins has hostel and camping accommodation. Derry, Omagh, Armagh and Belfast all have hostel accommodation. Bed and breakfast and hotel accommodation is plentiful along the coast and available in inland towns.

Maps

The Ordnance Survey Ireland/Ordnance Survey Northern Ireland (OSI/OSNI) sheet Ireland

North covers the whole route at 1:250 000 scale. For 1:50 000 coverage you will need the following sheets from the OSNI Discover series: 15 Belfast, 9 Larne, 5 Ballycastle, 4 Coleraine, 7 Derry, 13 Sperrins, 18 Enniskillen (only for about 6km), 19 Armagh, 20 Craigavon.

The OSNI Sperrins Activity map covers the area from Derry to the west side of Lough Neagh, including the north coast as far east as Dunluce Castle, at 1:100 000. The mountains themselves are covered at 1:25 000, and this map is an alternative to sheets 18, 19, 4 and 7, if you don't mind the 1:100 000 scale or are exploring further in the Sperrins. The route described here only just nicks a corner on the 1:25 000 section.

Onwards

This route connects with Route 2 at Derry. Route 12 from Dublin also finishes in Belfast.

STAGE 1
BELFAST TO CARNLOUGH

62km Low coastal route; gentle climb to 150m between Carrickfergus and Larne.

This stage starts from the Lagan waterfront in the heart of the city and heads along the shores of Belfast Lough. The first 11km is on cycleways until you reach the Loughshore Park at Whiteabbey. The stage then follows the main A2 to Carrickfergus, with its fine Norman castle and small harbour.

The construction of the Antrim Coast Road, approved in 1832, opened up the Glens of Antrim, which previously had been in much closer contact with Scotland than the rest of Ulster.

From Carrickfergus the route climbs to follow a road parallel to the coast before dropping down to the harbour town of Larne. North of here the stage joins one of Europe's great coastal roads. The Antrim Coast Road (from 40km) is seldom more than a few metres from the foreshore, which varies between stony, bright sandy beaches and jumbles of rounded boulders. Cliffs often come right down to the road, and in places there are short tunnels through rock spurs. This is one of the most geologically interesting areas in Ireland, or Britain. The variety of landscape and colours produced by the mixture of dark volcanic basalts, red sandstones and white chalks – to name but a few – makes this a spectacular and beautiful coast.

There has been a castle at Glenarm (57km) since the 13th century and the site has been the seat of the Earls of Antrim since the 17th century. The castle was rebuilt in its current Palladian style in the 18th century,

Carrickfergus Castle

Glenarm claims to be the oldest town in Ulster, its charter having been granted in 1636.

and the walled garden – one of the oldest in Ireland – also dates from this period. The castle is rarely open to the public, but you can visit the walled garden from May until the end of September, daily from 10am to 6pm (028 2884 1203, www.glenarmcastle.com). This stage finishes at the pretty harbour village of Carnlough.

On the Road

There are plenty of small shops along this stage, and a shopping centre in Larne (37km) opposite the tourist information centre. Camping supplies can be bought at T R Fultons, 28 Pound Street, Larne (028 2826 0288, closed Tuesday afternoons).

After Larne the next major town, and the next obvious ATM, is Coleraine on Stage 4, so take plenty of cash with you, and make sure you have the camping supplies you need (gas etc) preferably before leaving Belfast. This stage has a scattering of public toilets – see route card.

Carnfunnock Country Park (44km) and Ballygally (46km), which also has a shop, are the best places to stop for a break, but there are other choices.

Accommodation

The Carnlough area is not great for camping or hostelling, but the popularity of the Antrim coast means there is no shortage of bed and breakfasts. The best campsite along the route is at Carnfunnock Country Park, open Easter to October (028 2827 0541, www.larne.gov. uk/carnfunnock), although this is only some 40km north of Belfast. There is also a small site in Larne (Curran Court Caravan Park, 028 2827 3797, open Easter to September), which is handy for ferry connections (38km). If you want to push on further there are campsites on Stage 2, at Cushendall (16km) and Cushendun (20km). There is a very small camping/caravan site at Loughshore Park, Jordanstown (11km), which is the closest camping to Belfast – booking here is essential (028 9034 0058)

Options

This stage passes within a few hundred metres of the Larne ferry port, which has connections to Scotland.

STAGE 2
CARNLOUGH TO BALLYCASTLE

71km Moor and mountain; some long climbs; (or 48km via the Torr Head road, which is very steep).

Cyclists are spoilt for choice north of Carnlough. The quickest and flattest (though not *that* flat!) route is to follow the A2 all the way to Ballycastle, but this main road leaves the coast at Cushendall, and there are more scenic alternatives. The preferred route described here takes you through Glenariff, one of the Glens of Antrim, and high on to the Antrim Plateau before a freewheeling descent down another glen, Glenshesk, into the seaside town of Ballycastle. For a challenge, try the Torr Head road north of Cushendall. This is probably the toughest road in Ireland, with a rollercoaster series of climbs and descents with 20 per cent gradients.

'The magnificent nine': the nine Glens of Antrim, south to north, are: Glenarm, Glencloy, Glenariff, Glenballyeamon, Glenaan, Glencorp, Glendun, Glenshesk and Glentaisie.

The route into the glens begins at Waterfoot (14km) with a turn into Glenariff. Despite ascending to over 280m, the road, clinging to the northern wall of the valley, is never steep. During the climb the views behind to Red Bay and the Scottish islands open up, while to the left the steep valley walls climb from bright-green riverside pastures high into the mountains before disappearing into grey scree and brown bog.

Closer to the head of the glen, Glenariff Forest Park looks like a patterned bedspread thrown into the valley, with the different plantings of trees each a different shade of green. For a quick look at the park and waterfalls, the

Waterfall in Glenariff, one of the Glens of Antrim

Glenariff opened as a tourist attraction in 1889, as the railway company operating services in the area looked for an alternative to the declining iron ore trade.

lower entrance is best – turn at 18.6km, see route card – or for a longer look around take the upper entrance. There is a charge (£1.50 adults, 50p children) for using the park, but out of season there is seldom anyone around, and the tearoom, shop and visitor centre may be closed.

Above the park the route crosses high moorland and peat bog, and passes the lonely abandoned iron and bauxite workings (27km) above Newtown-Crommelin. After the village the route crosses open moor and pine plantations before passing the site of the 1559 Battle of Slieve an Aura (42km), where Sorley Boy

In 1824 Nicholas de Lacherois Crommelin set about building the village of Newtown-Crommelin in an extravagantly unsuccessful development scheme, which included roads and a port at Cushendun – Port Crommelin. Nicholas ran up large debts and the harbour was never built.

MacDonnell tricked Edward MacQuillan and Hugh MacFelim O'Neill into attacking into a bog – part of a long and complex history of internecine rivalry for supremacy in Ulster. Sorley Boy is buried at Bonamargy Abbey (turn at 46.8km, Stage 2a) at Ballycastle, which is now the best-preserved Franciscan Friary in Ulster.

The way back to the coast passes the round tower at Armoy (56km) – the site of a fifth-century monastery – before making the narrow pass between Knocklayd and Croghan at the head of Glenshesk, and freewheeling most of the way to the sea. This stage finishes at the ferry terminal for Rathlin Island.

On the Road
Waterfoot (14km) has a small shop. The forest park is by far the most pleasant spot to stop for a break on this section. After this there are no obvious places, so a roadside picnic may be needed. For the Torr Head route, Cushendall (16km) is the most convenient place to load up.

Accommodation
Ballycastle has a pleasant hostel housed in a harbour-front Georgian house, Ballycastle Backpackers (028 207 63612, www.bally castlebackpackers.net). There is also a small

51

campsite at Maguire's Strand (028 20763294), a couple of kilometres to the east of town along the road past the golf club and friary (see below). Apart from that there is plenty of bed and breakfast accommodation. Early in the day on the main route there is camping at Glenariff Forest Park, but call ahead (028 2955 6000). Also early in this stage (15.8km) is Cushendall Caravan Park (028 2177 1699, www.moyle-council.org), on the alternative route via Torr Head, so this means backtracking to reach the main Glenariff route. Another camping option is Glenmore House, 5.5km along Stage 3 (028 207 63584, www.glenmore.biz.

Options

The alternative route via Torr Head includes the charming coastal towns of Cushendall (16km) and Cushendun (23km), followed by dramatic coastal scenery culminating in the basalt cliffs of Fair Head, which rise to almost 200m above sea level.

From Ballycastle, Stage 4 continues along the coast, or Stage 3 heads to Rathlin Island.

STAGE 3
TOUR OF RATHLIN ISLAND

26km Some extreme,
albeit short, gradients over 15 per cent;
roads mostly sealed, but deteriorating
to bumpy tracks near East and
South Lighthouses.

Rathlin Island is one of the jewels of the north coast. The island has an internationally important seabird colony where, in season, puffins, fulmars, guillemots and kittiwakes, amongst others, can be seen. The wild coastline is dramatic, and there are fine views back to the mainland, but if the weather is miserable, there are better places to be than on a treeless rock 9km out to sea. The best plan is to wait and see what the weather is doing, and maybe book a day or so ahead.

> Charles Kingsley dubbed Rathlin a 'drowned magpie' in the novel *Westward Ho!*, because of its black and white cliffs.

> On 6 July 1898, the first commercial radio transmission across water was made from Rathlin Island to Ballycastle. The transmitter mast was set up near the East Lighthouse by Guglielmo Marconi's assistant, George Kemp, along with Edward Glanville and islanders.

Rathlin Island is a stepped plateau of basalt and limestone locked in by cliffs. It has been inhabited since Mesolithic times (6000BC), and its strategic position in the North Channel – so close to the coast at Ballycastle and 22km from the Mull of Kintyre in Scotland – has made it the site of some historically important battles.

The island has only a few roads and directions are barely necessary. The ferry lands at Church Bay in the centre of the south side of the island, and from there roads run to the South, East and West Lighthouses. The RSPB's Rathlin Island Seabird Centre is at the West Lighthouse, and there are usually telescopes and binoculars on hand, and RSPB volunteers ready to help.

Cycling around the island can be slow and bumpy, so leave luggage at accommodation if possible. There are also some steep short climbs – the road to the West Lighthouse is the worst offender. Adequate roads head off towards all three lighthouses, but the final sections of track (especially to the South Lighthouse) are rough.

> It was in a cave on the east of the island in 1306 that the persistence of a spider building a web inspired a fleeing Robert the Bruce to try again to drive the English out of Scotland.

On the Road

Facilities are sparse on Rathlin Island. There is a small shop near the harbour, but it has short opening hours, so it's best to stock up at Ballycastle, where there is a medium-sized supermarket by the turn to the ferry. There is not much choice for evening meals, apart from the National Trust's Manor House Guesthouse (028 2076 3964), where bookings are required. The visitor centre on the east side of the harbour may not be open outside of peak times.

East Lighthouse, Rathlin Island, with Scottish coast in distance

The East and South Lighthouses are quiet spots for a picnic, with panoramic views. The West Light is busier, but does have a public toilet.

There are four ferries a day in each direction, although the 'fast ferries' do not take bicycles – check for the latest timetable information (028 20769299 www.rathlinbally castleferry.com).

Accommodation
Rathlin has a camping barn that is as cosy and well equipped as most hostels (Kinramer Cottage 028 2076 3948, 16km), as well as an independent hostel (Soerneog 028 2076 3954) and bed and breakfast accommodation. Book accommodation and ferries in advance.

Options
None.

STAGE 4
BALLYCASTLE TO PORTRUSH

36.5km Coastal hills

This short stretch of coast surely holds a record for the most tourist attractions per linear kilometre, with the Giant's Causeway the star act. This stage follows the coastline as far as possible along good-quality B and local roads.

The Causeway coast is popular, however, so expect some traffic, especially around the Causeway itself and the Carrick-a-Rede rope bridge. This stage is also hillier than might be expected, and any ride right down to the shore means a steep climb back to the main route.

The first of the day's attractions is the diversion to the Carrick-a-Rede bridge (9km). This is a swinging rope bridge, originally built to access a salmon fishery, but now run by the National Trust, so there is a fee, as well as a car park, teashop and toilets. Also worth a short diversion on this stretch of coast is the picturesque harbour at Ballintoy (10km).

The National Trust also operates the visitor centre and car park at the Giant's Causeway (21km), but cyclists and pedestrians are not charged. The Causeway, with its whaleback shape of stacked hexagonal basalt columns, is a magical place. Maybe the giant Finn McCool didn't build a land bridge across to Scotland, but standing on the ridge of what looks like a super-sized children's building set, it seems just possible. There is a 15-minute walk down to the Causeway from the car park.

When the tramway from Bushmills to Portrush and the Causeway was opened in the 1880s, it was the first in the world to be hydro-electric powered.

Giant's Causeway, County Antrim

Bushmills is the oldest licensed whiskey distillery in the world. The licence was granted in 1608, but whiskey had already been made here for some time.

West of the Causeway the route follows NCN93 (National Cycle Route Network 93) alongside the recently re-opened narrow-gauge railway (21km) into Bushmills. The dune system behind Bushfoot Strand was laid down between 4000 and 6000 years ago. Bushmills is a charming Ulster town with tidy streets of white-painted buildings around a central diamond. The Bushmills distillery is the only one of the famous Irish whiskey distilleries open to the public (Mon–Sat, 9.15am–5pm, plus Sunday afternoons in summer, 028 2073 33218, www.bushmills.com).

After Bushmills comes a cross-country route to the coast at Dunluce Castle (30km), one of Ulster's biggest medieval castles. The Spanish ship the *Girona* wrecked near here in 1588 following the defeat of the Spanish Armada by the English. This stage then follows the main A2 road, before finishing on the promenade of the lively seaside town of Portrush.

After a storm in 1639, most of Dunluce Castle kitchen fell into the sea, taking several staff to their deaths.

On the Road
This is a popular area for visitors, so there is no shortage of places to stop and buy snacks or meals, including at Carrick-a-Rede and the Giant's Causeway. There is also a scattering of picnic areas along the coastal route. For somewhere quieter, try Ballintoy harbour, where there are toilets and, at the time of writing, also a small café.

Accommodation
The resort town of Portrush is swimming in bed and breakfast accommodation, but cheap places to stay are thin on the ground in the town itself. There are a couple of council-operated campsites just through Portrush on the way to Portstewart, on Stage 4 – Carrick Dhu

(028 7082 3712) and Juniper Hill (028 7083 2023), see www.colerainebc.gov.uk for more information on both. Carrick Dhu (1.8km) has 20 tent sites, Juniper Hill (2km) has five. Early in the day, for camping there is Glenmore House (5.5km – 028 2076 3584, www.glenmore. biz), and also early on an independent hostel at Ballintoy (9km, Sheep Island View, 028 2076 9391 www.sheepislandview.com), which also has camping facilities, and a youth hostel at Whitepark Bay (13km, 028 2073 1745 www. hini.org.uk).

Options
Trains run from Portrush to Derry and Belfast, via Coleraine.

STAGE 5
PORTRUSH TO DERRY

79.8km Undulating coast, then steep climb over the hills to Limavady

West from Portrush to the mouth of Lough Foyle the coastline upholds the high standard set on the previous day. The view from the cliffs at the Mussenden Temple (22km), with the cliff-foot strand sweeping away to the grey-green Inishowen hills on the far side of the bay, is one of Ireland's most photographed. A climb over the hills to Limavady (41km) follows, and the entrance to Derry from the east is also hilly

The approach to Derry through housing estates to the east is a crash course in Ulster politics, with slogans, flags and painted kerbs defining Unionist (red, white and blue) and Nationalist (orange, white and green) areas. The city has, until very recently, been the site of considerable sectarian unrest, but don't be put off – the people are friendly and helpful, and Derry's turbulent recent history is now even being marketed as a tourist attraction, with 'Black Taxi' tours and guided walks through the Bog Side.

Derry is the most complete walled city in Ireland or Britain, and these are also the last city walls to have been built in Europe (1613–18).

Mussenden Temple and Downhill Strand

THE SIEGE OF DERRY

In the late 17th century, Ireland was one of the battlegrounds in the wars following the ousting of Catholic King James II of England by his Protestant daughter Mary and her husband William of Orange. When forces loyal to James were about to be let into Derry, 13 apprentice boys grabbed the keys from the main guard and hoisted the drawbridge at Ferryquay Gate, closing the gates. The siege proper began in April 1689, as King James's forces swept through Ulster. James offered terms to the surrounded city, but was greeted with cries of 'No surrender'. The 105-day siege was broken by a naval force on 28 July.

Derry is also very cycle-friendly, with plenty of dedicated cycle paths and places to lock your bike. The city centre and its historic walls are best explored on foot. Be careful with your bike and lock it up well – bags have been stolen from bikes here, so leave them at accommodation if possible.

On the Road

This is a long stage, and there are not many facilities after Downhill village (turn at 23.5km). There are toilets and picnic spots at the National Trust Downhill estate (22km), and after that Windy Hill (29km) has great views, but is well named. Limavady (41km) has shops, banks, ATMs and a park.

Accommodation

There is no camping close to Derry and the city has no official youth hostel, but the independent hostel scene is active. Paddy's Palace (028 7130 9051) is a friendly place in older buildings on the fringe of the city centre. Another option is the Derry City Independent Hostel (028 7128 0542, www.derryhostel.com). Book ahead, particularly at weekends. The two campsites near Portrush – Carrick Dhu and Juniper Hill – occur very early in the stage, and have been included in Stage 4.

Options

If going on into Donegal (Route 2), consider following the coastal road along Downhill Strand, then short-cutting across Lough Foyle on the Magilligan Point ferry to Greencastle and picking up the directions for Route 2, Stage 1. This saves over 100km, and avoids the busy and not particularly attractive 30km or so from Derry to Moville.

Derry city walls with St Columb's Cathedral behind

Derry has a train service to Belfast. The station is on the east side of the river and is passed on the route into town (76.9km).

STAGE 6
DERRY TO OMAGH

56.3km Long climbs over the Sperrin Mountains, but the gradient is not too severe

After four, or even five days of coastal riding, the change in scenery is dramatic, as this stage heads across the Sperrin Mountains to the County Tyrone town of Omagh. The only real problem for the day is getting out of Derry itself, which despite generally being a very cycle-friendly city, lets itself down when it comes to routes to the southeast. Currently there is little option but to cross the Craigavon Bridge and turn right on to the busy, fast and narrow A5 for a couple of kilometres until the cycleway starts. As this is the NCN93 route, however, the cycleway situation may improve.

Fortunately the rest of this stage is a delight. As soon as the route begins to climb away from the River Foyle, peace and calm are quickly restored, and the green valleys filled with cattle and birdsong are all the more beautiful in contrast to the bustle of Derry.

The Sperrins are the largest mountain range in Northern Ireland, and have been designated an Area of Outstanding Natural

Gorse in flower, Gortin Lakes, Sperrin Mountains

Beauty. The route described here gives a taste of the mountains, with a sympathetic traverse climbing close to 300m after Gortin (40km).

The day's ride finishes with a downhill stretch to Omagh, the county town of Tyrone. Omagh has a busy and historical commercial centre, including a fine neoclassical courthouse.

On the Road

Pick up a little cash in Derry, as ATMs are in short supply until you reach Omagh. There are shops in the pleasant foothills town of Dunnamanagh (18km), which also has a public toilet, as well as Aghabrack (25.6km), Plumbridge (33km) and Gortin (40km). Any of these settlements makes a pleasant enough refuelling spot. Gortin Lakes (42.1km) has a picnic area as well as toilets.

Accommodation

There is a youth hostel on the main street in Gortin (40km, 028 8164 8346, www.hini. org.uk). Further on, Omagh has a nice out-of-town independent hostel – turn at 52.9km (028 8224 1973, www.omaghhostel.co.uk). There is a campsite close to Gortin Glen

Forest Park – Sperrin Cottages Camping and Caravan Park (44km, 028 8166 2288, www. sperrincottages.com). As you ride towards the court house towards the top of the main street, the Omagh tourist office is down a walkway to the right.

Options

The 'Discover the Sperrins Region Cycle Route Map' from Sustrans (available as part of the Northern Ireland pack) is a good place to start looking for ideas for exploring the area further.

STAGE 7
OMAGH TO ARMAGH

64km Rolling farmland;
a few short sharp climbs over drumlins.

The countryside between these two inland towns is some of Ulster's prettiest. The area also has historic and prehistoric interest. Stage 6 also passes two family houses with connections to presidents of the United States – a reminder of the rich contribution made to the New World by Ulster emigrants.

St Patrick's Church of Ireland Cathedral, Armagh

EMAIN MACHA/NAVAN FORT

The circular hilltop enclosure of Navan Fort is an Iron Age site of European importance. One explanation of the fort's ancient name, Emain Macha, links to the foundation myth in which Crunniuc mac Agnomain boasted that his wife Macha could outrun a chariot. She protested she was about to give birth, but Conor, King of Ulster, said she must run. As the chariot raced to the end of the field, she gave birth alongside it, and screamed out that all who heard her would suffer the same pain for five days and four nights in their times of greatest difficulty. When Queen Maeve of Connacht made war on King Conor, his men were struck down and his champion, Cuchulain, was forced to hold back the attack single-handed.

The first presidential connection is the James Buchanan House (7.7km). This is not open to the public, but the Georgian house is close to the road. Buchanan was the 15th president of the United States (1857–61).

The ascent of the wide and peaceful Cloghfin valley to a small col, followed by a freewheel down through pastures bounded by gorse hedges, leading up to dark moorland hilltops, is particularly beautiful.

The second presidential ancestral home is more accessible than the first. The US Grant Homestead (31km) is open to the public, and has been restored as a traditional two-room, mud-floored cottage, which is interesting enough in itself. John Simpson, great grandfather of 18th US president Ulysses Simpson Grant, was born here in 1738, emigrating to Pennsylvania in 1760. There are displays exploring life in a typical Ulster homestead, as well as describing Grant's achievements in America.

Further on, Benburb (48km) is a picture-book village, with stone terraces set high above the Blackwater river. Down in the valley the Benburb Valley Heritage Centre is a restored Victorian linen mill by the Ulster Canal. It is a little off-route, so check in the village that it is open.

Emain Macha (60km), or Navan Fort in English, on the outskirts of Armagh, is important in the mythology of Ulster, and the view is panoramic. Off to the east are the towers of the

St Patrick decreed that Armagh would be the ecclesiastical capital of all Ireland after he had built a church here in AD445.

twin cathedrals of Armagh, Ireland's ecclesiastical capital. The older, Protestant cathedral is built on the drumlin-top site of St Patrick's original church, while the Catholic one makes up for its less impressive position with lofty spires. The older part of the city maintains a rather conservative air – rather like the smaller English cathedral cities.

On the Road
The US Grant Homestead (31km) has toilets and a picnic area. Brantry Lough (40km) is also a pleasant place to take a break. There are shops at Sixmilecross (13km) and Benburb (48km).

Accommodation
Armagh has a youth hostel in the heart of the old town (028 3751 1800, www.hini. org.uk). The closest camping is at Gosford Castle Country Park (028 3755 2169, www. gosford.co.uk), which is approximately 11km southeast of the town on the Newry road (A28).

Options
The only onward route included in this guidebook is the next stage to Belfast.

The Battle of Benburb, fought to the west of the village in 1646, was the greatest military victory the Irish ever had over the British.

STAGE 8
ARMAGH TO BELFAST

80.9km Rolling farmland
and flat towpaths

This is a long stage, but the final 20km is along the flat and well-surfaced cycleway along the Lagan Canal. Despite the idyllic countryside early in the day, this is a stage on which Ulster's history – some of it troubled – is writ large.

Loughall (14km) – home of an apple blossom festival in May – is also where the Unionist Orange Order was founded in 1795 after sectarian fighting at the nearby Battle of the Diamond.

The Georgian mansion Hillsborough Castle, at the head of Hillsborough town (51km), is the official government residence in Northern Ireland, and has been the scene of protracted negotiations on the road to peace in the province.

A few kilometres further on, this stage passes the site of the former Maze Prison (55km), which was used to house paramilitary prisoners from 1976 to 2000. It was the scene of the 1981 hunger strikes. At the time of writing the prison was being demolished and the future of the site was uncertain.

> The Newry Canal, completed in 1742, was the first true summit-level canal (that is, a canal that climbs across a summit level or watershed) to be built in Ireland or Britain.

This area played an important part in the island's industrial history. The Newry Canal – which is followed for a few kilometres south of Portadown – was intended to move coal from the Tyrone coalfields to Dublin, but along with the Lagan Navigation (completed 1763) it played an important part in the development of the linen industry, and an economic upturn in Ulster in the latter part

of the 18th century. These two waterways provide some easy, traffic-free cycling. The Lagan Navigation is both historically interesting and, in places, very beautiful, as it passes through farmland and beneath overhanging trees right into the heart of Belfast.

On the Road
The service station on the way out of Armagh (800m) has a supermarket attached and is a handy place to pick up supplies. Loughall (9km) has a village shop. After that Portadown (20km) is the last big town before Belfast, and it does have public toilets and a tourist information centre. Crossing the A1 approaching Hillsborough needs to be done with care. Improvements are planned in this area and may affect the directions slightly. Hillsborough (51km) has some shops, but after that there is very little until you reach Belfast.

Options
The Newry Canal towpath cycle route can be followed from the 25.9km mark at Knock Bridge all the way to Newry, to join with Route 12 to Belfast via Strangford Lough. From Knock Bridge it is approximately 26km to the end of the cycleway towpath at Newry. Follow the A2 Warrenpoint signs in Newry to join Route 12, Stage 3 at the 18.8km mark, the Kilmorney Street turn.

Accommodation
The Belfast International Youth Hostel (028 9031 5435, www.hini.org.uk) has a cycle parking area (in the open) inside the secured car parking area. To reach it, turn off this route along the cycleway/footpath under the railway at the old gasworks (turn at 79.5km). Turn left on reaching a road, then continue straight on to a busy road junction at Shaftesbury Square (about 1km from the gasworks). The hostel is straight on through this junction, about 100m on the left. All Belfast hostels are busy, especially at weekends.

ROUTE 1 – BELFAST TO DERRY

Stage 1 Belfast to Carnlough

0.0		Belfast, Lanyon Place, by the quay, next to the vented tower. Head north (river to your right) along NCN9. There is some development in progress along the river so keep an eye out for signs
0.8	→	Cycleway passes through iron gate and passes in front of Clarendon Dock building
1.0	←	Pass down right-hand side of building then follow cobbled road zigzagging through old docks
1.4	←	Cycleway passes through blue iron gate on left – signed NCN93 but easy to miss
1.6	→	Cross road and continue along signed cycleway
4.5	↑	Cross busy road to the port and look for cycleway on far side signed NCN93 Whiteabbey
8.3	→	At Hazelbank Park, cycleway turns right and continues along foreshore
11.3	▲ WC	Loughshore Park toilets and camping
11.4	←	Cross road at lights and join A2 to Carrickfergus
13.3	♦	Spar Shop
17.4	O↑	Unsigned
17.6	⇨	Turn right if you want to visit the harbour and castle
17.7	←	'Castle Street'
17.9	←O	'Antrim Street'
	☆	Tourist Information
18.2	→	Station is on left, after turn
20.5	→	'Marshallstown Road B90'
23.4	←	'B149 Glenoe'
25.5	☆	Vale National School in ruins
27.7	→	'Raiganee Road'
	←	'Ballyhone Road'
31.9	↑	'Glenford Road'
32.2	→	'Carrickfergus Road'
36.4	→	'Casement's Brae', now in Larne suburbs
36.7	→	At T-junction
37.0	↑	'Station Road'
37.2	O↑	'A8 Belfast'

Stage 1 Belfast to Carnlough

37.5	O↑	'Ferries'. For tourist information turn left into shopping centre car park here
37.8	→	'Harbour'
38.4	▲	Campsite
38.5	←	'Bay Road' – continue straight on if you are heading for the ferry
38.9	←	Follow shore
39.1	☆	Chaine Tower
39.3	→	Join cycleway
40.3	→	'Glenarm' NCN93 join Antrim coast road
42.0	☆	Tunnel
43.4	WC	Drains Bay
44.4	⇦▲ WC	'Carnfunnock Country Park' 1km return trip, camping, gardens, café
46.7	♦	Ballygally shop
57.7	O→ ♦	At Glenarm. Shop on this corner
57.9	☆	'Glenarm Castle' 50m down road on left
	WC	On right at harbour
62.3	☆	Tourist information at McKillop's Shop
62.4		Arrive Carnlough. Stage ends at white stone bridge over road

Stage 2 Carnlough to Ballycastle

0.0		Carnlough Bridge, continue north along A2
0.1	♦	Spar shop
6.4	☆	View of rotational sheer, chalk landslip on coast to north
14.0	←	A43 Glenariff
18.6	⇦	Side trip to Glenariff waterfalls – signed 'Laragh Lodge' – bear right after 400m to stay on the glen road
21.1	▲	Campsite
21.4	⇦	To Glenariff Forest Park
23.3	→	'B14 Cushendall'
23.8	←	Unpromising road through the trees
27.4	☆	Statue on the left is 'The Drum' by Needsmyth – commemorates the iron workings on this site

Stage 2 Carnlough to Ballycastle		
29.7	→	'Cushendall/Cushendun Scenic Route'
29.9	↑	Ignore turn to left
41.7	←	Turn left and follow road to left over bridge signed 'Magherahoney'
42.7	☆	Look for a gap in the trees on left – this is where the Battle of Slieveanorra took place in 1559
52.3	→	This road was closed for most of 2008 – distance may not be exact
56.8	→	'Ballycastle B15' – round tower on corner (left)
70.1	☆	Tourist Information on left
70.3	O→	'Ferries'
70.5	▲→	'Ferries'; Ballycastle Backpackers on left
70.7		Arrive ferry terminal

Stage 2a Carnlough to Ballycastle via Torr Head (altern)		
14.0	→	A2 Ballycastle
15.8	▲	Cushendall Caravan and Camping Park
16.7	→	Cushendall clocktower, 'Layd Church'
17.0	←	'Layd Church'
18.3	☆	Layd Church on right
22.5	→	'Cushendun'
23.6	WC	Arrive Cushendun. Toilets are May to September. Also shop
24.0	WC	Plus beach access on right
24.4	→	'Torr Head road'. Straight on to Ballycastle via B92/A2
32.0		223m summit
33.9	☆→	'Torr Head ½'
34.5	↑↓	Car Park
35.5	→	'Ballycastle 7'
35.6	→	
37.4	▲	Summit 257m
37.8	→	
40.3	⇨	Side-trip to Murlough Bay
41.7	→	'Ballycastle 4'
44.1	→	'Ballycastle B92'
46.8	▲☆⇨	Turn for Bonamargy Friary and campsite
47.3	→	'Causeway coastal route'

Stage 2a Carnlough to Ballycastle via Torr Head (altern)		
47.5	☆	Tourist information on left
47.7	O→	'Ferries'
47.8	▲→	'Ferries'; Ballycastle Backpackers on left
48.1		Arrive Ferry Terminal

Stage 3 Tour of Rathlin Island		
0.0	→	At top of ferry ramp, head right
0.3	←	
0.4	→	Now on road to South Lighthouse
2.1	☆	Sealed road ends, gravel at first, slowly deteriorates
4.3	↑↓	Stop and walk last few hundred metres to South Lighthouse
8.4	↑	(Back at 0.4 crossroads) Now on road to East Lighthouse
8.6	→	'East Lighthouse'
9.8	→	'East Lighthouse'; becomes bumpy track
10.6	↑↓	At lighthouse
11.3	↑	Continue straight on at road
12.5	→	At school, signed 'West Lighthouse'
16.8	▲	Camping barn
17.6	☆	Enter nature reserve
17.8	☆	End of sealed road
18.9	↑↓	Arrive West Lighthouse
21.1	☆	Back at Kinramer Camping Barn
25.3	→	'Harbour ½'
25.8		Arrive harbour

Stage 4 Ballycastle to Portrush		
0.0	→	Start at harbour car park on North Street. Turn right out of car park
0.3	☆	Marconi memorial on right
2.3	→	'Ballintoy B15'
3.0	⇨	'Kinbane Head'. 2km round trip, 50m climb back
5.5	▲	Glenmore House B&B and camp site
7.4	☆	Portaneevy picnic area on right, sometimes mobile café here
9.2	⇨	Carrick-a-Rede 2km return and steep climb

Stage 4 Ballycastle to Portrush		
9.6	WC	at Ballintoy village
9.9	▲	Sheeps Island View Hostel
10.2	⇨	Ballintoy harbour – small café, WC. 2km return steep climb back
13.4	▲⇨	White park Bay Youth Hostel about 200m
14.0	⇨	To Port Bradden
14.9	→	'Causeway Road'
16.5	☆	Dunseverick Castle on right
21.0	→	'Giant's Causeway' follow signs to carpark
21.2	↑↓	Arrive car park
21.3	→	'Heritage Railway'
21.6	↑	Pass through railway car park
	→	'NCN93'
21.8	←	'Bushmills'. Follow sealed track along rail line
24.8	←	Cross station car park and turn left along shared cycle/ pedestrian path
25.0	↑	Ignore NCN93 sign to right and head straight on into town on bike track
25.5	O→	Copper Kettle on left is popular with cyclists. ATM and bank across street
25.6	→	'Bridge Street' (distillery is straight on)
25.8	←	'B17 Coleraine' (back on NCN93)
26.1	→	'Portrush 6 NCN93'
27.7	→	'Ballyclogh Road'
28.3	☆	Views over open farmland to Causeway coast
30.3	→	'Ballytober Road'
30.5	←	A2 (ignore NCN93 turn just before main road). Straight on for Dunluce Castle
31.0	☆	Magheracross viewing area on right
32.4	☆	White Rocks beach has WC on right
34.0	☆	Cycleway starts
34.9	←	Just before roundabout sign
35.1	←	Cross road and turn left on cycleway
35.7	O→	Leave cycleway and turn right
35.9	O↑	Turn left for tourist information centre
36.2	←	'Harbour'

Stage 4 Ballycastle to Portrush		
36.5	←	Just past toilets signed 'NCN93'. Route ends by beach information sign

Stage 5 Portrush to Derry		
0.0		From beach information sign at north end of Portrush strand, follow promenade (NCN93) along shore (sea to your right). This is where Stage 3 ended
0.4	☆	Dismount for 100m narrow section of shared cycle/ footway
0.8	☆	Cycle racks if you want to lock up and go to beach
1.0	↗	Follow cycleway up hill
1.8	▲	Carrick Dhu Caravan Park on left
2.7	▲	Juniper Hill Caravan Park on left
3.9	→	Follow main A2 – leave NCN93 cycleway, unsigned
5.9	O↑	'Coleraine A2'
6.7	O↑	Follow 'Coleraine A2' at Burns Road roundabout
7.1	☆	NCN93 rejoins – follow into Coleraine, watch for road crossings
11.7	→	At traffic lights continue on on-road cycleway
10.8	↑	Cross road join on-road cycleway
12.9	→	'NCN93' then cross Millennium Bridge cycle bridge
	→	After bridge 'NCN93'
13.1	←	'NCN93'
13.4	←	'NCN93'
	→	Unsigned. Join road (still NCN93)
13.7	O↑	Unsigned.
13.8	O↑	Unsigned. Join off-road cycleway after roundabout
14.9	→	'Cranagh Road NCN93'
20.1	☆⇨	Side-trip to Barmouth 1km return
21.4	→	Onto cycleway. Unsigned.
21.6	☆⇨	Side-trip to Castlerock 2km return
21.8	☆	Hezlett House – 17th-century thatched house and garden, National Trust, 028 2073 1582

63

Stage 5 Portrush to Derry

22.9	←☆⇨	'NCN93' through gate on left through woods. Turn right through Bishops Gate for Downhill Castle and Mussenden Temple
23.0	↗	Veer right at junction
23.5	←	Turn left after gate. If you want to visit lovely Downhill Strand and Downhill village go straight on and turn left at the main road; 1.5km return. Also hostel here. If you are heading to Magilligan Ferry continue on A2 at Downhill Village
24.7	→	'NCN93'
25.6	←	'Bishops Road'
28.9	☆	Windy Hill picnic area
32.4	⇨	Alternate route to Magilligan Point
33.7	↑	Ignore NCN93 turn (to right)
37.4	→	'Limavady B201'
39.6	←O	'Limavady'
41.4	→	'Town Centre' then Pass Tesco on the left and follow one-way system round to left
42.2	→	'Londonderry A2'
42.3	☆	Roe Valley Cycles on right
43.0	←	'Claudy B69'
44.0	☆	Roe Valley Country Park on left
51.3	☆▲	Summit 276m. Climb through tidy farms and villages
56.5	→	'Ness Wood Country Park 4'
58.6	↑	Continue straight on at crossroads
62.4	↗	Bear right, left goes to country park
63.6	←	Unsigned crossroads
65.2	☆	Ervey Wood Country Park
66.1	←	'Birch Road'
66.3	←	'A6 Belfast' – take care, fast and busy downhill section
67.0	→	'Ardmore'
73.4	←←	'Church Brae'
74.6	O↑	'Irish Street'
75.0	O↑	Unsigned
75.7	↑	'Fountain Hill' – very steep, short descent. Walk or take alternative route if unsure
76.0	←	Unsigned, at bottom of hill

Stage 5 Portrush to Derry

76.2	→	At traffic lights, Craigavon Bridge and River Foyle are in front of you
76.5	←	Side entrance to station
76.9	←	Turn left into car park then pick up path to left of station building which leads to quayside and bridge
77.9	→	Turn right to join cycleway along quay after bridge
79.8		Arrive quayside, across from Guildhall Clocktower

Stage 6 Derry to Omagh

0.0		Lough Foyle quay, on cycleway by water, from opposite Guildhall, with its distinctive clocktower, head towards bridge
0.9	←	Turn left over Craigavon Bridge
1.2	→	After bridge – fast dangerous section of A5 – consider using footway
2.4	→	'Prehen Boathouse'
	←	Join cycleway through park
2.5	☆	Foyle Search and Rescue
2.7	☆	Loughs Agency Visitor Centre
4.9	☆	Picnic area
5.2	☆	Picnic area
5.5	→ ATM	Cross road and continue right along cycleway. Shop and ATM at garage on left
5.7	←	'Woodside Road NCN93' – separate cyclepath ends
5.8	↘	'Rock Road NCN93'
5.9	←	'Foyle Crescent'
6.3	←♦	'NCN93'. Grocer, baker, PO and pharmacy across road
12.3	↑	Ignore NCN93 turn to left
18.1	→	'Plumbridge 9'. WC across road. Dunnamanagh has shop and pharmacy
18.1	←	'Lisnaragh Road'
23.0	⇦☆	Lough Ash Wedge Tomb 2km round trip
25.6	☆♦	Aughabrach – service station, shop, tea and coffee
29.1	⇦☆	'Clogherny Wedge Tomb'
33.8	←	'Heritage centre'
33.9	→	'Gortin Omagh B48'

Stage 6 Derry to Omagh		
40.2	↑	'B48'
40.3	▲	Gortin Hostel on right
42.1	⇦ ☆	Gortin lakes 2km return. Toilets and picnic area
44.8	☆	Gortin Glen Forest Park on left
44.9	▲ ⇨	Sperrin Cottages, Camping and Caravan Park
45.3	☆	Ulster History Park on right
51.1	♦	Gortnagarn has shop
52.9	⇦ ▲	Turn to Omagh Hostel – follow signs
55.3	↑	Cycle route turns left – continue into town on road
55.6	←	At traffic lights
55.9	→	'Town centre'. Continue up hill to courthouse
56.3		End in front of court house

Stage 7 Omagh to Armagh		
0.0		Omagh court house – head down main street
0.1	←	'Council offices'
0.4	→	'All other routes'
0.7	←	'Cooktown'
1.3	O↑	'Carrickmore B4'
1.9	O↑	Unsigned
2.8	☆	NCN92 joins from left
2.9	O↑	'Arvalee'
4.4	↗	'Sixmilecross 6' – bear right, no turn
7.0	☆	Deverney Bridge – Camowen River
7.7	☆	James Buchanan House
8.0	→	At crossroads
10.5	↑	At crossroads
13.9	→ ♦	'Beragh'. This is Sixmilecross village. Toilets, shops to the left
	←	'Ballygawley'
14.3	←	'Cloghfin Road'
16.3	↖	At fork in road
19.6	↑	'Cloghfin Road' (at crossroads)
27.2	↗	Bear right – no turn
28.1	↑	Cross busy A4 – careful
28.9	→	At T junction
29.3	←	'Grant Homestead'
31.7	☆	Grant Homestead on right
32.2	←	'Dergenagh Road'

Stage 7 Omagh to Armagh		
33.9	→	'Augnacloy'
34.6	→	'Augnacloy'
35.0	←	'Castletown Road'
35.6	↑	'Carricklongfield Road' (cross B35)
37.7	↗	Bear right only – no turn
38.6	↑	'Carrycastle Road'
38.8	↗	Bear right only – no turn
40.6	☆	Brantry Lough has walks
44.0	↑	'Drumflugh Road' (B45 crosses)
44.8	↑	'Drumflugh Road B128 Benurb'
46.2	☆	Battle site on right
48.9	☆ ♦	Benurb centre, castle on right. Shops and WC in town
49.5	→	'Armagh 7'
50.1	←	'Maydown Road'. To visit Benurb Valley Heritage Centre continue straight on here to 51.2km and turn right 3.8km; return to this point
52.7	←	Unsigned
55.4	←	'B115 Armagh' – can follow into Armagh if you are in a hurry
55.6	→	'Lisdown Road'
56.5	☆	Under old narrow-gauge railway bridge
57.6	←	'Navan Fort Road (NCN91)'
58.7	←	'NCN91'
59.5	⇦	'Kings Stables'
60.1	☆	'Navan Fort'
61.4	→	'NCN91'
61.6	←	Join cycleway
62.3	←	Cycleway leaves road
62.9	←	Cycleway joins road then turns left up steep hill
63.5	← ▲	'NCN91' – up steep hill. Entrance to youth hostel is on left
	←	'NCN91'
63.6	→	'NCN91 Cathedral'
63.7	☆	Church of Ireland Cathedral
63.8	←	'NCN91' - turn left through Market Place car park
63.9	←	'Upper English Street'
64.0	⇨	NCN91 turns off

Stage 7 Omagh to Armagh		
64.0		Arrive tourist information centre

Stage 8 Armagh to Belfast		
0.0		From Armagh tourist information centre, head north (towards spire of Roman Catholic cathedral)
0.2	O↑	'Loughhall B77'
0.8	←	At unsigned junction
	O↑♦	'Loughall B77'. Well-stocked shop before this roundabout
8.6	☆	Loughhall Country Park
9.0	♦	Village shop
9.6	⇦	'Battle of the Diamond' – use next turn
14.2	⇦	'Battle of the Diamond' – best turn to visit site
14.4	♦	Convenience store in garage
19.3	O↑	Now entering Portadown
19.9	O↑	'Portadown Centre'
20.3	→	Cross footbridge
20.4	↖	Continue on road at end of bridge heading towards church tower
20.6	→	At T-junction turn right and follow one-way, continuing to head towards church down Market Street
20.8	☆♦WC	Town centre, benches. Tourist information down street on right, also WCs
	↑	Through lights
21.0	→	Get off bike. Cross road at lights and walk up far side of Bridge Street (wrong way on one-way!)
21.2	→	Turn onto cycleway NCN9 and NCN94
21.3	→	'NCN9 Newry', along canal
24.9	☆	Moneypenney Lock
25.9	←	Leave towpath – onto road at Knock Bridge – carry straight on here for Newry via towpath, approx 26km
26.6	O→	'A50 Gilford' – can join cycleway on right before this roundabout
26.9	←	'Newmills'
27.3	☆	NCN 10 heads off to left
28.5	←	'Newmills'
29.9	←	'Plantation Road'

Stage 8 Armagh to Belfast		
30.0	→	'Waringstown 3'
34.5	→	'Annaghanoon Road'
35.3	↖	Road swings to left
36.3	→	'Banbridge A26'
36.4	←	Turn almost immediately left
38.0	→	'Banbridge B9'
38.3	←♦	'Lisnasure Road', 'Dromore 6'. Service station with shop on corner
40.3	→	'Dromore 4'
42.5	←	'Hillsborough'
50.6	↑	Cross busy and fast A1 – there is a central reservation but use extreme care. This junction is scheduled for improvement in 2009
51.5	☆	Hillsborough Forest on right, tourist information and Government House on left
51.9	↖	Bear left at bottom of hill
52.3	↖	'Culcavy Road'
55.4	☆	Site of former Maze Prison on left
55.5	→	'Blaris Road – NCN9'
58.4	←	'NCN9' – leave road; cycleway joins Lagan Navigation at Union Locks
60.8	↑	Towpath blocked. Follow NCN9 across car park, turn right at main road, keep heading in same direction as you cross junction at lights and rejoin towpath (on the same side of the navigation)
61.3	→	Cross river on bridge – small NCN9 sign
	←	Turn left after bridge
61.4	→	Past side of Island Arts Centre
	←	Turn left and join road over canal bridge
61.5	←	After bridge rejoin towpath – waterway now to your left
76.6	↖	Path leaves river by rowing club – follow NCN9 signs
76.9	→	'NCN9' – now on road
77.1	→	Cycleway starts again and continues right into city centre
79.5	☆	Gasworks area on left
80.3	↑	Cross road at lights and continue on cycleway
80.9		Arrive Lanyon Place, in front of Waterfront Hall

ROUTE 2
DERRY TO DONEGAL TOWN –
TOUR OF DONEGAL

Stage		Terrain	Distance (km)	Summit (distance from start/height)
1	Derry to Culdaff	Stiff climb from Greencastle; coastal hills	77.5	60km/275m
2	Culdaff to Clonmany	Low coastal terrain	55.1	6km/120m
3	Clonmany to Letterkenny	Steep climb over Mamore Gap	79.4	14km/240m
4	Letterkenny to Portsalon	Climb over Knockalla Mountains	47.9	40km/150m
5	Portsalon to Downies	Coastal hills	55.8	2km/80m
6	Downies to Bunbeg	Gentle climb into Derryveagh Mountains	67.5	49km/260m
7	Bunbeg to Portnoo	Some easy climbs	52.6	12km/150m
8	Portnoo to Carrick	Long climb up Glengesh	59.9	40km/280m
9	Carrick to Donegal Town	Coastal hills	45.6	40km/120m
		Total	**541.3**	

For route map, see pages 46 and 47

This is by far the longest route in the book, and also the toughest. The roads will hammer your spokes and spine into submission, accommodation is hard to come by, the road signs are rubbish, and if you break down there are precious few bike shops. In short, this is wild Ireland at its very best, but it's not for the faint-hearted.

Donegal is a geographical oddity, being part of the Irish Republic ('the south of Ireland' to some), yet it extends further north than Northern Ireland. Malin Head's latitude of 55°22'N would put it as far north as the Alaskan Panhandle, but the Gulf Stream keeps this coast a little warmer than it should be, and summer days seem endless – by late May the sun will be up by 4am and set around 9pm.

Options

To keep the distance down, consider bypassing Letterkenny by taking the Lough Swilly ferry from Buncrana (Stage 3) to Rathmullan (Stage 4), thus saving 76km in total. Likewise, if coming from the Northern Ireland coast, the Lough Foyle ferry from Magilligan Point to Greencastle will save 56km from the start of Stage 1, although this also skips Derry city (see Route 1, Stage 4, Options for details).

Another short-cut is to miss the Inishowen peninsula and Malin Head altogether, and instead go from Derry, via the Grianan of Aileach, directly to Lough Swilly, picking up the route from the 45km mark of Stage 3.

Getting to the Start

Below are the options to consider for this route.

By Air
Derry has an airport (www.cityofderryairport.com) about 11km out of the city on the way to Coleraine on the A2. This is a good centre for low-cost flights to and from England and Scotland.

By Sea
None.

By Rail/Bus
Derry has regular passenger rail services from Belfast and Coleraine, with connections to Dublin and Belfast. At the end of the route, Donegal Town has regular bus services to Dublin.

When to Go
It's hard to pick the weather up here, and there may be many fine spring days as well as awful summer ones. Consider travelling in May and early June, especially if you want to wild camp, as there are fewer people around.

Accommodation
To get the most out of the trip, seriously consider taking a tent. Cycle-camping isn't for everyone, but in this far northwest corner of Ireland there are some beautiful spots to pitch a tent. Hostels are also thin on the ground in some areas, particularly on the Inishowen peninsula (apart from Malin Head) and Fanad peninsula (Stage 4) – so you may have to resort to bed and breakfast in these areas.

Booking ahead is advisable for the towns, especially Letterkenny. Outside the peak season it's not unusual to find campsites not really expecting visitors, so call ahead to check they are open.

Maps
The whole route is covered by the Ordnance Survey Ireland North sheet at 1:250 000. For 1:50 000 coverage, the following sheets are needed: sheet 7 Londonderry, from the OSNI Discoverer Series, and from the OSI Discovery Series sheets: 1 Donegal, 2 Donegal, 3 Derry Donegal, 6 Donegal Tyrone, 10 Donegal, 11 Donegal Fermanagh Tyrone.

Onwards
This is one of the few routes in the book that is not circular, but it is easy to find a way back to Derry city.

Route 3 starts from Donegal Town and heads further down the coast and into the Fermanagh lakes.

Kinnago Bay, County Donegal

STAGE 1
DERRY TO CULDAFF

77.5km Coastal, stiff climb from Greencastle; hilly along coast.

Shipquay Street is the steepest commercial street in Ireland or Britain.

This is a long and tiring stage that begins with a heart-starting climb up Shipquay Street. After that it is off to the inland hills, with a climb to the ancient fort of the Grianan of Aileach. If this is too much climbing, skip the visit to the fort, instead taking local Cycle Route One north along Foyle Embankment, and either picking up the directions at Ballyarnett Country Park (26km) or along the A2 at Muff (30km). But the fort has great views of the route ahead into Inishowen – which will either inspire or intimidate. The imposing circular stone fort, or cashel, was a stronghold of the northern Ui Neill dynasty from the fifth to the 12th centuries.

Leaving Derry this stage passes the famous Derry murals and the Free Derry corner wall. This is the area where 26 people were shot, 13 fatally, by British Army paratroopers sent in to close down a Civil Rights Association march.

The entry into Inishowen is not too promising – the R238 is fast and busy – but things improve after Greencastle (56km) where, after a climb over the coastal mountains, this stage enters one of the most beautiful sections of the Irish coast. Kinnago Bay (65km), with dark-grey cliffs dropping to a semicircle of golden sand, is stunning. To the north of here the mountains flatten out to be replaced by a low, rocky, wind-blasted coast all the way to Culdaff.

It was along the cliff-bound coast to the west of Inishowen Head, at Kinnago Bay, that the Spanish galleon *La Trinidad Valencera* foundered in 1588.

Amelia Earhart landed at Ballyarnett to complete the first solo transatlantic flight by a woman – she was heading for Paris.

On the Road
Take plenty of cash (euros) – ATMs are thin on the ground from now on. There are shops at Moville (52km) and Greencastle (56km). Moville also has a bike shop (Ballynally Cycles, 074 9382410). After Greencastle the roads are slow going – while they are sealed, they are bumpy, and in some places badly potholed.

Accommodation
There is no hostel accommodation on this stage. Culdaff has a limited choice of other accommodation, but McGrory's (074 9379104, www.mcgrorys.ie) is popular. Wild camping is possible along the coast – see the section on camping in the introduction – but don't wait until you are close to Culdaff, where it is too populated.

Options
The Lough Foyle Ferry (074 9381901, www.loughfoyleferry.com) at Greencastle (56km) takes cycles and links to the County Derry coast at Magilligan. The whole of Inishowen can be short-cut by carrying straight on at the turn for the Grianan of Aileach (8.6km). When you reach the N13 (about 700m), continue straight on (the crossroads is staggered to the right). After another 600m you reach the turn at Stage 3, 46.7km.

STAGE 2
CULDAFF TO CLONMANY

55.1km Low coastal terrain

From Culdaff this stage climbs through a pass (180m) in the coastal mountains to enter the central valley in the finger of land leading out to Malin Head. The low rocky headland itself is far from beautiful, but has the kudos of being mainland Ireland's most northerly point.

The true Malin Head, down a bumpy track at the far western end of the peninsula, is less visited than the old Lloyd's signal tower, which has a road going to it, and is as far north as you can get without walking. The southern side of the peninsula is the better sheltered from the Atlantic, and there are a couple of sandy beaches – Five Fingers Strand and Back Strand. The village of Malin, with its buildings facing in onto a central diamond, is a fine example of a plantation settlement.

After Malin the route crosses the low sandy isthmus that now connects Doagh Isle to the mainland, before finishing at the neat town of Clonmany, just a stone's throw from the sweeping beach at Tullagh Bay.

On the Road

The approach to Malin Head is exposed and windy and can be extremely tiring. The route described here goes clockwise around the headland. The area around the Lloyd's signal tower, where there is usually a spot out of the wind, makes a dramatic lunch stop, watching the surging Atlantic.

There are a couple of small shops on the way out to the head, but it's best to get your day's supplies at Culdaff. Late in the day there is a rare ATM at Ballyliffin (53km), and an equally rare cycle shop (McEleney's Cycles, 077 76541).

Accommodation

Clonmany has a few bed and breakfasts, and there is a campsite a couple of kilometres down the road to Tullagh Strand at the start of the next stage (Tullagh Strand Bayside Caravan Park, 074 9376729). The 'No Camping' signs haven't appeared on the beaches around here yet, and it is quiet enough to consider wild camping. Accommodation might be tight during the annual Clonmany Festival at the beginning of August. Further back on the route there are two independent hostels on the Malin peninsula – the Malin Head Hostel (17km, 074 9370309, www.malinheadhostel.com) and Sandrock Holiday Hostel (18km, 074 9370289, www.sandrockhostel.com).

Options

If pushed for time, consider continuing along the R238 to Buncrana (17km approximately) and skipping the Gap of Mamore and Dunree Head coming up in Stage 3.

STAGE 3
CLONMANY TO LETTERKENNY

79.4km Steep climb over Mamore Gap

This stage takes in some stunning beaches at the start of the day, the historically interesting Fort Dunree in the middle, and the lovely shoreline of Lough Swilly towards the end.

Tullagh Strand is an early highlight – in fact consider visiting the day before. The sight of the long arc of dune-backed beach with the rock-strewn Urris Hills towering behind can be breathtaking in the evening light. Soon after the strand the road turns towards the Gap of Mamore (summit at 14km) – one of the steepest climbs in the book. It rises 280m over the 2km from the turn to the climb, with a few extremely steep switchbacks near the start. The views are back towards Malin Head and on to the long inlet of Lough Swilly.

Lough Swilly's suitability for large ships and its remoteness have made it the site of many pivotal scenes in Irish history – notably the Flight of the Earls (see Stage 4) and the capture of Wolf Tone. The lough was one of the three Irish Treaty Ports, and the impressive fortifications at Fort Dunree (turn at 19.8km) were part of the port's defensive cordon. You can often see porpoises here.

South of Buncrana (29km) the roads get busier, but this stage manages to get off-road, following an old railway embankment across tidal flats in the lee of Inch Island.

Donegal's largest town, Letterkenny, sits at the head of Lough Swilly. After the wilds of Inishowen, the bustle and the one-way system can be hard to take, but there is pretty much any sort of shop you could imagine here, as well as a wild and raucous social scene – particularly on Friday and Saturday nights.

Dublin-born barrister Wolf Tone, co-founder of the United Irishmen, took part in two French-backed invasion attempts (1796 and 1798). On the second he was captured at sea, off the mouth of Lough Swilly, and landed near Buncrana. He was sentenced to death by a Dublin court martial, but died in prison before the sentence could be carried out.

Fort Dunree guards the entrance to Lough Swilly

On the Road

Buncrana (29km) is a friendly place to stop for a break. There is a decent-sized supermarket as well as ATMs, and a picnic area with toilets by the foreshore (30km). A little earlier on Fort Dunree (19km) has picnic tables, toilets and a small café, in season.

Accommodation

For budget accommodation, Letterkenny has a hostel (Port Hostel, 074 9125315, www.porthostel.ie), but as it is often full with hen/stag parties, book ahead. The town is also well off for motel/hotel accommodation, and there is a cycle shop (Church Street Cycles, 074 9126204) and camping supplies at Aladdin's Outdoor Sports (78km, 074 9177905). Stocking up on fuel, especially gas cartridges, is a good idea.

Options

Letterkenny has bus connections through Bus Eireann (074 912130, www.buseireann.ie) to Dublin, Derry, Galway and Sligo. Consider taking the short-cut from Buncrana to Rathmullan on the Lough Swilly ferry (074 9381901, www.loughfoyleferry.com) – the turn is at 30.8km. However, be aware that this is a summer service only, and it is not certain whether it will continue to operate.

STAGE 4
LETTERKENNY TO PORTSALON
47.9km Gentle coastal ride, until Knockalla Mountains approaching Portsalon

North of Letterkenny the western shore of Lough Swilly, with its lush, gently sloping pasture and small patches of woodland, has a gentler aspect than the eastern shore. The sting in the tail of the ride is the climb over the hard quartzite of the Knockalla Mountains, before the descent to Portsalon. These mountains are part of the same structure as the Urris Hills (crossed at the Gap of Mamore in Stage 3), but the ranges have been separated by a glacial breach, now occupied by the sea lough, which is a true fjord.

Earlier in the day comes the faded glory of the port town of Ramelton (Rathmelton, 16km), which grew rich from the linen trade, and the strategically important town of Rathmullan (27km), where the Flight of the Earls took place. Also worthy of mention is Killydonnell Friary

> During its 19th-century heyday, ships from the Caribbean docked at Ramelton.

The Flight of the Earls marked the end of the old Gaelic order in Ulster. On Friday 4 September 1607 the Earls of Tyrconnell and Tyrone and the cream of Ulster's aristocracy sailed out of Lough Swilly into continental exile.

(turn at 12.1km) on the shores of the lough south of Ramelton. There are more impressive Franciscan ruins in Ireland, but few are in such a beautiful location. North of Rathmullan this stage enters the Gaeltacht – an officially Gaelic-speaking area.

The Portsalon area has some sandy, protected beaches. The village itself is attractive

enough, but it does get swamped with visitors on summer long weekends. During the week, outside holiday periods, many of the businesses are closed.

On the Road

Letterkenny is by far the biggest town in County Donegal, so stock up with any hard-to-get supplies before heading north or west. The next decent-sized town on the route is Donegal, in four days' time. ATMs are hard to come by en route, so take plenty of cash as well. Ramelton (16km) and Rathmullan (27km) both have reasonable-sized shops to buy lunch and places by the water to eat it, and are good for stocking up on supplies for the evening or next day.

The Urris Hills loom over the fortified entrance of Lough Swilly

Rathmullan, in particular, is popular with day-trippers, and so has good facilities. Portsalon does not have many shops.

Accommodation
There are no hostels in this part of the Fanad peninsula, but there is a grandly positioned camping and caravan park near Warden Beach (43km – Knockalla Caravan and Camping Park, 074 9159108). Note that there are 'Camping Prohibited' signs on nearly all the beaches in this area, and fewer bed and breakfasts than you might expect.

Options
The Lough Swilly Ferry (074 9381901, www. loughfoyleferry.com) from Buncrana (see Stage Three) lands at Rathmullan (Stage 4) during the summer months.

STAGE 5
PORTSALON TO DOWNIES

55.8km Coastal hills

The Fanad peninsula north of Portsalon is a world of gorse, heather and wild Atlantic breakers crashing onto golden strands. In the stretch before the Fanad lighthouse, Lough Swilly offers some protection, but after 'turning the corner' at the lighthouse, the coastline faces northwest into the full force of the ocean.

Along this shore are the sandy beaches of Ballyhiernan Bay (15km), before a swing south up the long inlet of the Broadwater to skirt the town of Milford (36km). After Milford the way heads north again, on the other side of the Broadwater. It was along this road that one of Ireland's most notorious murders took place – that of the much-hated landlord Lord Leitrim. Just north of Milford this stage passes close to a 'mass rock' (see note below).

> The notoriously predatory Lord Leitrim was bludgeoned to death on the road between Manorvaughan and Milford on 2 April 1878. The murder made news around the world, and served to highlight the harsh treatment of the tenantry in Ireland.

> At times of religious oppression in Ireland, Catholics resorted to celebrating mass in the open air, often on lonely hillsides, with a rock used to hold the sacred vessels. These rocks still retain their religious significance.

The day finishes with a visit to the tidy Gaeltacht town of Carrickart (or Carraighart) across the windswept tombolo of the Rosguill peninsula, and on to the fine sandy bay at Downies. (Note that the name Downings is also used for the town.)

On the Road
There are a few small shops en route (see route card). The way rather skirts Milford (36km), but if you take a detour to the centre of town there is a choice of food shops. There are also some picnic tables at the top of the town. The prettiest places to stop for a break are early in the day along the north-facing coast – try either the Fanad lighthouse (10km) or the beaches along Ballyhiernan Bay (15km).

Accommodation
There is a youth hostel 7km from Downies. Tra Na Rosann (074 9155374, www.anoige.ie) is signposted on the right just before reaching the town. Apart from that there is a beachfront campsite and caravan park in Downies itself, a few hundred metres past the stopping point of this stage (Caseys Caravan Site, 074 9155376).

Options
One alternative route from Fanad Head to Downies would be to continue straight on along the coast at the Kerrykeel turn (16.7km), visit Rinboy and then cut across the western Fanad to Leat Beg to join the Mulroy bridge (opened 2009) that connects with the main R245 road 1.5km east of Carrickart. This would give an approximate total distance of 36km from Portsalon to Downies (a saving of some 20km), and also allow more time closer to the attractive coast around Ballyhiernan Bay. If your map does not have the new bridge, the grid reference is 150 382, or just pick out the narrowest stretch of the bay immediately to the east of Carrickart.

The view from Errigal Mountain is worth the climb

STAGE 6
DOWNIES TO BUNBEG

67.5km Coastal hills;
gentle climb into Derryveagh Mountains.

This stage begins with a tour of the beaches and holiday homes of the Rosguill peninsula, before heading to the open moorlands and quartzite peaks of the Derryveagh Mountains, then turning back to the coast at the quiet fishing village of Bunbeg.

During the first part of the day the Rosguill peninsula encapsulates the best and worst of Donegal – some beautiful unspoilt coastline is interspersed with sprawling caravan parks and over-optimistic holiday homes. But the beautiful bits – just to the east of Rinnafaghia Point (5km) and the beach at Tra Na Rosann – are fantastic.

After the highs and lows of the coast it is refreshing to turn inland for a while and head for the hills. An unassuming turn off the highway at Cresslough (32km) leads through one of the prettiest valleys in the north. The climb is gentle, spinning along between meadows flecked white and yellow with wildflowers, the air is sweet with gorse and pine and the sky rings with birdsong. The white quartzite mass of Muckish Mountain rises to the right, and the valley opens out onto a high moorland of heather and gorse before narrowing to a low

Errigal (752m) is Donegal's highest mountain. Quartzite summit screes make the top look like a snow-capped cone all year round. It is a three-hour return trip to the summit from the car park at 51.6km.

U-shaped valley of small farmhouses, rich green pasture and fat sheep.

There is still a little more climbing to be done across the flanks of Errigal Mountain. By now the landscape, with its bare mountains and deep glacial valleys, has a very Scottish feel, which continues along the descent past the Poisoned Glen, Dunlewy Lake, Lough Nacung and on to the picturesque harbour at Bunbeg.

On the Road
There are few shops on the Rosguill peninsula, so stock up for at least the morning at Downies. A couple of lovely beaches towards Melmore Head are the best swimming spots (turn at 9.7km, and close to the road at 12.2km).

If you want to climb Errigal, consider skipping the tour of the Rosguill – saving approximately 18.5km – to ensure you have enough time.

Accommodation
Early in the day you pass Ireland's most northerly hostel, Tra Na Rosann (turn at 10.6km

– 074 9155374, www.anoige.ie), off the road to Melmore Head. In 2007 and 2008 it didn't open until late May, and was also not well signed – so check locally for directions. Also up here is Rosguill Caravan and Camping Park (11km, 074 9155766). The new Errigal Youth Hostel (55km) is the best place to stay later in the route. Bunbeg, at the end of the day, has bed and breakfast accommodation.

Options

None.

Every year 'Marys' from Ireland and emigrant Irish communities compete to be crowned 'Mary From Dungloe'. The pageant and international music festival attracts tens of thousands of visitors from late July to early August.

STAGE 7
BUNBEG TO PORTNOO

52.6km Some gentle climbs

Some of the coastal sections on this stage are a rather grim mixture of ribbon development, power lines and undistinguished houses. But on the plus side, the climb over the low pass from Crolly to Dungloe is a gem, while the descent passes a lovely, dark-watered lake studded with low islands. Dungloe (21km) is a tidy and friendly commercial town.

The area bounded by the Gweebarra river to the south, the Gweedore to the north and the Derryveagh Mountains to the east is known as the Rosses. This is an area of undulating granite with small lakes and windswept heathery moors, where glaciers have dumped thousands of large boulders.

Traditionally, the Rosses had a relatively high population density, and maintained the subsistence agriculture characteristic of much of the west of Ireland in the 19th century. Ireland's recent development boom has robbed the area of much of its traditional charm – although with better housing and more prosperous towns it is a much nicer place to live!

The area to the south of Dungloe – which by some definitions doesn't even count as the Rosses – maintains some of the traditional landscape. The day finishes at the small fishing and holiday village of Portnoo.

On the Road

There are a few shops in Bunbeg, including a pharmacy – just turn left at the R257 crossroads after leaving the pier (1km). Crolly has a big supermarket (6km) and Dungloe has a choice of shops, including a big 'Cope' (Co-op). Lough Craghy (19.2km) is a pleasant spot for a break,

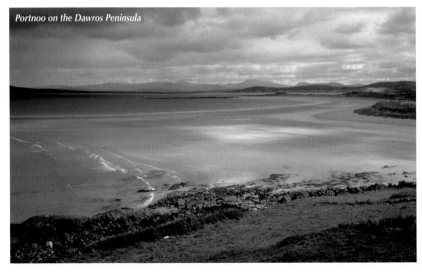

Portnoo on the Dawros Peninsula

as is Dungloe (21km), which has some benches in front of the Bank of Ireland, where there is also an ATM. At the end of the day Narin and Portnoo both have shops, but they sometimes close early out of peak season.

Accommodation

Narin (50km) has a small caravan and campsite, Dunmore Caravans, which manages to evade the telephone directory. There is a larger site further round the peninsula on Stage 8, at Tramore Strand – turn at 7.3km (Tramore Caravan and Camping Site, 074 9551491) – but this is a little out of the way. The nearest hostel is the Drumbaron Hostel, 18km along Stage 8 on the diamond at Ardara (074 9541200). Narin and Portnoo have bed and breakfast accommodation.

Options

None.

STAGE 8
PORTNOO TO CARRICK

59.9km Long climb up Glengesh

The small peninsula between Gweebarra Bay and Loughros More Bay is a temperamental beast. On a warm sunny day you might be in the Mediterranean, but when squalls pile in from the west, the wind, which has been gathering speed since Newfoundland, drains away body heat in an instant.

At the base of the peninsula, Ardara (18km) is a pleasant settlement town with a central diamond and a choice of supermarkets on the main street. After this, a long climb through Glengesh dominates the remainder of the day. The valley follows the typical Irish pattern of a steady climb along the floor of a glacial valley followed by a series of switchbacks and steep sections over the valley head.

After the pass comes the descent into scenic Glencolmcille (44km) – a place of spiritual importance because of its links with one of Ireland's most important saints, St Columba (or Colm Cille in Old Irish). There are plenty of places to stay here, and plenty of good reasons too – nice beaches in particular – but there has been a fair amount of development in recent years, so consider pushing on to the rather more established village of Carrick.

St Columba (Old Irish – Colm Cille) is one of Ireland's three patron saints (along with St Patrick and St Brigid). In the sixth century he founded monasteries at Derry, Durrow and Iona in Scotland.

Slieve League Cliffs, County Donegal

On the Road

Ardara (18km) is the best place to stock up on supplies for the day, but bear in mind that they will have to be carted over Glengesh. There is also internet access at the Spar supermarket and a bike shop (Byrne Bikes, 074 9541658 – on the way out of town towards Glengesh). Glencolmcille has a couple of shops, as does Carrick – which is a good base for visiting the Slieve League Cliffs, by some accounts the highest sea cliffs in Ireland. Directions to the cliffs are provided in a separate route card.

Accommodation

On the previous stage you might have pushed on to the caravan and camping park at Tramore Strand (70.3km, 074 9551491). Ardara (18.8km) has a hostel (Drumbaron Hostel, 074 9541200). The Glencolmcille area is spoilt for choice, with the Dooey Hostel (44.6km, 074 9730130) and the Malinbeg Hostel (turn at 48.6km, 074 9730006, www.malinbeghostel.com). Just through Carrick (on Stage 9) is one of Ireland's best hostels, the Derrylahan Independent Hostel (3.1km, 074 9738079, derrylahan@eircom.net), which also has good facilities for campers.

Options

To save time, cut across from Ardara to Killybegs (Stage 9) via the N56 and R263 (17km). Continue straight on at the Glencolmcille turn (21km).

Alternatively, taking a day to climb Slieve League and see the cliffs is a good way to give cycling legs a change (see route card). The detour to Malin Beg is worth a look, as there is a stunning sheltered beach and bay at Silver Strand.

STAGE 9
CARRICK TO DONEGAL TOWN

45.6km Coastal hills

After a week or more on the road the call of civilisation grows, and it's strange how Donegal Town (population about 2500) actually seems like a big place after days in the wilds. But before reaching the town there is some pleasant scenery to pass through, as well as the fishing port of Killybegs (19km).

One of the most interesting features of the route is the slow transition in the landscape from the metamorphic rocks and bare mountains of Atlantic Ireland to the lower relief produced by glacial deposition. The westward limit of debris from the last glaciation is just to the west of Killybegs, and by the time you reach Donegal, upland Ireland seems far behind.

On the Road

There are plenty of shops on this stage, including Kilcar (6km) and Killybegs (19km). The latter is a pleasant place to take a break and have a look at the fishing boats. Donegal has a good bike shop – The Bike Shop, on Waterloo Place – turn left just before the river (074 9722515).

Accommodation

For budget accommodation, try the Donegal Town Independent Hostel (074 9722805, lincunn8@eircom.net). There is an An Óige franchise hostel about 8km to the north-west of town at Drimarone (Blue Stacks Hostel, 074 9735564 www.anoige.ie). On

---

DONEGAL TOWN

Donegal Town's fine central diamond marks it out as an Ulster plantation town, but its history goes back further. The town was home to the O'Donnells from the 15th to the early 17th century. After the Flight of the Earls in 1607 the castle and lands were given to Basil Brooke, an English captain, who added a Jacobean wing to the castle, which had been begun by the O'Donnells in 1505. Earlier still, there was a Viking fort here.

For more recent history there is the Donegal Railway Heritage Centre in the old railway station building, which tells the story of the narrow-gauge railways that were once a vital part of the Irish economy.

The name Donegal (in Irish Dun na nGall) means 'fort of the Gall', or foreigners – this may relate to the Viking settlement that was once here.

route (27km) is the Blue Moon Hostel and Camping at Dukineely (074 9737264).

Options

The stage is a simple one that could be speeded up by staying on the R263 and then the N56 after Killybegs. The route described here takes the coast road from Carrick, as well as following a quiet track (turning at 21.7km), which is slightly rough in places, over the peninsula to the east of Killybegs. The route ends only 70km from the start at Derry. Donegal Town has five or more buses a day to Dublin.

ROUTE 2 DERRY TO DONEGAL TOWN

Stage 1 Derry to Culdaff		
0.0		Derry, Shipquay Gate. Head uphill through the gate
0.2	O→	At the Diamond, turn right into Butcher Street
0.4	☆◆	Pass through Butcher Gate. Bees Cycles just to the right
0.6	↑	At crossroads. This is a good place to see the murals and 'Free Derry' wall
0.6	→	Almost immediately right
0.7	←	Unsigned street – Bloody Sunday Memorial is straight on here
1.0	←	'Rosemount, Creggan'
1.2	↑	Need to be in right-hand lane for straight on
1.4	☆	Pass Brook Park
1.7	O↑	Rosemount roundabout
2.2	←	'Glenowen'
2.4	→	'Groarty Road'
6.0	☆	80km/h speed limit signs – crossed into Republic
6.4	↑	At crossroads
7.4	↑	At crossroads
8.0	☆	Views of Lough Swilly to front
8.6	←	'Grianan of Aileach'
10.5	←	'Grianan of Aileach '
11.1	↑↓	Arrive car park at Grianan of Aileach
11.8	←	Back at road turn left
12.8	←	Unsigned
14.0	↗	Road veers right
15.3	→	Back on road you came in on

Stage 1 Derry to Culdaff		
15.5	↑	At crossroads
16.9	←	'Whitehouse Road'
19.2	→	Unsigned crossroad
22.9	←←	Turn left and almost immediately left again at roundabout onto cycleway
23.4	→	Cycleway crosses road at lights
	→	At lights
23.8	↖	Cycleway forks – take the left
24.3	↖	Bear left on cycleway
25.7	←	Cross road and continue on cycleway to right
25.9	←O	'Ballyarnett' – easier to join road here
26.2	→	'Cornshell Fields'
26.3	←	Join cycleway and stay on main, wide cyclepath through Ballyarnett Country Park
26.8	←	Join road
26.9	←	Through stone gateposts
27.1	→	At road
28.6	☆	Cross border
30.9	←	Onto R238 at Muff
43.3	◆	Service station with shop
45.0	⇦	Short-cut to Culdaff
52.3	◆	Moville has shops and bank (no ATM)
52.6	◆	Ballynally Cycles on left
56.1	☆	Greencastle Maritime museum and planetarium
56.4	☆	Foyle Ferry from Magilligan Point on right
56.5	◆ WC	Views across Lough Foyle
56.8	⇨	Turn to see castle – but no access
57.4	↑	'Ballymacarthur Road'
60.7	△(277)	Summit – views forward into Inishowen
62.2	←	'Kinnago Bay'
63.1	→	'Kinnago Bay'
64.9	→	Turn to bay – steep
65.2	↑↓	Kinnago Bay car park
65.5	→	Back at turn to bay – 'Carrowmenagh 6'
68.9	↗	'Tremone Bay 1'
69.8	↗	Unsigned
70.2	⇨	Leads to pretty bay, rocky foreshore
72.2	→	'Culdaff'

Stage 1 Derry to Culdaff		
76.8	→	'Culdaff R238'
77.5		Arrive Culdaff centre by old pump

Stage 2 Culdaff to Clonmany		
0.0		Culdaff by memorial pump, head towards the shops
0.1	→	'Bunagee Pier'
1.0	⇨	Side-trip to Bunagee Pier – 2km return
2.7	↗	'Malin Head 16' – road swings right
4.5	♦	Food shop
4.7	→	Unsigned
5.1	↖	'Malin Head 15'
5.8	↖	
12.7	→	At T-junction
15.3	↑	'Malin Head R242' (at crossroads)
17.2	▲	Malin Hostel
17.4	↖	Malin Head
18.4	→▲⇧	At crossroads continue straight on for Sandrock Hostel, about 1km
20.3	☆	Picnic area
21.9	⇦	Rough track to left is to real Malin Head – 3km return
22.3	←	Towards Lloyd's Tower
23.1	↑↓	Top of car park
23.8	←	Back at road
25.3	♦	Old Curiosity Shop
26.0	☆	Malin Head meteorological station
26.7	↑	'R242 Carndonagh'
29.1	↗	'R242 Carndonagh'
31.6	↗♦	'Malin R242'. Small shop on corner
33.9	⇨	Five Fingers Strand turn
39.2	♦▲	Malin village, central diamond. Shop, Malin Hotel across diamond
39.3	→	'R242 Carndonagh'
42.1	→	Just after Glennagannon river bridge
43.8	↑	'Ballyliffin 9'
45.1	→	'Ballyliffin R238'
50.1	⇨	Doag Famine Village (8km return)
52.5	♦	

Stage 2 Culdaff to Clonmany		
	⇨	Pullen Strand 2.5km return
52.6	♦	Shop at Ballyliffin
53.1	♦	McEleney's Cycles 074 9376541
53.2	♦ ATM	Service station with shop and ATM
54.0	↖	Road bears left
54.7	→	'Mamore Gap'
55.1		Stage ends at Diffley Garden – rest area, benches etc. Tourist information sign. Mcdonald's Bar is across the road and there is a small shop

Stage 3 Clonmany to Letterkenny		
0.0		Diffley Garden – head left along road
0.1	↖	Bear left at car parking area
0.4	↗	'Tullagh Bay'
1.6	☆	Glenelvin Waterfall
2.3	⇨▲	To Tullagh Strand 3km return. Tullagh Strand Caravan Park 200m down this road
4.1	↑	'Lenan Pier'
6.3	♦	Dunaff has PO and shop on right
7.4	↗	Bear right
9.5	←	At crossroads
10.8	↑	To beach car park
	↑↓	Turn around at car park
10.9	→	After leaving car park
12.3	→	Signed 'Viewpoint'
14.1	☆	St Eigne's Well shrine
14.3	△(238)	Steep climb
15.2	→	Unsigned turn
19.3	→	At T-junction
19.8	⇨	To Fort Dunree (2km return)
	↖	Bear left if not going to the fort
22.3	♦	Shop on left
23.5	♦	Service station and small shop
24.4	↗	'Buncrana'
27.1	↗	'Buncrana'
29.1	→	At T-junction
29.6	↖	Road swings round to left through Buncrana centre
29.8	♦	Large supermarket through alley on right
29.9	→	'Church Street'

Stage 3 Clonmany to Letterkenny		
30.1	↑	At crossroads
30.5	WC	Toilets and picnic area in park on right
30.8	⇨	To Rathmullan Ferry 0.4km
30.9	→	At T-junction
31.1	♦ ATM	At service station
31.6	O↗	'Derry R238'
37.9	♦	Service station and shop
39.1	→	'Inch Island'. If R238 is not too busy you can carry straight on
40.6	←	Just before Inch Island causeway
43.7	→	'Burnfoot R238'
44.1	♦	Shop on right
44.3	ATM	At service station
44.6	→	'R239 Letterkenny'
46.7	→	Where R239 turns left, take small road to right
47.7	←	Through gate and onto gravel track
48.0	↑	Through another gate, views of Inch Island as track climbs to top of embankment
50.4	↑	Continue straight on down track – no access problems for bikes
50.9	←	Unsigned
51.0	→	Unsigned
51.9	→	Unsigned
52.3	↑	At crossroads
55.4	→	Towards Lough Swilly – signed Burt Gun Club but access OK
55.6	↗	Bear right at junction
55.8	←	Turn left to cross old railway causeway – watch out for walkers
56.6	↖	End of causeway bear left
59.1	→	At T-junction
60.6	←	Signed 'Dillon Car Sales'
66.0	→	On to N13
67.8	☆	Picnic area on left
68.1	←	Small road takes you off N13
	→	At T-junction Newtown Cunningham Post Office in front
68.3	↖	Straight on would take you to main road
69.1	←	Unsigned
69.8	→	At N14, turn right
69.9	←	Turn left after 60m

Stage 3 Clonmany to Letterkenny		
71.5	↗	Road bears right by concrete plant
75.5	↑	At crossroads
76.3	→	At crossroads just before concrete plant
77.3	←	Onto busy road by tourist information sign
77.6	O↑	Port roundabout. Turn left for tourist information centre
78.0	♦	Aladdins Outdoor Sports
78.6	↖O	'Town Centre' – one-way system starts
78.8	▲⇨	Port Hostel down street on right
79.1	↑	At lights
79.4		Arrive Market Square – benches and picnic area

Stage 4 Letterkenny to Portsalon		
0.0		Letterkenny Market Square. Follow one-way down Main Street
0.1	←	'Oliver Plunkett Road' – before library
0.3	←	One-way system
0.4	↑	At lights
1.0	O↑	'Ramelton R245'
1.3	O↑	'Milford'
1.5	←	'Gortlee'
2.2	♦	Handy small supermarket
2.5	←	'Auganinshin Abbey'
3.5	⇦	Turn to abbey
4.1	↑	'Letterkenny Golf Club' (at crossroads)
5.8	←	Unsigned
7.1	→	At T-junction
10.6	↑	'Killydonnell Friary 2'
12.1	⇨	Killydonnell Friary 500m return
13.2	☆	Views of Derryveagh Mountains
13.4	←	'Ramelton 3'
13.5	→	'Ramelton 3'
13.9	←	'Ramelton 2'
16.1	↑	'Milford 9'
	↖	Road swings left
16.4	↗	Road swings right
16.6	♦	Shop on left
16.7	→	'Rathmullan 10' just over bridge

Stage 4 Letterkenny to Portsalon		
17.2	⇨	Turn here for good view of town across river
27.2	↑	'Swilly Ferry'
27.4	↑	Towards ruined priory
	☆	Rathmullan Priory
27.6	☆	Flight of the Earls of Rathmullan Heritage Centre
27.7	←	Turn left; ferry and foreshore area to right
28.0	→	At T-junction
28.3	→	'L5442'
30.1	→	'At T-junction'
37.7	☆	An Gaeltach
42.9	WC	Warden Beach
43.3	⇦▲	Knockalla Camping 1.2km
43.6	→	'Portsalon R268'
45.3	→	'R246 Portsalon'
46.5	→	'R246 Portsalon'
47.9		Arrive Portsalon Pier, Swells shop on right

Stage 5 Portsalon to Downies		
0.0		Portsalon quay by Swells Watersports – head up the hill
0.2	→	At T-junction
2.2	→	Unsigned
2.6	←	Unsigned
3.4	→	At T-junction
5.6	↖ ♦	Road veers left – avoid road to right. Small shop at this junction
6.6	→	'Pollet Great Arch'
6.9	⇨	'Pollet Great Arch' 2km return and a 2km walk
9.1	→	'Cionn Fhanada'
10.7	↑↓	Lighthouse car park
11.7	♦	Lighthouse Tavern does some food
12.3	↑	'Kerrykeel'
15.4	⇨	'Beach' (Ballyhiernan Bay) 1.5km return
16.7	←	'R247 Kerrykeel'
18.1	♦	Small supermarket
22.8	→	'R247 Kerrykeel'
	♦	Small shop on corner
23.8	♦	Shop and post office
27.1	↗	'L1092'
27.9	→	'Kerrykeel R246'

Stage 5 Portsalon to Downies		
30.3	♦	Shop
	→	At crossroads
30.3	♦	Shop on corner
34.9	→	'Milford town centre'
36.4	→	'R245 Carrickart' (turn left for Milford town)
38.4	☆	Mass rock
40.6	☆	Site of Lord Leitrim murder – Glen turn
47.5	→	Just before service station
52.0	♦	Carrickart has choice of shops, pub, hotel
52.2	→	'Downies'
53.7	▲⇨	Tra Na Rosann Hostel, turn here
55.8	WC ▲♦	Arrive Downies, beach, WC, shops

Stage 6 Downies to Bunbeg		
0.0		Centre of Downies by turn to beach. Head uphill past caravan park
0.5	⇦	Side road leads to small park and memorial to lost at sea, and McNutts Tweed factory – 300m return
1.3	↖	Signed 'Fish Shop'
2.4	←	Unsigned
3.0	↑	At crossroads
3.5	←	'Atlantic Drive'
5.3	⇦	To beach
8.8	←	'An Meail Mor'
9.7	⇦	To surf beach 1km return
10.6	⇦▲	Turn to Tra Na Rosann Hostel approx. 150m
11.2	▲	Parc Rosguill – caravan and camping
12.2	☆	Pleasant beach close to road
12.4	↑↓	Turn around at entrance to caravan park
16.1	←	Back at road – T-junction
16.2	☆	Rest area on left – views over Mulroy Bay
17.4	☆	From small summit views of Mulroy Bay Bridge
20.3	↑	Back at road to Carrickart
21.1	↗	'Cresslough'
22.5	→	At T-junction rejoin main road by church

Stage 6 Downies to Bunbeg		
29.9	⇐	Side-trip to Doe Castle
31.4	→	At crossroads
31.9	☆	Pass nature reserve
32.1	↑	Road joins from left
32.5	→	Join N56 at T-junction
	♦	Cresslough has post office and shop
33.3	←	Unsigned turn, just past house with columned front porch
40.8	←	'Kilmacrenan' – at T-junction
42.1	→	'Goath Dobhair'
49.0	△(295)	
51.6	☆	Car park for Errigal Mountain
52.9	☆	View of deserted village and Poisoned Glen
53.8	⇐	Side-trip to Poisoned Glen and Dunlewy Lake
55.1	▲	Errigal Youth Hostel
55.2	♦	Roarty's foodstore and takeaway – open until 9pm
58.5	←	'N56 An Clochan'
61.8	→	'R258 Bunbeg'
66.5	↑	'Pier'
67.5		Arrive Bunbeg pier

Stage 7 Bunbeg to Portnoo		
0.0		At corner of pier, by stone steps
1.0	→	'R257' (turn left here for shops)
5.4	→	'N56 Croithli'
6.7	♦	Crolly has shop at service station
7.0	←	'Cro na nCuigeadh' (just before bridge)
11.5	→	Unsigned road
11.6	☆	Pass former National School
19.2	☆	Nice spot for a break by Lough Craghy
20.7	↑	Cross N56
21.2	♦	Lidl on right
21.8	☆	Tourist information
21.9	→♦ ATM	Down Dungloe main street. Shops, bank and ATM
22.1	←	'An Machair'
23.8	↗	'An Machair'
24.8	←	'Min na Croise'
28.0	←	'Glenties' (at crossroads)
31.2	→	'Glenties'

Stage 7 Bunbeg to Portnoo		
34.2	→	'N56 Glenties'
38.8	♦	Shop in service station
39.9	♦	Shop
40.5	☆	Cross Gweebarra river
45.3	→	'R261 Narin'
49.9	→	'Narin, Portnoo'
50.5	♦	Shop
50.7	⇒	Access to each and small campsite at Narin
52.4	♦	Shop
	→	'Harbour' (steep road)
52.6		Arrive Portnoo harbour

Stage 8 Portnoo to Carrick		
0.0		Portnoo harbour, top of slipway, head uphill
0.2	↗	'Rossbeg'
0.9	↖	'Rossbeg'
5.1	⇒	Turn to pier and small beach. Pier has tap if you need one. 300m return
7.3	▲⇒	To Tramore Beach Camping and Caravan park
7.9	☆	To left, view of Kiltooris Lough, castle and crannog
8.4	→	At T-junction
10.4	→	'Ardara'
12.3	→	'Ardara R261'
18.3	♦	Service station and shop
18.4	→	At T-junction
18.7	☆	Tourist information M – Fr 10am – 2pm, Sat 2pm – 6pm
18.8	☆ ▲ ATM	Benches, car park, ATM at Ardara. Drumbaron Hostel. Spar has internet access
19.4	♦	Shop and service station
21.0	→	'Glencolmcille'
35.6	→ ♦	'Glean Cholm Cill'. Shop 200m straight on
38.9	△(187)	Views of glen and ocean
42.0	←	'Glencolmcille'
43.5	←	Unsigned road
44.3	♦	Shops in Glencolmcille
44.6	→	'Malainn Mhoir'
	⇐▲	Dooey Hostel
45.4	☆	Father McDyer's Folk Village Museum

Stage 8 Portnoo to Carrick		
48.6	←	Unsigned. Carry straight on for Malin Beg, Malin Beg Hostel and Silver Strand – 9km return
55.9	→	'An Charraigh R263'
59.9		Arrive Carrick car park, near telephone boxes

Extra side-trip – Carrick to Slieve League Cliffs		
0.0		Carrick car park, by phone boxes, head towards centre of village
0.1	→	'Teileann L1095'
2.4	←	'Teelin Pier'
2.9	→	'The Cliffs'
3.3	♦	Cafe Ti Linn
4.9	☆	Pass through gate
6.8		Cliffs car park. Three to four hour return walk to summit

Stage 9 Carrick to Donegal Town		
0.0		Carrick car park, by phone boxes – head towards centre of village
0.1	⇨	Turn to Teelin
0.2	→	'Coast Road' – just after bridge
1.8	→	'Coast Road'
3.1	▲	Derrylahan Hostel & camping
6.0	♦	Shop at Kilcar
6.1	→	(Straight on is R263 – main road)
12.1	➚	Road veers right
12.6	→	'R263 Killybegs'
14.1	☆	Picnic area
15.8	⇨	Fintra Strand
19.3	↑	'Killybegs'
19.5	O→	Unsigned
19.6	←	At T-junction
19.8	☆	Killybegs, car park and quay
19.9	⇦	Turn here for town centre
20.8	♦	Shop in service station
21.2	♦	Shop in service station
21.7	→	'Carrick House B&B'
22.2	←	About 50m past bridge
22.4	←	'Carrick House'
22.5	➚	Bear right at junction
22.8	➚	Bear right at junction. Track becomes stony but very rideable

Stage 9 Carrick to Donegal Town		
24.2	←	T-junction
24.5	➚	Road veers right
25.0	➚	Bear right as road swings to the left
25.1	←	Turn left towards main road
25.3	→	'N56 Donegal'
	♦	Spar shop opposite
26.5	⇨	Side-trip to St John's Point – 20km return
27.8	▲	Blue Moon Hostel and Camping
27.9	♦	Convenience store
32.2	♦	Shop and café
32.5	♦	Shop
43.2	♦	Shop
43.4	⇨	Beach
44.3	▲	Donegal Independent Hostel
44.7	O➚	'Donegal'
45.6		Arrive Donegal central diamond

83

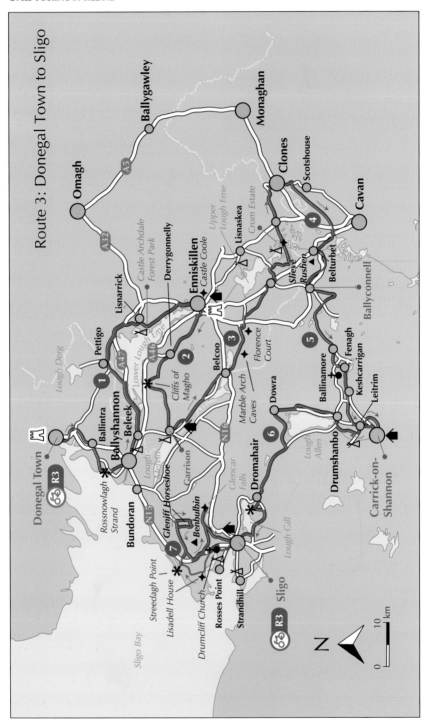

Route 3: Donegal Town to Sligo

ROUTE 3

DONEGAL TOWN TO SLIGO – THE IRISH LAKELANDS

Stage		Terrain	Distance (km)	Summit (distance from start/height)
1	Donegal Town to Castle Archdale	Gentle coastal and lakeside hills	76.6	23km/120m
2	Castle Archdale to Garrison	Stiff climbs to Cliffs of Magho	64.5	45km/330m
3	Garrison to Crom Estate	Fast and flat lowland cycling	62.1	46km/60m
4	Crom Estate to Ballyconnell	Lowland route; some drumlins	57.9	52km/75m
5	Ballyconnell to Carrick-on-Shannon	A few small hills, no long climbs	62.5	56km/90m
6	Carrick-on-Shannon to Sligo	A few small hills, no long climbs	84.7	23km/110m
7	Tour of Sligo	Coastal riding; climb into the Gleniff Horseshoe	(84.3)	43km/240m
		Total	**408.3**	

During recent times, these borderlands between Northern Ireland and the Irish Republic were not always the safest of places, but further back in history Fermanagh was one of the most stable and prosperous regions in Ulster. The Normans had found the area unconquerable, and from the 14th to the 16th centuries the ruling clan of the Maguires managed to hand on the kingdom from father to son without the sibling squabbles that turned to bloody conflict in other parts of Ulster. Here, amongst the hills, lakes and mountains of the Gaelic sub-kingdom, poetry, scholarship and culture flourished.

The relatively flat terrain, along with the quiet roads, makes this area ideal for cycle tourism, and Ireland's first long-distance cycle route, the Kingfisher Trail, was opened here. This cross-border route consists of around 370km of signposted roads and trails, along with many link routes and side-trips. The route described here often follows the Kingfisher Trail, but also deviates, sometimes to pass accommodation, but mostly to pick out places of particular interest. An extra day trip, Stage 7, has been included to take in some of the fine scenery to the north of Sligo.

Options

This is not a route to get you anywhere in a hurry, and the lazy, looping trail creates many potential short-cuts. For a quick route from Donegal to Sligo, take this route as far as Belleek (35.2km), then head south on the B52/R282 to Manorhamilton. West of Manorhamilton pick up the R286 around the north side of Lough Gill to reach Sligo, or head towards Glencar Falls, also from Manorhamilton, and pick up Stage 7 at 71.6km. When looking for alternative routes around Sligo, avoid the N15 – much too fast and busy for pleasant cycling.

Getting to the Start

Below are the options to consider for this route.

By Air
None.

By Sea
None.

By Rail/Bus
From Donegal Town there are several Bus Eireann services to and from Dublin daily. Sligo has a rail service, but cycles are not currently carried.

When to Go
The area is very quiet outside peak season – travel any time from Easter to September.

Accommodation
Campsites are some of the best places to stay in the lakelands, with many enjoying idyllic lakeside locations. The backpacker boom hasn't really happened here, and so there are, unfortunately, only a handful of hostels. County Fermanagh has only one hostel (Enniskillen, Stage 2) and Cavan and Leitrim also have only one each (Ballyconnell, Stage 4, and Carrick-on-Shannon, Stage 5, respectively), so non-campers will have to rely on bed and breakfast accommodation.

Maps
This is one of those annoying routes that always seems to be on the edge of a map sheet. At 1:250 000, the Ireland North and Ireland West sheets from the Ordnance Survey series will be needed, although the West sheet is only needed for the area from Drumshanbo

to Carrick-on-Shannon (15km). In 1:50 000 the OSI Discovery Series, sheets 11 Donegal Fermanagh Tyrone, 25 Sligo Leitrim Roscommon, 26 Cavan Fermanagh Leitrim Roscommon Monaghan, as well as 16 Donegal Fermanagh Leitrim Sligo (only for about 4km to the northwest of Ballyshannon) will be needed. From the OSNI Discoverer Series, sheets 17 Lower Lough Erne and 27 Upper Lough Erne complete a long map list. The Kingfisher Trail map from Sustrans, at 1:100 000, covers the entire route from just north of Ballyshannon. It is detailed and accurate and saves a lot of map shuffling.

Onwards
Stage 4 and the wild west beckon, otherwise it's back to Dublin by train from Sligo.

STAGE 1
DONEGAL TOWN
TO CASTLE ARCHDALE

76.6km Gentle coastal and lakeside hills

This is a long day in distance, but the terrain is generally easy and the roads smooth and fast. The area to the immediate south of Donegal is not particularly attractive, but by Rossnowlagh (18km) things have improved. Here the stage follows the beach for about 1.5km, and the sand is generally firm enough to support a fully loaded touring bike. There is an alternative road just behind the beach (both are signed as cycle routes).

Ballyshannon, County Donegal

During the Second World War, flying boats based at RAF Castle Archdale patrolled the Atlantic approaches. One airman dubbed Lower Lough Erne, 'the most beautiful runway in the world'.

The biggest town of the day, Ballyshannon (27km), is an attractive settlement on a steep hill above a stone bridge over the River Erne. This is the last town in the Irish Republic for a couple of days. Within an hour of here there is some of the finest lake scenery in Europe, where long stretches of silver water lap against a myriad of low, wooded offshore islands, and grand Georgian country houses nestle against a backdrop of hills and cliffs. The first of these fine estates is at Castlecaldwell (43.1km). The house is in ruins, but the foreshore and woodlands give a fine taste of typical lakeland scenery. The pottery clay used at nearby Belleek Pottery, which you may have visited earlier, used to be mined here. If you do visit the pottery, it's best to take a tour. It's open 9am–6pm, Mon–Fri in summer; there are no tours at weekends, but the shop is open (028 6865 9300, www.belleek.ie).

After Castlecaldwell there is a fine stretch of road alongside the lake, before a short diversion 'inland' to Pettigo, and then on to Kesh, finishing at the lakeside Castle Archdale Forest Park.

On the Road
This stage crosses the border into Northern Ireland at Belleek (35km). There is an ATM and supermarket here, so stock up on cash and supplies – food is generally cheaper in Northern Ireland. Public toilets are also far more common, and there are some at Kesh (64km). Rossnowlagh beach (18km) is patrolled. Castlecaldwell (turn at 43.1km), or somewhere along the lake immediately to the east, are other pleasant places to stop.

Accommodation
There are no hostels on this stage – the nearest is on Stage 2, at Enniskillen (17km). Castle Archdale (73km) has a pleasant camping and caravan site, and the beautiful surrounding woods and lakeshore make this the best place

to stay in the area. There are minimum stays for public holidays and 12 July week. Book ahead in peak times (www.castlearchdale.com, 028 6862 1333). The site has a shop and takeaway in high season, or there is a small shop back towards Lisnarrick. There are bed and breakfasts in the area, including the Cedars Guesthouse (028 686 21493, www.cedarsguesthouse.com), which is 1km along Stage 2.

Options
From Belleek this stage follows some sections of the Kingfisher Trail, which is also signposted as NCN91, so if you have the Sustrans cycle route map you may prefer to follow the Kingfisher Trail as an alternative route. The Kingfisher Trail is, however, more than 22km longer between Belleek and the end of the stage (64km compared to 41.4km).

The main differences between the NCN91 and the route described here are that, east of Belleek, the Kingfisher Trail diverts away from the A47, taking some long detours away from the lake. The lakeside main road is, however, quicker and very scenic. Similarly, east of Pettigo the Kingfisher Trail heads away from the lake to avoid the A35, although this main road is generally not very busy.

STAGE 2
CASTLE ARCHDALE TO GARRISON

64.5km Stiff climb to the Cliffs of Magho

This stage starts heading southwards along Lower Lough Erne to Enniskillen. There are few views of the lake, but the woodland scenery is attractive, and the roads fast and smooth with very little heavy traffic.

Enniskillen is an interesting historic town set on an island drumlin at the head of the lough. There is a castle here that dates from the 15th century (17km).

Nearby is Castle Coole (8km round trip), now owned by the National Trust, which may be the finest classical building in Ireland. The grounds are open during daylight hours all year, and the house at weekends from mid-March to September, and during the week in July, August and Easter week, as well as some weekdays in June (www.nationaltrust.org.uk).

Cliffs of Magho overlooking Lower Lough Erne

Castle Coole is a neoclassical mansion designed by James Wyatt and built in the late 18th century. It is constructed entirely of Portland stone, quarried in Dorset and brought to Ballyshannon by ship and then by bullock cart to the site.

The scenic highlight of the day is the visit to the Cliffs of Magho (45km). From 240m high above Lower Lough Erne, there is a bird's-eye view of the intricate pattern of islands in the lough, while to the east is Ballyshannon and the Atlantic, which, with any luck, will be shining in the afternoon sun. The descent through the pine plantation and open country to Lough Melvin and Garrison is a chance for a breather, and fine views open up over the hill-bound lough.

Lough Melvin is home to the gilaroo (*Salmo stomachicus*), a species of trout that is rare in that it has a gizzard. According to legend, St Brigid was angry at being offered chicken to eat on a Friday, and threw the bird into the lake, where it turned into a fish.

On the Road
Enniskillen (17km) is the largest town for a few days, so make the most of it. For bike-related matters, try Lakeland Bikes (028 6632 2511), which is about 4km east of the town centre on the B80. Enniskillen also has extensive parkland by the river. Derrygonnelly (33km) has a few shops at around the halfway mark. There is a shop close to the stage end at Garrison.

Accommodation
Garrison has the Lough Melvin Holiday Centre (028 6865 8142, www.melvinholidaycentre.com), which has camping and other accommodation – book ahead. A new hostel, Leitrim Lakes Hostel (Irish Republic number 072 54044), which also advertises camping facilities, has opened at Kiltyclogher (turn at 5.1km into Stage 3). For accommodation queries, check at the tourist information centre in Enniskillen (see route card). There is also a new youth hostel at Enniskillen (028 6634 0110, www.hini.org.uk), in Belmore Street.

Options
The route is based on scenery rather than distance. At Garrison the stage is only 40km away from Belleek from early in Stage 1.

STAGE 3
GARRISON TO CROM ESTATE

62.1km Fast and flat lowland cycling

From Garrison the route turns easterly and shadows the border to the foot of the Cuilcagh Mountains. There is the option of climbing into the mountains to see stalactites and other formations in the Marble Arch Caves (www. marblearchcaves.net, 028 6634 8855). It is, however, a tough climb up to the caves, and the lowland route along the base of the escarpment is also very pretty.

> The Marble Arch Caves and surrounding mountains are a UNESCO-recognised global geopark. The limestone slopes have some of Ireland's best karst landscape and there is an important area of blanket bog.

Another fine 18th-century house, Florence Court, nestles at the foot of the mountains (turn at 33.9km). The grounds are open all year, and the house, by guided tour, at weekends from mid-March to September, all week during

> Florence Court is where the yew tree that is the source of all Irish yews grows.

Easter week and June, July and August, except Tuesdays in June (028 6634 8249, www. nationaltrust.org.uk).

The day finishes with a short ferry ride across Lower Lough Erne to the National Trust Crom Estate, a fabulous example of a demesne landscape set amongst the inlets and small islands of the lough; there is also boat hire here. Grounds open daily mid-March to early November, visitor centre at weekends from mid-March to early November, and weekdays during March and May to mid-September (028 6773 8118, www.nationaltrust.org.uk).

On the Road
For this stage it is necessary to plan ahead and book the ferry to the Crom Estate. The crossing is actually part of the National Cycle Network, but must be booked 24 hours in advance with the visitor centre (028 6773 8118). The absolutely latest time for the ferry is 4pm.

This stage is generally flat and quite fast, so time should not be a problem. An alternative route, also signposted as NCN91, crosses Upper Lough Erne by bridge (see route card, 51.4km).

Belcoo (21km) has a choice of shops, a pharmacy and a riverside park. If staying at the Crom Estate, the closest shops on this stage are at Derrylin (46km), where there is also an ATM.

Stage 3 is all in Northern Ireland, apart from a few hundred metres at Blacklion (21km).

Crossing Lower Lough Erne by boat

Accommodation

The Crom Estate has a small camp ground near the visitor centre, with access to the centre for toilets and showers. In the evening it is possible to wander the estate as you please (apart from the private 19th-century castle). An option earlier in the day is the Rushin House Caravan Park (028 6638 6519, www.rushinhousecaravanpark.com) at 19km.

Options

The Marble Arch Caves (turn at 24.4km), as well as the bridge alternative to the Crom Ferry, are discussed above. This route loops back towards Enniskillen, which is only 15km away at the closest point (near Florence Court). One option is to set up a base at Enniskillen and combine Stages 2 and 3 into an 80km, pannier-free day trip.

STAGE 4
CROM ESTATE TO BALLYCONNELL

57.9km Lowland, some drumlins

Stage 4 is an enjoyable run through pleasant countryside. Along the way there are two of the most traditional towns you will find in Ulster – Clones and Ballyconnell – as well as places of historical interest, including a railway museum and a castle site at Belturbet.

The River Erne and Upper Lough Erne spread out through an archipelago of small islands into a myriad of channels. Fermanagh is reputedly one-third covered with water, and in this waterlogged landscape it is the low summits of glacially deposited drumlins that are prime sites for settlement.

The approach to Clones is not promising, but the heart of the hilltop town (17km) is largely unaffected by recent development, and this was clearly once a prosperous 19th-century commercial town. Clones is best known

Patrick McCabe's 1992 novel *The Butcher Boy* is set in 1950s Clones. The film *The Playboys*, also from 1992, was filmed at nearby Redhills, and its co-writer, Shane Connaughton, was born in the village.

for its lace production, and the Ulster Canal Stores has some exhibits. Also in the town are a fine Celtic cross and a round tower, and there are other historic sites to see. Check the map in the marketplace for directions.

Belturbet (45km) is a busy crossroads town set high on a drumlin over the River Erne. If you want to find out more about Ulster's once thriving railway network, try the Belturbet Station visitor centre (www.belturbet-station.com). On a small island in the river is a well-preserved 12th-century Norman motte and bailey fortification.

At stage end, Ballyconnell is a sleepy town sitting at the foot of Slieve Rushen and astride the Shannon–Erne waterway.

On the Road

The drumlin landscape creates sinuous roads and repetitive short climbs, making this stage more tiring than might be expected. Clones (17km), Redhills (31km) and Belturbet (45km) are all good places to have a break – all have shops. The first place to get some euros after crossing the border is Clones – there are ATMs in town, including one at the diamond.

Accommodation

Sandville House, 4km from Ballyconnell, is one of Ireland's prettiest hostels, and booking is advisable (049 9526297, sandville@eircom.net). The directions are to take the N87 southwards from town, turn right after 2.8km and follow the signs. Ballyconnell also has bed and breakfast accommodation.

Options

None.

STAGE 5
BALLYCONNELL TO
CARRICK-ON-SHANNON

62.5km A few small hills;
no long climbs.

In many ways the lake-studded landscape here, with its low, rounded hills, distant spires, meadows and woodlands, is similar to the previous few days. But a change is afoot – the dark forested slopes of Slieve Rushen hover behind

Carrick-on-Shannon, County Leitrim

Until the Grand Canal closed in 1960, Guinness was shipped to Carrick-on-Shannon via the canal and the Shannon Navigation.

Ballyconnell, and the high plateau of Slieve Anierin rises to the west, heralding the magnificent limestone scenery of northern Leitrim and Sligo further ahead.

Fenagh Abbey (turn at 33.7km) is one of the oldest monastic sites in Ireland, believed to have been founded in the fifth century by St Caillin.

Fenagh was the home of the writer John McGahern for many years, and the area figures heavily in his short stories, and in novels such as That They May Face the Rising Sun (2002).

Leitrim (52.6km), despite sharing the county's name, is little more than a village. Carrick-on-Shannon, in contrast, is a busy, commercial riverside town on the Roscommon border. It is in a delightful setting and has many historic buildings, but the traffic in the narrow streets can be terrible, and the one-way system is tortuous. Tourist information is in the old barrel store at the quay.

On the Road

This stage is easy to navigate, as it follows the Kingfisher Trail all day. The signposting is not, however, always obvious, and signs do sometimes go missing. There are public toilets alongside the Shannon–Erne Waterway (25.7km and 41.6km – a rarity in the south). Ballinamore (24km) is a traditional market town with shops and ATMs – stop here or a little further on along the canal. Keshcarrigan (41km) is also a pleasant place for a break.

Accommodation

Carrick has one hostel (An Óiche Hostel, 071 9621848), but it does book up. It is on Bridge Street, which leads to the river bridge from the north side close to the tourist office. The town is also very rumbustious at weekends, which may or may not suit you. Camping is limited nearby – the closest site is 8km away, at the riverside Beirnes of Battlebridge (071 9650824, www.beirnesofbattlebridge.com) – see Stage 6 for directions.

Options

Stage 6 can be picked up at Leitrim village. Pushing on to Carrick means doubling back this way in any case. From Leitrim to Carrick, the way follows the hilly Kingfisher Trail route. If the traffic is not too bad, the R280 is a quick and quite simple way into town – just follow the signs.

Another route option is to head northwest over the mountains from Ballinamore and pick up Stage 6 at Ballinagleragh. This is marked as an option on the Sustrans Kingfisher Trail map.

STAGE 6
CARRICK-ON-SHANNON TO SLIGO

84.7km A few small hills;
no long climbs.

Anthony Trollope's novel *The MacDermotts of Ballycloran* (1844) includes some rare descriptions of the mountains around Lough Allen during pre-famine Ireland.

The final stage into Sligo is a long one, but at least it manages to weave its way through the surrounding mountains without too much climbing.

North to Drumshanbo (16km) the route is fairly flat. Then follows a section along a rough road high above Lough Allen, which despite being the route of an old railway line, somehow manages to be annoyingly hilly, although the views across the lough make the effort worthwhile. At Dowra (34km) the stage turns west towards Sligo, waving good-bye to the Kingfisher Trail, which continues north towards Blacklion. From here on the landscape continues to lose the lushness characteristic of the Shannon lowlands. By Drumkeeran (45km) the limestone mountains of north Leitrim and County Sligo have started to close in.

The mountain to the east of Lough Allen is Slieve Anierin – literally 'mountain of iron'. This area was once home to a smelting industry, and there were also coal mines in the Arigna valley on the far side of the lake.

Before the hustle and bustle of Sligo, there are two beautifully peaceful sites to visit. The first is the well-preserved Franciscan foundation at Creevelea Friary near Dromahair (60km). The second dose of quiet contemplation comes at Traware Bay on Lough Gill, gazing out on the Lake Isle of Innisfree (64km), made famous by the WB Yeats poem of that title. When the noise and traffic of Sligo start to close in, Yeats' poem of peaceful retreat from the world will have all the more resonance. Further on is Dooney Rock (76km), from another Yeats poem, 'The Fiddler of Dooney'.

This route brings you into the heart of Sligo along the river, avoiding the unfathomable traffic signs, and leaving some sense of the geography of the place. The town is very confusing, but take heart, it is a lively and friendly place, with a fine mixture of old and new, and surrounded by some of Ireland's most beautiful countryside.

On the Road
There is no shortage of shops on this stage. The picnic area above Lough Allen (26km) is a scenic place for a break, as are any of the small towns along the way.

Lough Allen, north of Drumshanbo

For cycle repairs in Sligo, try Cranks (087 9564086), which offers a mobile service and will pick up your bike in the Sligo area, including from the campsites at Strandhill and Rosses Point.

The way into Drumshanbo was suffering from extensive roadworks at the time of writing, so the directions/distances may change slightly. If in doubt, once in the town (it's very small) find the central diamond (16.9km) and pick up the directions and Kingfisher Trail signs from there.

Accommodation

Sligo has two very good campsites close to town. The Strandhill Caravan and Camping Park (071 9168111) is on the coast about 8km west of town. It's next to the airport (only small planes, and noise is not a problem), making it easy to find. From the end of the stage, at the Douglas Hyde Bridge turn left – initially it's one-way in the wrong direction, so walk a short distance. This road heads straight out to the village of Strandhill (see Route 4, Stage 1, 7.6km), which has a couple of shops, a pub and a café or two.

Greenlands Caravan and Camping Park (071 9177113) is at Rosses Point to the northwest – the R291 will take you there. Both are great sites, but Strandhill village has more going on, and the tent sites here are well protected by the sand dunes. Sligo has a choice of independent hostels, including the Railway Hostel (071 9144530).

Options

From Carrick to Leitrim village the route follows the main R280. The Kingfisher Trail follows an alternative route and this is covered, southbound, in Stage 5. From Dowra it is possible to follow the Kingfisher Trail back to Blacklion. Sligo has Bus Eireann services to pretty much anywhere in Ireland.

| STAGE 7 |
| TOUR OF SLIGO |

84.3km Coastal riding;
climb into the Gleniff Horseshoe.

Leaving Sligo without enjoying some of the fine scenery to the north and west of the town

---

Countess Markiewicz was second in command of the forces at St Stephen's Green during the Easter Rising. In 1918 she became the first woman elected to the British Parliament, but like the other members of Sinn Féin, did not take her seat.

---

would be a pity, so this day trip takes in some of the highlights of the area.

Two names loom large in the history of the Sligo and its surrounds – WB Yeats and Countess Markiewicz. Most visitors have heard of Ireland's foremost poet, while the countess is better known in Ireland than abroad for her role in the Easter Rising of 1916. The first Yeats homage of the day comes at Drumcliff church (8km), where the poet is buried. Across the road is the ruin of St Columba's monastery.

The histories of Yeats and the countess intersect at Lissadell House (15km), and the 'exceedingly impressive house' of Yeats' memory is open to the public daily (www.lissadellhouse.com). This is the ancestral home of the Gore-Booth family (the countess was Constance Gore-Booth before marriage). The location, overlooking Drumcliff Bay, is breathtaking, the gardens impressive, and the house and exhibitions interesting.

Nearby Streedagh Point (25km) is a fine spot to look back towards the mountains, especially the tabletop shape of Benbulbin, much loved by Yeats.

Many Spaniards drowned off Streedagh Point in 1588 when three Armada ships, anchored in Sligo Bay, were driven ashore. One account reports more than 1100 corpses on the five-mile strand.

Two further scenic delights lie ahead. The first is the climb into the deep glacial corrie of the Gleniff Horseshoe (38km), the second the Glencar Falls (71km), also written about by Yeats: 'Where the wandering water gushes/ From the hills above Glen-Car'.

93

Glencar Waterfall, County Leitrim

ROUTE 3 DONEGAL TOWN TO SLIGO

Stage 1 Donegal Town to Castle Archdale		
0.0		Donegal diamond by Magee clothing store. Take the R267 leading off the diamond straight in front of you
0.7	→	Just past a school
5.9	←	At T-junction
6.2	◆	Large Eurospar supermarket on the right
	↑	Make sure you head straight on as main road swings off to left
12.1	◆	Ballintra has convenience shops
	→	'Rossnowlagh'
12.3	↑	Cross N15 with care
16.3	→	'Rossnowlagh'
18.3	←	Turn left along beach – sand is nice and firm
19.8	↑	Leave beach via slipway
19.9	→	Top of slipway turn right
20.7	←	'North-West Trail Cycleway, Rossnowlagh'
21.1	◆	Small shop
21.2	→	'North-West Trail'
23.4	△	Views of Ballyshannon and hills beyond from this low summit
25.2	→	At T-junction
25.4	←	'Ballyshannon'
25.8	O↗	'Ballyshannon'
26.8	←	Start of one-way system
26.9	↗	'Town centre'
27.0	→	'Town centre, Kingfisher Trail', at crossroads
27.2	←	At crossroads at top of steep part of main street – for shops etc go straight on
27.7	→	'Kingfisher Trail'
	O←	Unsigned
28.3	☆	Ballyshannon hydro-electric plant on right
34.0	→	'Belleek'
35.2	←	'T-junction at Belleek – turn right for pottery
	ATM ◆	Now in Northern Ireland
39.5	☆	Kingfisher Trail turns left here, but A47 is pretty along lake so stay straight on
40.1	☆	Picnic area (OK)

On the Road
There are a few shops on the route, but it is easiest (and cheapest) stocking up at one of the Sligo supermarkets first. Streedagh Point (25km) is a good break spot, while Lissadell House (15km) has a café.

Accommodation
Day trip – see Stage 6.

Options
The extra 7km or so out to the waterfall (the route doubles back) may seem a bit much at the end of the day, but it is very pretty. You could also skip the Gleniff Horseshoe, but the cliff-bound head of the canyon is rather atmospheric.

Stage 1 Donegal Town to Castle Archdale

43.1	⇨	Turn to Castlecaldwell
44.9	☆	NCN91 heads left here – continue straight on
46.7	☆	Lakeside picnic area
48.6	←	'B136 Pettigo'
53.9	→	'R232 Pettigo'
54.0	♦	Shop in service station
55.7	→	'Enniskillen', at T-junction
62.8	↑	'A35 Kesh'
63.0	ATM ♦	Shop at service station
64.3	O↑	At Kesh, bank, ATM, shops. Turn right here for the marina which has public toilets, showers
64.4	→	'NCN91, Enniskillen (scenic route)' Just over bridge
65.5	→	'NCN91, Enniskillen (scenic route)'
70.9	→	'NCN91', between stone gateposts
71.3	↑	'NCN91' through gate. Old Castle Archdale on left
71.9	↖	Road bears right
72.9	→	'NCN91', at T-junction
73.2	→	'NCN91', on to road
73.3	↑	'Caravan Site'
73.6	▲⇨	Turn to Castle Archdale Campsite
	←	'NCN91 Burma Road'
74.6	☆	Old bomb stores
75.0	→	At Duross Bay car park area
75.4	↗	'NCN91'
75.9	→	Turn right at T-junction
76.6		Stage ends at Castle Archdale exit onto B52. Lisnarick is 1.5km to left. Service station and shop about 1km on left

Stage 2 Castle Archdale to Garrison

0.0	→	Crossroads exit from Castle Archdale onto B82. Turn right – 'Killadeas B82'
1.0	▲	Cedars Guesthouse
9.8	☆	Enniskillen airport
10.7	O↗	'Enniskillen A32'
10.9	♦	Shop at service station
13.9	O↑	'A32 town centre car parks'
14.5	↑	Cross road and join cyclepath at Drumclay Park, continuing straight on

Stage 2 Castle Archdale to Garrison

15.1	☆	Cycleway ends, continue on road
	←	Turn left
	→	Almost immediately turn right down cycleway – Great Northern Way – running parallel to main road
16.0	↑	Leave cycleway and continue on road
16.5	→	'Town centre'. Hostel at bottom of this road before crossing river
17.1	←	Just past clocktower (on right) look for NCN91 sign. Join shared cycleway
	↑	Join cyclepath across road 'NCN91'
17.2	←	'NCN91'
	→	'NCN91' across road
17.3	☆ WC	Tourist information, bus station
	↑	Through gates of Lakeland Forum
	↖	'NCN91'
17.4	⇦	Side-trip to Castle Coole over bridge – 8km return
17.9	→	Just before Enniskillen Castle
18.0	→	Turn right onto road
	←	Immediately left
18.1	←	'The West A4'
18.3	→	Just over bridge – get in right-hand lane early
	←	'Belleek A46'
18.6	←	'Roscorry Terrace – Kingfisher Trail'
18.8	♦	Shop on right
20.4	→	'Derrygonnelly B81'
21.4	←	'Derrygonnelly B81' at T-junction
33.7	♦	Two shops
37.1	←	'Garrison' – at T-junction
40.0	→	'Lough Navar' Forest Drive
41.5	WC	Summer only
44.2	↑	'Viewpoint'
45.3	☆↑↓	Cliffs of Magho. Best view in Ireland. Turn around at car park
46.4	→	
48.3	↑	Carry straight on – look out for a couple of loose gravel sections on descent
51.7	→	Rejoin road

Stage 2 Castle Archdale to Garrison

56.2	↖	'Garrison'
58.8	→	'Garrison '
63.8	←	'Garrison', at T-junction
64.2	♦	Small shop in Garrison
64.3	→	At T-junction
64.5	▲	Lough Melvin Holiday Centre
	→ WC	Turn into lakefront car park. Toilets here

Stage 3 Garrison to Crom Estate

0.0	←	Garrison lakefront carpark. At entrance turn left
0.2	↑	Carry straight on (don't cross bridge)
5.1	← ▲⇧	'B52' Straight on for Leitrim Lakes Hostel
8.8	↑	'Belcoo' (scenic route to left is much more hilly)
19.8	▲	Rushin House Caravan Park
21.3	→	At T-junction, Belcoo
21.9	←	In Blacklion (now in Irish Republic)
24.4	⇨	Alternative route via Marble Arch Caves – hilly
27.3	☆	Cladagh Glen
29.9	⇨	To Marble Arch Caves 8km return – hilly. (Alternative route rejoins here.)
33.6	→	'Florence Court house and gardens'
33.9	⇨	To Florence Court – 2.5km return to house
35.3	↑	'Killesher'
35.9	→	'Kinawley' (at crossroads)
40.3	♦	Small shop at Kinawley
45.1	→	'A509 Derrylin'
46.2	♦ ATM	Shop on right has ATM
47.0	WC	In Derrylin
47.4	↖ O	'B127 Lisnaskea'
51.4	→	'Ferry NCN91' – carry straight on for alternative route via bridge
53.5	→	'Teelin'
54.6	←	'Derryvore' (at crossroad)
56.3	←	'Derryvore quay'
59.6	↑	Through gate
59.8	☆	Arrive slipway for ferry to Crom Estate
	→	At far jetty, follow road to right

Stage 3 Garrison to Crom Estate

60.5	→	At crossroads
61.6	→	At T-junction
62.1		Arrive visitor centre, Crom Estate

Stage 4 Crom Estate to Ballyconnell

0.0		Crom Estate visitor centre, upper end of car park by main sign – head away from carpark
1.0	→	'NCN91'
2.7	→	'Newtonbutler '
5.6	↑	'Newtonbutler'
7.0	↑ O	Unsigned
7.2	WC	In Newtonbutler
7.5	♦ ATM	Small shopping centre with ATM at Newtonbutler
7.9	←	'B143 Magheraveely'
12.7	→	'NCN91'
	↑	'Clones'
14.6	←	'Clones'
15.5	☆	Cross border
16.7	→	Unsigned
17.4	↑	At crossroads, enter main street, Clones
17.7	←	Arrive Clones diamond, turn left
17.8	→	Take first right
	↑	Leave the diamond, keeping Lennard Arms Hotel on your left
22.2	→	'Kingfisher Trail'. Hard to spot – look for green posting box in wall
23.1	←	'Kingfisher Trail', at T-junction
23.4	↗	'Kingfisher Trail'
24.2	→	'Kingfisher Trail'
24.4	←	'Kingfisher Trail' (at T-junction)
29.3	↑	At crossroads
31.3	☆	Diamond at Redhills village. Benches
31.4	←♦	'Kingfisher Trail' , at T-junction. Shop on right
32.0	→	'Kingfisher Trail' (first of two right turns next to each other)
35.1	☆	Pass old railway station
35.2	→	'Kingfisher Trail'
36.4	←	'Kingfisher Trail', short distance on N54
	→	'Kingfisher Trail'

Stage 4 Crom Estate to Ballyconnell		
40.7	→	'Kingfisher Trail' (500m on N3 – busy, so take care)
41.3	←	'Putiaghan' 'Kingfisher Trail'
41.9	→	'Kingfisher Trail'
42.4	↖	Road veers left
45.1	☆	Note campsite on Kingfisher Trail map is now a holiday park
45.3	←	Turn left at Belturbet centre
	♦	Shop opposite
	⇨	Side-trip to Belturbet Station visitor centre
45.6	⇦ WC	Park with toilets and picnic tables a few hundred metres on left

Stage 4 Crom Estate to Ballyconnell		
	→	Kingfisher Trail (just over bridge, be careful – this is a busy road)
	⇦	Turn sharp left straight after bridge for Turbet Island Motte and Bailey
46.0	←	'Kingfisher Trail'
46.6	↗	Veer right onto cycleway
46.7	↑○	'Ballyconnell'
47.3	←	Unsigned turn by new housing development
48.4	↑	'Kingfisher Trail' (at crossroads)
50.1	↑	'Kingfisher Trail' (cross N87)
52.0	☆	Look for crannog in lake on the left
52.8	→	'Kingfisher Trail'
55.8	←	Unsigned T-junction
57.1	→	'Ballyconnell'
57.7	♦ ATM	In service station
57.9		Arrive Ballyconnell post office

Stage 5 Ballyconnell to Carrick-on-Shannon		
Stage 5		Ballyconnell to Carrick-on-Shannon
0.0	←	Ballyconnell main street – at crossroads turn left onto N87
0.3	→	'Carrigellen'
4.3	→	'Bellaheady Bridge'
6.9	←	'Ballinamore'
7.8	→	'Kingfisher Trail, Bawnboy'
9.6	←	'Kingfisher Trail'
10.9	→	'Kingfisher Trail'
12.4	←	'Ballinmore, Kingfisher Trail'
18.2	→	'Aughnasheelin, Kingfisher Trail'
19.6	←	'Ballinamore, Kingfisher Trail'
21.3	→	'Kingfisher Trail'
22.0	←	'Kingfisher Trail, R202'
24.7	→	'Carrick-on-Shannon', now in Ballinamore
25.3	→	'Aughnasheelin'
	♦	Supermarket on corner
25.6	↖	'Kingfisher Trail'
25.7	WC	Public toilets by waterway
29.7	←	'Kingfisher Trail'
31.4	→	'Lough Reane, Kingfisher Trail'
33.3	→	'Kingfisher Trail at T-junction'
33.6	↑	'R209 Carrick-on-Shannon'

Celtic Cross at Clones, County Monaghan

Stage 5 Ballyconnell to Carrick-on-Shannon		
33.7	⇦	To Fenagh Abbey 200m
33.9	☆	Fenagh visitor centre
41.6	WC	At parking by canal
41.8	♦	Shop at Keshcarrigan
43.6	→	'Kingfisher Trail'
44.0	←	Just after crossing canal
44.4	↑	At crossroads
46.8	↑	'Kingfisher Trail'
50.2	←	'Leitrim R280'
52.3	⇨	Can turn here to join Stage 6 at 7.1km
52.6	♦	Shop in service station at Leitrim
53.1	←	'L7391 Kingfisher Trail' – can continue straight on for Carrick, but busy
53.3	↗	Road veers right
54.3	↑	'Kingfisher Trail', at crossroads
56.0	→	'Kingfisher Trail'
57.3	→	'Kingfisher Trail'
57.5	←	'L3408 Carrick-on-Shannon'
59.3	→	'Kingfisher Trail'
59.5	←	'Kingfisher Trail'
61.1	←	Have to turn – one-way system ahead
61.4	→	'Kingfisher Trail', just after school
61.7	↖ O	'N4 Sligo'
62.0	←	Turn on to cycleway
62.4	↑	At car park, tourist information is straight ahead
62.5		Arrive tourist information

Stage 6 Carrick-on-Shannon to Sligo		
0.0		Tourist information, Old Barrel Store, Carrick. Head across car park and pick up cycleway along the river
0.7	←O	'R280 Manorhamilton'
1.2	→	'Leitrim'
1.4	♦	Service station and shop
7.1	←	'R284 Ballyfarnon, Kingfisher Trail'
8.0	→ ▲⇧	'R284 Ballyfarnon'. Beirnes of Battlebridge camping is straight on, 300m
10.5	←	At bridge
13.4	←	'R280 Drumkeeran, Kingfisher Trail'
14.6	→	'L3378 Drumshanbo'

Stage 6 Carrick-on-Shannon to Sligo		
15.1	→	'R208 Drumshanbo'
15.7	WC	'Drumshanbo Lock '
16.1	←	'Dowra N3' (see 'On the Road' for note about Drumshanbo)
16.5	→	'Town Centre'
16.8	←	'R208 Ballinamore'
	♦	Supermarket on right
16.9	← ATM ♦	At Drumshanbo central square
17.0	↑	'Aghacashel 7'
	♦	Moran's Motorcycles and Cycles
17.4	←	'Lough Allen, Kingfisher Trail'
19.1	↑	'Kingfisher Trail' (at crossroads)
20.6	↑	'Kingfisher Trail, Leitrim Way'
24.3	↑	'Kingfisher Trail, Leitrim Way'
24.5	↑	Through gate, now firm grassy track
24.6	↑	Cross footbridge
24.7	↑	Rejoin road
	↑	'Kingfisher Trail'
26.4	←	Picnic site straight ahead
26.6	→	At T-junction, onto R207
28.7	⇦	'L8300' road leads to stony beach by lake, nice views – 4.5km return
29.5	↑	Kingfisher Trail wanders off to right to visit Ballinagleragh village, keep straight on
34.0	←♦	'R200 Drumkeeran'. Shop at Dowra
45.2	→♦	'R280 Manorhamilton', Drumkeeran has small shop on this corner and another up the hill to left
51.0	↖	'R289 Dromahair'
57.0	↑	'L4165' (main road swings left, continue in a straight-on direction)
58.5	←	At T-junction
58.9	←	'R288 Drumshanbo'. Turn right for shops and Dromahair centre
	♦ ⇨	
59.3	→	'R287 Sligo'
60.1	→	'Creevelea Friary'
60.5	←⇨	Side-trip to Creevelea Friary – 600m, return
62.4	→	At T-junction
	←	Unsigned, after about 80m
62.7	→	Unsigned

Stage 6 Carrick-on-Shannon to Sligo		
64.4	WC	At Innisfree car park
64.5	↑↓	Jetty at lake – view of island and lake
67.1	←	At T-junction
68.6	→	At T-junction (on to R287)
71.5	☆	Enter Slishwood Gap
74.0	☆	Slishwood Country Park
76.3	☆	Dooney Rock
77.8	→	Signed 'Holy Well'
81.3	→	'Cleveragh Retail Park'
82.5	↗	Join cycleway through car park on right
84.2	↑	Cycleway heads right – stay straight ahead on road
84.5	↑	Straight ahead is no entry to vehicles, walk or ride with care final 200m
84.7		Arrive Douglas Hyde Bridge, Sligo town centre

Stage 7 Tour of Sligo		
0.0		Sligo, north side of Hyde Bridge across from Ulster Bank, follow R291 Rosses Point
0.1	↑	'(R291) Rosses Point' at traffic lights
0.5	→	'N15 Lifford'
0.7	↖	'R291 Rosses Point' (go through lights then bear left)
2.3	→	Unsigned turn (Rosses Point straight on)
6.2	←	'Bundoran'
6.5	☆	Countess Markiewicz statue
8.2	☆	Drumcliff church on right
8.8	←	'Lissadell House'
10.8	♦	Carney has a shop
12.9	←	'Lissadell House'
14.7	☆	Pass through entrance to grounds
15.3	←	'Car Park'
15.5	←	Coach house in front
15.6	☆	Lissadell House car park
16.7	↑	At crossroads with church opposite
17.4	↑	At crossroads
18.4	→	At crossroads
22.4	←	'Streedagh'

Stage 7 Tour of Sligo		
24.0	☆	Armada memorial
24.1	→	Unsigned
24.6	→	Straight on is dead end
25.2	↑↓ WC	Streedagh Point car park (turn around and backtrack to Streedagh turn)
27.9	←	At T-junction
29.1	←♦ ATM	Join N15 – care, Grange has shop plus ATM in service station
29.4	→	Signed 'North-West Trail (NWT)'
29.5	←	'NWT', just past school
32.9	←	'NWT'
38.0	→	'Gleniff Horseshoe'
38.4	☆	Picnic area in barytes mill site
42.1	⇦	Road to RTE transmitter – might be tempting
46.8	☆	Views of coast and Mullaghmore
47.5	←	Back at road
52.5	☆	Now 'closed the loop'
54.4	←	Unsigned
	→	Unsigned
57.1	↑	Cross N15
59.6	←	Before give way sign (now at Carney again)
61.3	↑	Cross N15
65.9	⇨	Could take NWT here for Sligo and miss lake
68.5	←	'Glencar Lake'
70.0	☆	Co Leitrim border
71.2	☆	Picnic area
71.6	↑↓	Glencar waterfall car park – bike racks
74.6	→	Unsigned, retracing your steps to NWT turn
77.2	←	'Sligo NWT'
79.5	↑	'NWT' (at crossroads)
81.1	↑	'NWT' (at crossroads)
82.0	←	(NWT heads right here)
83.6	↑○	Unsigned
84.0	←	At T-junction
84.1	↑	Officially this is not straight on – so walk/cross with care
84.2	→	To cross Hyde Bridge
84.3		Arrive back at start

Route 4: Sligo to Achill Island

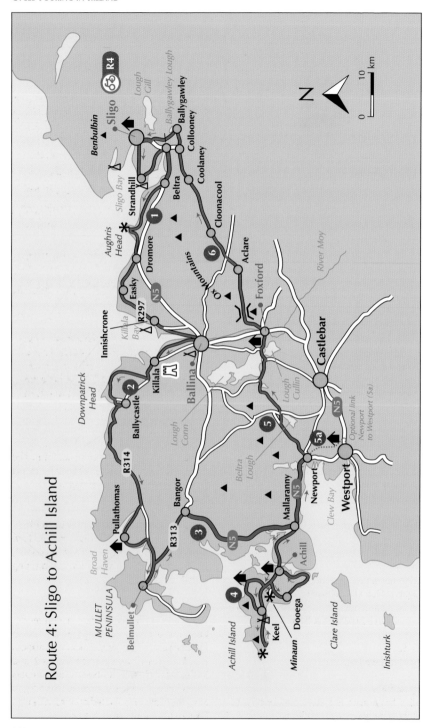

ROUTE 4
SLIGO TO ACHILL ISLAND – INTO THE ATLANTIC

Stage		Terrain	Distance (km)	Summit (distance from start/height)
1	Sligo to Ballina	Low coast, can be windy	88.4	21km/50m
2	Ballina to Belmullet	Gentle coastal hills	100.1	50km/120m
3	Belmullet to Achill	Low coast; gentle climbs	64.9	52km/60m
4	Tour of Achill Island	Hilly	75.1	22km/160m
5	Achill to Foxford	Low hills	68.5	47km/80m
5a	Link from Newport to Westport (Route 5)	Flat with a few drumlins	(14.6)	14km/210m
6	Foxford to Sligo	Stiff climb over the Ox Mountains	69.9	14km/210m
		Total	**466.9**	

This circular route from the lush fields and limestone scenery of Sligo to the ancient rocks and pounding Atlantic of Achill Island can feel like a trip to the end of the Earth and back. Indeed, on a stormy day Achill and, to the north, Belmullet do feel like the end of the known world. Along the way there are the unspoilt beaches of western County Sligo, the beautiful mountain-bound sea inlet of Broad Haven, the glacial glens leading to the twin loughs of Conn and Cullin, and the quiet lanes and roads nestling behind the Ox Mountains.

Options
Stage 5a links to Route 5 at Westport, see Onwards, below.

Getting to the Start
Below are the options to consider for this route.

By Air
Sligo has an airport with regular commuter flights to Dublin. Cycles are carried, but should be booked in advance (www.aerarann.com, Ireland 0818 210210, UK 0870 876 7676).

By Sea
No direct services.

By Rail/Bus
Sligo has a main line service to Dublin, but at the time of writing bicycles are not carried on trains – check before you make plans. The town is well connected to other major towns and cities via the Bus Eireann network.

When to Go
Achill is popular with visitors from Northern Ireland, and noticeably busier from mid-July, but nowhere on this route is a 'tourist hotspot', so consider travelling at any time from spring to early autumn.

Accommodation
West of Ballina the budget accommodation thins out. There is, however, a hostel at Pullathomas (Stage 2), which actually balances the distances better between Stages 2 and 3. On Achill Island, hostellers and campers have plenty of choice, but on the return leg to Sligo there are only limited options, although Foxford has a hostel and camping.

Dunmoran Strand is a well-kept secret

Maps

The Ordnance Survey 1:250 000 Ireland West sheet covers the whole route. At 1:50 000, sheets 24 Mayo Sligo, 25 Sligo Leitrim Roscommon, 23 Mayo, 22 Mayo, 30 Mayo, and 31 Mayo are needed from the OSI Discovery series.

Onwards

This route links to Route 5 via a short extra section from Newport (on Stage 5) to Westport. This is called Stage 5a.

STAGE 1
SLIGO TO BALLINA

88.4km Low and coastal; can be windy.

The stub of land to the west of Sligo is dominated by the 327m limestone mountain Knocknarea, with delightful Strandhill at its foot. From this mountain-foot village, another limestone massif, Benbulbin, dominates the

> On top of Knocknarea is the tomb of Queen Maeve – a warrior queen of Connacht in Celtic mythology.

> Post boxes are one of the few remnant signs of British rule. The box at 71.6km on this stage is a hybrid. It carries Queen Victoria's royal cipher, VR, but the door has been replaced by one with the initials of the Irish Free State, Saorstát Éireann.

view across Sligo Bay. Both these mountains are visible for many miles along the coast heading west, but it is the far older Ox Mountains that soon dominate the scenery.

Some of Sligo's prettiest coastal scenery hides along the strip of land between the Ox Mountains and the coast. Along the 3–4km wide fertile plain between the bare grey quartzite and gneiss ridge and the Atlantic, cattle graze languidly amongst hay meadows, in neat rectangular fields marked by blackthorn-smothered stone walls. Protected by Aughris Head is untouched kilometre-long Dunmoran Strand (38km).

The fine coastline continues as the way turns to the southwest, towards the head of Killala Bay, although the road tends to drift away from the shore until the seaside resort of Inishcrone/Enniscrone (74km). The strand makes it tempting to stay here rather than push on to Ballina, just across the County Mayo border.

On the Road

There is a short section (200m or so) of rough track behind the beach to the east of Aughris Head. It can be a bumpy to ride, but is not a problem to push. The turn that commits to this is at 42.2km. As an alternative, take the next right (about 400m) and pick up the directions by turning left at the first crossroads (44.6km on the main route). Note that a change to the Ballina one-way system has been mooted – this may affect the directions.

Accommodation

The Blind Brook Activity Centre (096 76838, www.blindbrook.ie) has hostel accommodation and camping facilities, about 4km out of Ballina on the main Sligo road (N59). Just north of town is the excellent Belleek Caravan and Camping Park (096 71533, www.belleek-park.com), which is on the edge of the Belleek Demesne. Stage 2 goes past the site (3km), or head out of town on the R314 towards Killala and look for the signed turn on the right a couple of kilometres out of Ballina.

Options

There are upwards of five Bus Eireann services a day to Dublin.

STAGE 2
BALLINA TO BELMULLET

100.1km Low coastal hills

It is a long way out to northwest Mayo, and if a northwesterly wind springs up, either or both of the first two days can be tiring. Accommodation is also sparse along this coast, and the first hostel is at Pullathomas (Kilcommon Lodge, 78km). This is a day to get an early start, and if time permits, stop and visit some of the interesting sites along the way.

On the way out of Ballina are the fine Gothic gates of the Belleek Demense and house, built in 1831 and now the Belleek Castle Hotel. Further along, the Franciscan Moyne Friary (13km) has a fine tower and almost intact cloister. Ecclesiastic architecture is the order of the day, and Killala has a round tower (16km). It was in this area that General Humbert landed with his French forces to support the 1798 rebellion by the United Irishmen.

French forces under General Jean Joseph Amable Humbert landed near Killala on 22 August 1798 to support the United Irishmen. Humbert beat the British at Castlebar, but was later defeated at Ballinamuck.

Downpatrick Head, County Mayo

Archaeologists have mapped the Neolithic sub-peat walls at Ceide Fields to reveal regular fields similar to the surrounding aboveground field systems in the area today.

As this stage leaves Killala Bay the country begins to open up, slowly the field sizes increase, there are fewer trees, and the landscape foreshadows the windswept rocky Atlantic coastline of the far west. In this transition zone to the west of beautiful Downpatrick Head is Ceide Fields (50km) – Europe's most extensive Iron Age monument. This field system, buried in bog, has been mapped to over 1000 hectares.

By the time Pullathomas is reached, mountains, moor and sea dominate the scenery, and this is clearly Atlantic Ireland. Belmullet, with about 1200 inhabitants, is the most significant settlement hereabouts. It lies at the neck of a tombolo joining the Mullet Peninsula to the coast.

A consortium led by a subsidiary of Royal Dutch Shell is developing the Corrib natural gas field, some 80.0km offshore, with the gas to be processed at the Bellanaboy Bridge terminal, alongside this route.

On the Road
There are shops at Killala (16km), Ballycastle (42km) and Belderrig (57km), but after that not much until close to Belmullet. Civilisation is sparse out here, so do not get caught running out of supplies. Pullathomas (78km) has a small shop, but if staying in this area it is better to stock up at Ballycastle or earlier.

Accommodation
Pullathomas (78km) has the pleasant Kilcommon Lodge Holiday Hostel (097 84621, www.kilcommonlodge.net). Belmullet has bed and breakfast accommodation.

Options
Rather than turning off for Pullathomas at 71.6km, continuing via the R314 and R313 to Belmullet saves about 9km. If heading straight

to Achill Island, Belmullet can be skipped by turning left at 95.7km and taking up Stage 3 from the 4.3km mark.

STAGE 3 BELMULLET TO ACHILL

64.9km Low coast; gentle climbs.

South to Achill Island is a potentially fast stage through lonely windswept boglands, which despite a certain melancholy, also hold a captivating beauty. Bangor (19km) is the only town of note along the way, and even here a frontier atmosphere prevails, as the grey slash of a gravel quarry hangs over the town, and the rounded green summits of the Nephin Beg range swell up to the south.

Close to the turn to Achill Island, Claggan Mountain almost pushes the road into a quiet inlet, where neat rectangles of small buoys mark out aquaculture pens. The stage then swings north and west to the foot of the bridge across Achill Sound, with the glories of the island still to come.

Clutching a return rail ticket to London, Belfast-born artist Paul Henry arrived at Achill Sound station in 1910. He stayed for nine years on the island, producing famous works such as *Launching the Currach* (1910–11) and *The Potato Diggers* (1912).

On the Road
This is a simple route to follow with few surprises. Bangor (19km) is the obvious place to stop for supplies, and there is a picnic area by the river and a supermarket on the way into town. There is a big supermarket at Achill Sound, just across the bridge, along with an ATM. While this route was being measured for this guidebook, extensive works were being done on the Achill bridge – hence this stage stops on the mainland side of the bridge and the next starts on the other.

Accommodation
The Railway Hostel (098 45187) at Achill Sound, based in the old railway station, is a comfortable place to stay with fine views over

the sound. The entrance to the hostel is on the right just before the bridge across the sound. There are bed and breakfasts scattered around the island – for an up-to-date list, see the Achill tourism website www.achilltourism.com.

Options

The main decision to make here is whether to push on and stay on the island proper, or to base yourself at Achill Sound and take a day trip around the island. The far-flung corners of the island are mountainous, and a lightly loaded bike is a definite plus, particularly if you fancy the 330m climb up Minaun Mountain (Baran Mhionnain). Pushing on takes you closer to the beaches however.

STAGE 4
TOUR OF ACHILL ISLAND

75.1km Hilly

From Achill Sound this stage follows a lazy figure-of-eight, by heading straight out to the far west of the island along the R319, before backtracking a little way and heading to the north shore. From here it crosses the outward leg to tour anticlockwise along the southern section of the island. Heading to the far west

first means a probable tail wind back to Achill Sound, but on a fine morning consider heading straight to the 330m climb of Minaun Mountain. This is the best view you can ride to in Ireland. The road to the top services a transmitter and is well surfaced and not too steep. The turn is just before the tourist information office, heading west.

The Deserted Village (34km) is a popular and photogenic destination. Tours start arriving by mid-morning, after which it is unlikely to be deserted.

The beaches on the north shore are sandy and attractive, although none quite measures up to the dune-backed strand at Keel (15km) on the south shore. Keem Bay (24km) at the far west of the island is a sandy cove protected by the knife-edged ridge of Achill Head – which can be explored on foot. The island's most scenic road is the southern loop from Dooega (Dumha Eige) (56km) round to Achill Sound.

On the Road

The best shop on the island is the supermarket at Achill Sound – there are other choices, but this has the best selection of fresh food. Across the car park is the island's only ATM. Most signs around the island are in Irish, and spellings vary considerably, so take care.

Achill Head

THE DESERTED VILLAGE

The Deserted Village consists of the ruins of between 80 and 90 mainly one-room cottages along a mile-long section of an ancient trackway crossing the back of Slievemore. Archaeological evidence suggests that the buildings were lived in permanently for little more than a century, from the mid-1700s until the 1850s, but the cottages were used as a 'booley' settlement into living memory, being occupied for the part of the year when livestock were moved to summer grazing. The ridges and furrows of the 'lazy-beds' where potatoes were once grown are visible around the settlement, and a wander through the un-roofed cottages on this lonely hillside give some insight into life in 19th-century rural Ireland.

Accommodation

There are campsites at Keel (14km, Keel Sandybanks Caravan and Camping Park, 098 43211, www.achillcamping.com) and Dugort (41km, Lavelle's Golden Strand Caravan & Camping Park, 098 47232). Also on the north side of the island is the Valley House Hostel and Bar (42km, 098 47204, www.valley-house.com), where tents can be pitched – for the quick way there, turn on to the L1406 at the 8.1km mark and follow the signs for about 3km.

Options

At the time of writing new local cycle routes were being signed on the island, although no other information was available.

STAGE 5
ACHILL TO FOXFORD

68.4km Low hills

From Achill it is a pleasant two-day run back to Sligo. Away from the coast, this is a road less travelled – cyclists are rare and, away from the main towns, so are cars. While there are no spectacular attractions along the way, the quiet roads and the wide, lake-filled glacial valleys make Stages 5 and 6 ones to savour.

During the first part of the day, Stage 5 retraces Stage 3 to Mallaranny crossroads, then pushes eastwards along the north shore of Clew Bay. The stage misses the centre of Newport, but it's worth a slight detour to visit the town, with its wide main street set high above the river.

The back-to-back glens of Glen Hest and Glen Nephin provide an escape route through the mountains to the bridge over the narrow confluence of loughs Conn and Cullin (62km). Nearby Foxford is a hospitable and interesting town, where fishing is a big tourist activity – Foxford sits on Ireland's most famous salmon river, the Moy.

William Brown, born in Foxford in 1779, is an Argentinian hero for his role in the war of independence, including defeating the Spanish in the Battle of the River Plate (1814). Find out more about the 'father of the Argentine navy' at the Admiral Brown Centre.

On the Road

There are no ATMs until the end of the stage at Foxford. Newport is the best place to stop. To reach the town, carry straight on at the R317 turn (31.1km) and the town centre is a few hundred metres further on, then there is a park by the river.

Accommodation

Gannon's Hostel (094 9256101) at Foxford also has camping – it is at the post office on the left as you leave town on the N26 towards Swinford.

Options

Ballina is only 20km to the north, for an alternative route back to Sligo via the coast (Stage 1 in reverse).

STAGE 5A
LINK FROM NEWPORT TO WESTPORT (ROUTE 5)

14.6km Flat with a few drumlins

See the route card for Stage 5a for the link to Westport and Route 5. No further description is needed for this short extra stage.

If you need bike repairs, J P Breheny's garage (098 25020) at 45km is the best bet in the area

STAGE 6
FOXFORD TO SLIGO

69.9km Stiff climb over the Ox Mountains

The Ox Mountains are survivors. They began as marine sediments over 1000 million years ago, before being pushed deep into the Earth's crust and reforming as the hard gneisses and quartzites that are now some of mainland Ireland's oldest rocks. Approaching their rounded summits from the west is another survivor – an old Irish country lane (at 4.5km). This grassy track winding between moss-covered rough stone walls and tunnelling through overgrown hedges is a step back into the 19th century.

After an initial climb into the mountains, this stage follows a gently sloping plateau through fertile farmland in the lee of the hills. The ridge thins out towards the west, but the Ox Mountains are still a barrier all the way to Lough Gill, making the wide col, filled by Ballygawley Lough, a welcome route into Sligo. Keep an eye out for the old handball court at Kilmacteige (18km).

On the Road

Outdoor handball courts are a distinctive feature of the west of Ireland. Irish handball is traditionally played in a 60 foot by 30 foot 'big alley', such as the one at Kilmacteige.

Aclare (19km) and Coolaney (46km) both have shops. Coming from the south is the easiest way into Sligo – just follow the signs.

Accommodation
See Route 3, Stage 6 for Sligo accommodation.

Options
As an alternative way into town, turn right at 68.3km and after 700m take a left turn, signed 'Cleveragh Retail Park' (Route 3, Stage 6, 82.1km) which leads to the cycleway along the river.

Author crossing the Ox Mountains above Foxford

ROUTE 4 SLIGO TO ACHILL ISLAND

Stage 1 Sligo to Ballina		
0.0		Sligo, Knappagh Road opposite bus station outside the Gateway Bar
1.0	↑	At traffic lights
7.6	↖ O ◆ ▲	'R292 Ballysadare' (bear right here for shop (600m) and Strandhill Caravan Park)
10.6	⇦	To Knocknarea
14.1	O➡	'R292 Ballysadare'
17.9	➡	'N59 Ballysadare'
18.1	➡	'N59 Ballysadare'
19.6	O↗◆	'N59 Ballina', shop on corner, more in Ballysadare
19.9	O➡	'N59 Ballina'
27.2	◆	Service station has small shop
29.3	➡	'Aughris Head'
37.3	➡	'Dunmoran Strand' (could skip this)
38.3	↑↓ WC	Car park at strand
39.3	➡	Rejoin road
39.6	➡	'Aughris Head', just over bridge
42.3	➡	'Corcagh church and burial ground'
44.1	↑	Road ends, follow track behind shingle
44.3	↑▲	Cross footbridge next to small campsite
44.4	↑	At Maggie Maye's Beach Bar join road
44.6	↑⇨	At crossroads, side-trip 500m return to small harbour and walk to headland
47.4	➡	At T-junction
54.5	➡	'Easkey'
60.8	↗	Road swings right after bridge
61.0	◆	Easkey has a few shops
65.6	◆	Rathlee has small shop
71.6	☆	Irish Free State letter box
74.3	◆ ATM	Food store. Service station has shop and ATM
74.5	☆	Tourist information at Inishcrone/Enniscrone
74.9	⇨	To sweeping, dune-backed beach
75.2	▲	Atlantic Caravan Park
76.9	➡	'Coast Road'
85.9	⬅	(Straight on is no entry)

Stage 1 Sligo to Ballina		
86.5	➡	'Town centre'
87.7	➡	Swing to right across river
88.4		Arrive Ballina PO

Stage 2 Ballina to Belmullet		
0.0		Ballina Post Office – head down Casement Street (with back to PO, head to your right)
0.1	⬅	At T-junction
	➡	At T-junction
0.3	⬅	'N59 Sligo' – just over bridge
0.6	⬅	'Town centre'
0.8	➡	'Nally Street' – just before Ballina civic offices
1.4	⬅	Through stone gates – Belleek Forest Park
2.3	☆	Belleek Wood
2.5	⇨	Belleek Castle Hotel
3.2	⬅	Road turns left
3.8	▲	Ballina Caravan and Camping Park
4.3	➡	Follow cyclepath at main road
4.6	➡	'Tour d'Humbert'
9.6	⇨	Side-trip to Rosserk Friary – 3km return
11.3	↑	At crossroads. Have right of way but be careful – visibility poor
13.3	☆	Moyne Friary – 300m walk down track to right
15.2	➡	On to R314
15.8	☆	Killala tourist office in centre on left
16.1	☆	Humbert statues
16.3	⇨	Killala round tower, 150m return
	➡ ◆	'Ballycastle', shop opposite
16.4	⬅	'Ceide Fields'
16.5	◆	Service station and shop
20.8	➡	'Tour d'Humbert', immediately over bridge
23.3	⬅	At crossroads
24.8	↑	Road joins from right. For Humbert's landing, turn right
25.1	➡	'Ballycastle via coast road', at T-junction
26.8	↑	Ignore fork to right

Stage 2 Ballina to Belmullet		
29.9	⇨	To Lackan Bay
37.3	⇨	To Downpatrick Head, 4km return
39.2	→	At unsigned crossroads
40.5	☆	Pass sandy beach backed by dunes
42.2	→♦	At T-junction (turn left for Ballycastle, which has a shop)
50.1	☆	Ceide Fields
57.4	♦	Belderrig has small shop
57.7	⇨	There is an alternative, mountain route along coast
71.6	→	'Poll a tSomais'
78.1	⇦	Turn past shrine for small shop and post office at Pullathomas
	▲	Kilcommon Lodge Holiday Hostel, Pullathomas
78.9	▲	McGrath's has accommodation
86.2	⇨	To small beach and pier, 2.3km return
89.4	→ ♦	At main road – R314. Supermarket about 50m on left
95.8	→	'Beal an Mhuirthead R313'
100.1		Arrive Belmullet central roundabout

Stage 3 Belmullet to Achill		
0.0		Belmullet central roundabout, outside Shelvins shop, head towards Bangor (past phone boxes)
16.4	☆	Picnic table on old bridge
19.6	♦ →	'N59 Mallaranny', supermarket on corner
19.7	☆	Bangor tourist information and internet café
19.9	☆	Picnic area by river
30.2	☆	Picnic area and access to river
34.5	☆	From low summit, views towards Achill Island
37.7	♦	Very small shop
47.8	☆	Pass Claggan Mountain
51.3	☆	Old Achill Island railway bridge
51.6	→	'R319 Achill'
52.0	☆	An Ghaeltacht
64.9		Arrive Achill Island bridge, Achill Sound

Stage 4 Tour of Achill Island		
0.0	→	Exit shop car park on island side of Achill bridge and turn right
5.2	☆	Lavelle's Garage and shop and Achill Tourism
8.1	▲⇨	Turn for Valley House Bar
10.8	⇦	Rough track has view of crannog (approx 200m)
12.4	⇨	Dugort turn
14.7	←	'Beach'
14.9	▲	Keel Sandybanks Caravan Park
15.0	→	Follow road along back of beach
15.3	WC	On left
15.4	←♦	Shop across road
18.5	⇦	Small stony beach with picnic table
24.1	↑↓ WC	Arrive Keem Strand
32.9	←	'L1407 Dugort'
34.9	⇦	To deserted village, 1km return
39.3	☆WC♦	Access to Dugort Strand, small shop across road
41.4	☆	Nice beach
41.6	▲	Lavelles Caravan and Camping Park
42.9	→	At crossroads
	⇦▲	For Valley House 300m
47.4	←	Atlantic Drive, at T-junction
50.6	→	'Dumha Eige' (Dooega)
52.2	⇨	To 'Baran Mhionnain' – turn here for climb to Minann
56.5	↖	'Cycle Route 1'
56.9	←	At T-junction
57.2	→	At T-junction
57.3	↑	'Gob an Choire'
57.5	☆WC	Pretty Blue Flag beach
59.9	→	'Cursana Farraige'
61.5	☆	Picnic table – fine views
65.1	☆	Best view on stage
66.3	←	'Atlantic Drive'
66.9	☆	Caislean Ghrainne
72.8	♦	Small shop
74.0	→	'Gob an Choire'
75.1	←	Arrive shop car park

Stage 5 Achill to Foxford

0.0	←	Achill Sound, mainland side of bridge, entrance to small car park to quay, turn left
13.1	↑	At Mallaranny crossroads
14.2	♦	Supermarket at service station
14.3	♦	Supermarket
29.2	⇨	Burrishoole Abbey 1.5km return, pretty spot
31.0	♦	Shop in service station – but plenty of shops in Newport at top of the hill ahead
31.1	←	'R317'
36.6	☆	IRA memorial
41.0	→	'Beltra'
43.9	←	At T-junction
	→	After 20m
50.5	←	Castlebar signed to right
51.4	♦	Shop Bofeenaun
51.7	♦	Shop
52.0	→	'Pontoon'
55.2	→	'Pontoon'
60.5	←	'R310 Foxford'
62.3	☆	Pontoon bridge
63.9	→	'R318 Foxford'
64.5	☆	Access to lake beach
65.1	☆	Access to lake beach
65.3	☆	Access to lake beach
67.0	⇦	To Foxford Station
68.3	→	'Swinford'
68.5		Arrive Foxford town centre

Stage 5a Link from Newport to Westport

31.1	↑	At R317 junction, carry straight on into Newport
31.4	♦	Supermarket
31.6	←	After bridge
34.1	↑	'Western Way' (WW) at crossroad
37.1	↑	'Fahy'
38.0	→	'WW', at Fahy
44.0	→	Join N5 just outside Westport, continue straight on to head of town
45.0	♦	Breheny's services bikes
45.5	→	At clocktower
45.6	→	At St Patrick statue
45.7	▲	Arrive tourist information, hostel adjacent

Stage 6 Foxford to Sligo

0.0		Foxford crossroads, corner N26 and Lower Main Street, head down Lower Main Street
0.1	↑	Past Admiral Brown Centre
	☆	Foxford Woollen Mills
2.0	←	'Foxford Way (FFW)', at T-junction
2.5	←	'FFW', at T-junction
2.7	→	'FFW', at crossroads
3.1	←	'FFW', at T-junction
4.4	←	'FFW', at T-junction
4.5	→	Down grassy lane, bit stony but very rideable
5.4	↑	Meet better road
5.7	→	On to sealed road
6.9	→	'FFW', at T-junction
8.1	△(134)	Bench if you need a rest
9.5	☆	Monastic site, fifth/sixth century – not much to see
9.9	↖	'Aclare'
11.6	☆	Bridge is Sligo county border
14.0	△(199)	
18.0	☆	On right is handball court, left is Kilmacteige famine cemetery
19.8	←♦	'Tobercurry'; Aclare has shop
23.7	←	'R294 Ballina'
23.9	→	'Cloonacool'
31.7	↑	'Coolaney'
33.3	☆	Pass Knocknashee Common – distinctive hillfort
39.4	↖	Take left fork
45.2	☆	Rockfield...has a rock in a field
46.2	←	At T-junction by IRA memorial in Coolaney
46.5	♦	Shop
47.6	→	'Collooney'
54.6	→	At T-junction, continue on main road through Collooney
55.4	←	'Sligo'
55.5	O↑♦	'R290 Dromhair' – careful, busy roundabout – shop at service station
56.1	☆	Markree Castle
58.8	←	'R284 Sligo'
58.9	♦	Shop in service station at Ballygawley
62.8	☆	Views of Benbulben and Knocknarea

Stage 6 Foxford to Sligo		
65.6	←	'N4 Sligo'
65.7	→	After 50m
	○→	'R287 Sligo'
66.5	☆	Cycle way starts
	○↑	'R287 Sligo' (cycleway ends after roundabout)
68.1	↑	'Town centre' – need to be in right-hand lane at lights
68.3	⇨	Alternate route to Hyde Bridge

Stage 6 Foxford to Sligo		
68.9	☆	Pass court house
69.0	←	'All routes', at lights
69.5	→	'Town centre', at lights
69.7	←	'All other routes', at lights
69.8	↑	'Station', at lights
69.9		Arrive at start point outside bus station

Strandhill sunset

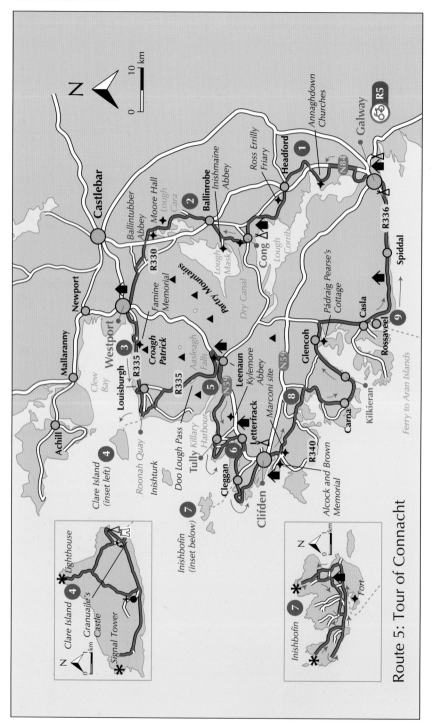

Route 5: Tour of Connacht

ROUTE 5

TOUR OF CONNACHT – PILGRIMS AND ISLANDS

Stage		Terrain	Distance (km)	Summit (distance from start/height)
1	Galway to Cong	Flat	63.6	42km/30m
2	Cong to Westport	A few gentle hills	53.0	45km/60m
3	Westport to Roonah Quay	Flat coastal	31.5	23km/50m
4	Tour of Clare Island	Small hills	21.9	10km/110m
5	Roonah Quay to Tully	Hilly	59.1	43km/70m
6	Tully to Clifden	Low hills	49.7	8km/80m
7	Tour of Inishbofin	Low hills	15.7	8km/50m
8	Clifden to Kilkieran	Low coastal	45.0	40m
9	Kilkieran to Galway	Flat coastal	68.1	30km/30m
		Total	**407.6**	

From Galway the immediate temptation is to head west into Connemara, but taking a northward route is a better alternative for several reasons. Firstly, the prettiest scenery immediately around Galway is along the shores of Lough Corrib and, further on, Lough Mask and Lough Carra. Also, the best coastal scenery in western Connacht is in the northwest, from Louisburgh, south to Clifden. So if you set off west from Galway you face two days of good but unremarkable scenery, probably pushing a headwind, and risk using up all your energy and time before reaching the really good stuff.

Connacht is one of the four provinces of Ireland, and consists of the counties of Galway, Leitrim, Mayo, Roscommon and Sligo. Like the other provinces, it owes its origins to one of the great Irish dynastic families, in this case the Connachta, who claimed descent from the mythical king Conn. This far western corner of Ireland is home to some of the island's most beautiful and deserted wild places.

The highlights of the northwards part of the trip described here include the old village of Cong and the High Georgian ruin of Moore Hall. Westport is a rare Irish example of an architect-planned town, and nearby Croagh Patrick has one of the best views in the country. This route includes optional trips to two fine islands; if you only have time for one, visit Inishbofin – it is a real treasure.

After the trip north, the way into the heart of Connemara is through melancholic Doo Lough Glen. The coast from here south to Clifden, with its low headlands and mountain-backed beaches, is idyllic.

To the south and east of Clifden the miles of bogland and lakes, so often associated with the Connemara landscape, take over. The final stretch of road into Galway from Casla is the only disappointing part of the route – see Options for alternatives – and as you sail downwind along the coast, passing cyclists slogging their way west, you can decide which is the better route into the west.

Options

On Stage 9, as an alternative to the busy and fast R336 from Casla back to Galway, consider taking the ferry to the Aran Islands from Rossaveel – the turn is at 30.8km. This will take a couple of extra days, but from the islands it is possible to return to Galway via Doolin and the Burren or continue south to Limerick or County Kerry (see Route 6 map for all these options).

The full tour is detailed as nine stages, and is just over 400km. The tours of Clare Island (Stage 4) and Inishbofin (Stage 7) can be omitted if time is short, and Stages 3 and 5 combined into a Westport to Tully stage (approximately 77km) giving a 356km six-day tour. A further short-cut is possible from Clifden to Galway, via Oughterard (78km), which knocks another 35km off the total.

Getting to the Start

Below are the options to consider for this route.

By Air

Galway Airport is 8km to the northeast of the city. There are connections to UK regional airports – Manchester, Luton and Edinburgh – Dublin and Waterford in Ireland, and Amsterdam Schiphol (www.galwayairport. com).

By Sea

No direct services.

By Rail/Bus

There are seven rail services a day to and from Dublin Heuston, with the journey taking under three hours. The bus takes slightly longer – about three hours 40 minutes. Buses and trains depart from the same central location – just off Eyre Square.

When to Go

Connacht seems big enough to soak up the tourists at any time, but the roads into and out of Galway to the west are very busy during holiday weekends, so avoid these if possible. Galway itself is hectic for the two weeks of the Galway Arts Festival, from mid-July, and the following week of the Galway Races. The hostels are often full, and buses and trains can be very busy.

Accommodation

There is budget accommodation most of the way along the route and in Galway city. The only tricky stretch is Stage 8 from Clifden to Kilkieran. Here there are no hostels, no official campsites and limited bed and breakfasts, so it is best to sort out a booking before leaving Clifden.

Maps

The Ordnance Survey Ireland West sheet covers the route at 1:250 000. At 1:50 000 the following OSI Discovery sheets are required: 45 Galway, 46 Galway, 38 Galway Mayo, 31 Mayo, 30 Mayo (for Clare Island and the strip of coast Westport to Louisburgh), 37 Mayo Galway and 44 Galway. Galway city is positioned right on the edge of sheet 45, which makes navigation to the north more awkward than it might be.

Onwards

Rather than returning to Galway, it is possible to head off to the Aran Islands and Route 6 – see Stage 9 below for details.

STAGE 1
GALWAY TO CONG

63.3km Flat terrain

After clearing Galway, this stage follows the picturesque farmland on the eastern shore of Ireland's second largest lake, Lough Corrib. The mountain barrier of Connemara looms to the west, and the strip of land along the lake, with its golden cattle, long thin bright-green fields and white limestone walls, feels like the last bastion of civilisation before the uncompromising granite of the far west.

The importance of this barrier country was not lost on earlier generations, and the area is littered with castles and ecclesiastic sites. Annaghdown (25km) has a fine collection of religious buildings, and is well known for its connections with St Brendan, who built a nunnery here for his sister Briga. Further on, Ross Errilly Friary (turn at 43.3km) is one of the best-preserved monastic sites in the country. It was a Franciscan foundation in the 14th century.

Galway's harbour fills with pleasure boats

The 1952 John Ford film *The Quiet Man*, starring John Wayne and Maureen O'Hara, was filmed in Cong.

Cong, a traditional-looking village guarding the neck of land separating Lough Corrib from its northern neighbour, Lough Mask, is a pleasant place to stay. There is plenty to see around town, including Ashford Castle, the ruined abbey and the Dry Canal. This monument to folly was built to carry steamer traffic between Lough Mask and Lough Corrib. Construction began in 1848, but the massive locks and the neat rock-cut channel remain unused to this day, as the porous limestone of the canal route swallowed up all the water.

On the Road
Getting out of Galway to the north is simple and, barring a rather unattractive 7km stretch through the industrial estates lining the N84, pleasant riding. There are a couple of shops and an ATM in the Cloonboo area (19km). It is advisable to take some cash with you, as ATMs are pretty thin on the ground from here, although Connolly's service station in Cong has one. The best access to Lough Corrib is quite early in the day (9km).

Accommodation
Cong Hostel and Cong Caravan and Camping Park (61.1km, 094 9546089, www.quietman-cong.com) are on the same site – not far from the lake and adjacent to the Ashford Demesne a kilometre or so from the village.

Options
If the mountains to the west are tempting, consider heading northwest on the R345/R336 towards the coast at Killary Harbour, Leenaun, and picking up directions from Stage 5, 36.1km.

STAGE 2
CONG TO WESTPORT

53km A few gentle hills

North of Cong the route follows the Dry Canal for a short distance before heading cross-country and looping around the north side of Lough Carra. The mountains retreat from view, at least until Ireland's holy mountain, Croagh Patrick, appears near Westport. Most of the through-roads in the area run 2–3km from the loughs, and with the low relief there are no panoramic views until the vicinity of Moore Hall (25km). This High Georgian ruin is worth

Moore Hall was built between 1792 and 1795

a walk for the architecture and atmosphere of faded grandeur.

North of the hall is Ballintubber Abbey (33km), the oldest royal abbey in Ireland that has been in constant use (established 1216). It is on an ancient pilgrim path that heads towards Croagh Patrick, and on a clear day the mountain is framed in the cloister arches.

At the end of the stage, Westport is a bright and lively town with wide streets and a tree-lined Mall along the river.

John Moore of Moore Hall was made president of the short-lived Republic of Connacht during the 1798 uprising. In 1961 he was officially recognised as Ireland's first president.

On the Road
Ballinrobe (12km) is the only significant town on the route. Moore Hall (25km), or the foreshore thereabouts, is the most pleasant place for a break.

Accommodation
Westport has a well-equipped hostel (Old Mill Hostel, 098 27045 www.oldmillhostel.com), but bikes have to be left outside in the courtyard. It is easy to find, right next to the tourist office. Westport House has camping (098 27766, www.westporthouse.ie), but prices are geared towards family holidays and there are other options further on.

Options
This is a short day, so pushing on towards Croagh Patrick on Stage 3 to climb the mountain, or Roonagh Quay for the ferry to Clare Island, are possibilities.

At the 7.2km mark there is a 5km side-trip to Inishmaine Abbey – the ruins are not spectacular, but it is finely positioned on a low lacustrine peninsula on Lough Mask.

STAGE 3
WESTPORT TO ROONAH QUAY

31.5km Flat coastal

The spin along the shores of drumlin-infested Clew Bay to the ferry at Roonah Quay is a pleasant one along a well-protected coast. The conical shape of Croagh Patrick dominates the scenery for most of the route. If time and weather permit, climb up Ireland's holy mountain for a view that is one of Ireland's best (10km). Across the road from the

St Patrick's association with Croagh Patrick dates from AD441, when he fasted on the summit for Lent, and also supposedly banished all the snakes from Ireland. Allow three to four hours for a return trip.

mountain is the National Famine Memorial, with its eerie famine-ship sculpture. Also of interest on the way to the ferry are the sand hills and sand cliffs of Carrowmore (24km). The coastal strip from Louisburgh around to the entrance to Killary Harbour is remarkably untouched, and has the wild and remote atmosphere which is increasingly rare on the Irish coast.

On the Road
Louisburgh (22km) has a well-stocked shop that opens around 8am. Stock up before going to Clare Island, where shopping is limited.

Accommodation
The route passes a couple of campsites. The Croagh Patrick Caravan Park (098 64860) is at the foot of the mountain (14km). A little further on, Old Head Forest Camping and Caravan Park (087 6486885) is near the beach (turn at 19.7km).

Options
Ferries depart from Roonagh for Clare Island and Stage 4. With an early start, it is easy to make the morning ferry (departures are currently at 10.45am and 11am) and spend the afternoon exploring the island, returning to the mainland the next morning. If you are rushing for the ferry, continue on the R378 at Louisburgh (junction at 23.2km), which leads straight to the ferry. The difference in distance is negligible, but the R378 is much faster than the road via the Carrowmore sand cliffs.

If you are not going to the island and heading on into Connemara, taking the R335 direct to Leenaun, at the same junction, saves about 4km and, again, this is a faster route. You can pick up the directions again after 6km, where Stage 5 rejoins the R335 at the 11.1km mark. If combining Stages 3 and 5 in this way, the total distance, Westport to Tully, is just over 77km.

STAGE 4
TOUR OF CLARE ISLAND
21.9km Small hills

Clare Island is easy to find the way around, as there are only a few roads. These directions take in the lighthouse at the northern point

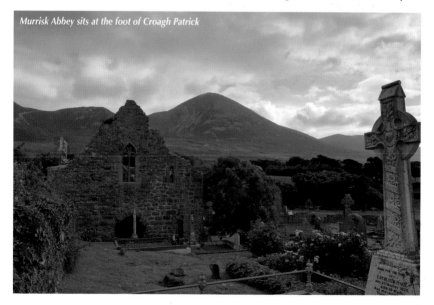
Murrisk Abbey sits at the foot of Croagh Patrick

Beautiful, and sad, Doo Lough Glen

of the island and the signal tower at the west end. The best beach is the one in front of the campsite. The medieval wall paintings at the island's abbey (11km), with their depictions of warriors, herdsmen, animals and dragons, are some of the finest in Europe. The abbey is locked, so ask around in the village for current access arrangements.

> The Pirate Queen, Grace O'Malley (Granuaile or Gráinne Mhaol in Irish), controlled the seafaring traffic on much of the west coast from her Clare Island fortress during the 16th century.

On the Road
The roads are reasonably good here and there is very little traffic. Pick up supplies at Louisburgh before sailing for the island, as the shop there is small. The community centre near the port offers food 9am to 9pm at the time of writing – though it would be best to check before relying on this.

Accommodation
The camp ground is little more than a paddock with a tap at the rear of the beach, but the position is fantastic, and there are showers and toilets at the community centre. There is other accommodation on the island, and the best place for a complete list is www.clareisland.info.

Options
There are two ferry companies running to the island – O'Malley Ferries (098 26976 www.omalleyferries.com) and Clare Island Ferries (098 28288 www.clareislandferry.com. At the time of writing, ferries leave Roonah Quay at around 10.45 and 110am, and as the crossing takes less than half an hour, Stage 5 can be completed in a day (the last ferry back from the island is around 5pm). There are extra sailings in summer.

STAGE 5
ROONAH QUAY TO TULLY

59.1km Hilly

The gateway into Connemara from the north is through the fabulous Doo Lough Glen, one of the most scenic passes in Ireland (18km). After passing Delphi Lodge, the pass ends at one of Ireland's few fjords, Killary Glen. Here, 10km from the open ocean, it is hard to credit that the quiet waters below are salty. Killary, less than a kilometre wide, causes a long diversion inland to its head at Aasleagh Bridge, just below a pretty waterfall (32km). A steady climb

In 1849, at the height of the famine, hundreds of men, women and children marched up Doo Lough Glen to to plead with the Famine Commissioners meeting at Delphi Lodge. Help was refused, and many died in the snow on the return march.

to the west of the crossroads town of Leenaun (Leenane) (36km) leads into the heart of the mountains, before another glacial pass ends among the sand dunes and beaches of northwest Connemara.

On the Road
The bridge at Leenaun was destroyed by floods in 2008 and a temporary bridge has been in place since, so directions/distances may change a little in the area – just follow the N59 out of Leenaun towards Clifden. There are no shops until Leenaun (36km) and no ATMs at all on this stage.

Accommodation
There are two hostels near Leenaun – Sleepzone Connemara (091 566999, www. sleepzone.ie) and the K2 Killary Centre (095 43411, www.killary.com), both 41km.

Further on, the turn to Harbour House at Rossroe pier is at the 48.2km mark, and it's about 4km to Rossroe (095 43933). For camping at 52km, there is the Connemara Caravan and Camping Park (095 43406), and just at the start of Stage 6 is Renvyle Beach Caravan and Camping Park (095 43462).

Options
The R336/R345 at Leenaun heads back to Cong (approximately 35km).

STAGE 6
TULLY TO CLIFDEN

49.7km Low hills

This far western part of Connemara is a disquieting mixture of the serene and the severe, with sandy beaches a few hundred metres from bog and rock-filled glens and glowering brown hills. In sheltered spots the vegetation can be almost tropical, while on the other side of the hills wind-lashed trees cower low, their roots grasping at little more than loose rock.

Amongst all the wild scenery, the towns are particularly well kept. Fine Letterfrack (13km) was actually founded by Quakers in

Off the beaten track approaching Cleggan

Kylemore Castle was built in the 1860s by wealthy Manchester politician and financier Mitchell Henry. Now a community of Benedictine nuns, the house and beautifully restored gardens stand in stark contrast to the surrounding mountains.

the 19th century. A little further up the valley is one of Ireland's top tourist attractions, Kylemore Abbey (turn at 13.8km, open daily 9am–5pm, gardens 10am–4.30pm, www. kylemoreabbey.com, 095 41146).

Connemara was once a land of many fine estates, and you can see the clues in the landscape – in the fine cut-stone field boundaries and iron gates, and in thick ornamental vegetation gone wild. For example, at around 22km the route passes the Shanboolard estate, hidden by the Victorian ornamental bush of choice – the rhododendron. Just past here is a turn to a quiet, protected beach.

Ferries to Inishbofin (Stage 7) leave from the small harbour at Cleggan (26km), which is itself a pleasant place for a break. From here the route skirts the low peninsula of Aughrus Head.The road towards Clifden then follows the shore of a narrow inlet before a short climb over the neck of another peninsula drops you into the lively town.

On the Road
The best shop on route is in Letterfrack (13km), where there is plenty of fresh produce, and also an ATM. If you are heading to Inishbofin, stock up at Letterfrack or Cleggan (26km), which also has a good shop. The beach reached by a turn at 23.4km is one of the prettiest spots in Connemara. In Clifden, the Video Vault on Main Street has internet access. Clifden also has a bike shop – John Mannion's, on Bridge Street (095 21160). The tourist information office is on Galway Road (095 21163).

Accommodation
Letterfrack (13km) has two hostels – Letterfrack Lodge (095 41222, www.letter fracklodge.com) and Old Monastery Hostel (095 41132, www.oldmonasteryhostel.com). For camping, at 39km Actons Beachside Caravan and Camping Park (095 44036) does what it says on the tin, while Shanaheever

Camping and Caravan Park (47km) is on a hillside location close to Clifden (095 22150, www.clifdencamping.com). At the end of the stage is the Clifden Town Hostel (095 21076, www.clifdentownhostel.com).

Options
At Cleggan you can take the ferry to Inishbofin for Stage 7, leaving the remaining 23km of Stage 6 for the following day. Check for the latest timetable at www.inishbofinisland discovery.com or telephone 095 45819. There is a late afternoon or early evening sailing daily. You can buy a ticket in town or on the boat, and they do take bicycles. It makes sense to sort out your accommodation before you depart for the island – see Stage 7.

If you fancy getting even further off the beaten track, access to Omey Island is across a sandy beach uncovered at low tide.

STAGE 7
TOUR OF INISHBOFIN

15.7km Low hills

Inishbofin measures barely 6km by 3km, but this small lump of dark rock manages to capture all that is best about the Connemara landscape in a package easily toured in an afternoon.

The protected beaches on the eastern side of the island are pristine (2km), while on the north and western shores the Atlantic has pounded the shoreline into cliffs and sea stacks. On the way out to the north shore (4km) is a stretch of rock, bog, lake and mountain that encapsulates the essence of the west of Ireland in just half a kilometre of track.

There is historical interest here too, with a fine Cromwellian fort guarding the harbour, as well as cultural interest. The island is a stronghold for traditional music, and hosts an arts and music festival in May. Traditional farming

The star-shaped fort guarding the harbour was built around 1656. It also was used to house captured Catholic clergy, declared guilty of high treason by statute in 1655, ready for transportation.

Unspoilt coastal scenery on Inishbofin's north shore

practices held out longer here than in many places in Ireland, making this one of the few places where the distinctive call of the ground-nesting corncrake can still be heard.

The directions here will get you round the island, but treat them as a rough plan – there is plenty to see. This is a friendly and welcoming place, so don't be afraid to seek out some local knowledge

On the Road
There is a shop on the island (15km) that has the basics and some fresh food. It opens 11am to 5.30pm (5pm on Saturdays) and 11am to 2pm on Sundays, but it's best to have at least some supplies when you arrive. There are three hotels on the island that serve meals. The community centre has an internet café.

Check for the latest ferry timetable at www.inishbofinislanddiscovery.com or on 095 45819. There is a 4pm departure from the island daily, as well as a morning sailings at 8.15am, 9am or 10am, depending on the day of the week. You can buy a ticket in Cleggan or on the boat, and they do take bicycles.

Accommodation
The Doonmore Hotel (9.5km 095 45804, www.doonmorehotel.com) and the Dolphin Hotel (1km 095 45991, www.dolphinhotel.ie) are both on the route card, while for the Inishbofin House Days Hotel (095 45809 www.dayshotel.ie) take the right fork at the junction at 0.3km.

Inishbofin Island Hostel (095 45855, www.inishbofin-hostel.ie) also does camping, and is in a beautiful high position on the island. There is a bed and breakfast, and hotel accommodation – www.inishbofin.com has up-to-date lists. Do sort out your accommodation before leaving the mainland.

Options
Talk to the locals and explore.

STAGE 8
CLIFDEN TO KILKIERAN

45km Low and coastal

South of Clifden the mountain spine of Connemara slowly recedes towards the horizon as bog, lake and rock take over. Before heading out across the wilds, there is a chance to visit the site of the old Marconi wireless station at Derrigimlagh Bog. To reach the Marconi station, carry straight on at 3.5km and look for a left turn at 4km, and follow the track to the site by a lake. When the facility opened in 1907 it was the first permanent transatlantic radio station. In those

The masts of the Marconi station guided Captain John Alcock and Lieutenant Arthur Whitten Brown through the fog to a soft landing at Derrigimlagh Bog, completing the first non-stop transatlantic flight in 1919.

days wireless transmissions involved massive masts strung with wire, and banks of capacitor plates releasing streams of sparks.

At Carna (36km) there is a discernible change in the landscape, as small optimistic fields with boulder-filled walls replace the miles of unimproved bog. Down the unsigned lanes are some of Ireland's best beaches. Seaweed-choked rocks are no more, and in the lee of Finish Island, bright white sands hold out against the suck of the Atlantic tides in Galway Bay (39km).

On the Road

Stock up on supplies in Clifden. There are no shops until Carna (36km).

The beaches in the lee of Finish Island are often deserted

Accommodation

There is precious little budget accommodation on this route. Consider wild camping along the coast somewhere. Alternatively, there are bed and breakfasts in the Kilkieran area. Stage 9 passes Hillside House (095 33420, www.connemara.net/Hillside) at 4.2km, but if you are planning on bed and breakfast, it is best to sort it out before you leave Clifden.

Options

For a one-day return route to Galway from Clifden, to take the N59 via Oughterard (51km) direct to Galway city (78km in total). This saves about 35km, although you will be following a busy main road all the way. That route also misses some wild landscapes and the fine coastal scenery opened up by the southern route described in Stages 8 and 9. A less drastic short-cut is to cross the peninsula separating Bertraghboy Bay and Kilkieran Bay. For this option turn left at 23.6km, from there it is approximately 10km to the R340, which is joined at about the 9km point of Stage 9 (the best place to re-set the cycle computer is at the turn to Pearse's Cottage, 12.4km). This short-cut gives a total Clifden-to-Galway distance of about 93km, but unless you plan to ride this in a day, accommodation options are very limited.

STAGE 9
KILKIERAN TO GALWAY
68.1km Flat coastal

The early part of this route back to Galway is by far the best riding. On the west side of Kilkieran Bay the road hugs a narrow strip of land between the razorback of the encroaching Cnoc Mordain mountain and the calm island-studded water. This coastal area and the offshore islands are a Gaelic-speaking stronghold, and this was one of the reasons Patrick

Patrick (or Padraig) Pearse was one of the leaders of the 1916 Easter Rising. Many of the key figures in the rising visited the cottage Pearse built here in Rosmuc.

The cycling on Stage 9 starts well, but the roads soon become busy

Pearse (see below) built a cottage here (turn at 12.5km, open 10am–6pm daily, end of May to September, also Easter; 091 574292, www.heritageireland.ie).

On the eastern side of the bay, the bog makes a brief reappearance before the road turns towards Galway. There are a couple of nice beaches along here, but the road (R336) is too busy, fast and narrow for comfortable cycling – see Options, below, for an alternative.

On the Road
Spiddal (49km) has ATMs, takeaways shops and public toilets. Glencoh (12.9km) has no facilities. If heading directly to the Aran Islands via Rossaveel, there is a large supermarket at Casla – turn at 29.1km – but there is also a good shop on the islands, at Kilronan on Inishmore (see Route 6, Stage 1).

Accommodation
Coming into Galway there are three campsites close together at Salthill (63km). These are Bayview Caravan Park (091 523316), O'Halloran's Caravan Park (091 590576) and Salthill Caravan Park (091 523972, www.salthillcaravanpark.com).

A little earlier on the route is the Seaview Lodge Holiday Hostel (091 593 888, www.seaviewlodge.ie) at 41.5km. Galway itself has a modern official youth hostel (091 566999, www.anoige.ie) close to the town centre, as well as a choice of independents. The closest camping is the Ballyloughane Caravan and Camping Park (091 752029), which is about 4km to the east of town. It is easy to find – take the R339 out of town, turn right at French roundabout (R338) and turn right at Dawn Dairies.

Options
Heading to the Aran Islands ferries at Rossaveel (the turn is at 30.8km) is a good way to avoid the busy R336 back to Galway. From the islands you could return to Galway via Doolin and the Burren, or continue south to Limerick or County Kerry (see Route 6 map for these options).

Galway has rail connections to Dublin, and is well connected to the Bus Eireann network.

ROUTE 5 TOUR OF CONNACHT

Stage 1 Galway to Cong		
0.0		Galway, Eyre Square, by Liam O Maoiliosa statue in northern corner, head uphill, away from square
1.1	O↑	'Sligo, Roscommon'
1.6	↑	At traffic lights
2.7	O←	'(N48) Castlebar' – cycle lane
4.6	O↑	'Menlo' – third exit
5.0	☆	An Gaeltach
5.3	→	At T-junction
7.4	←	'Monlach'
	→	After about 40m
7.9	→	At T-junction
8.8	☆	Lough Corrib appears to left
9.5	☆	Access to lake
10.3	←	Unsigned
11.3	←	At T-junction
12.6	←	On to N84 – care in traffic
12.7	♦	Shop
19.6	♦ ATM	Service station, shop, ATM at Cloonboo
19.8	←♦	Just past a bigger shop
20.2	←	T-junction
20.5	→	'Cloonboo Riding School'
22.6	↖	Road veers left
23.7	→	'Annaghdown'
24.6	←	'Annaghdown Pier'
25.1	⇐	Annaghdown Pier (also Annaghdown Priory) 1km return
25.1	☆	Annaghdown Cathedral
30.3	→	On to N84
30.5	←	'Caherlistrane'
32.3	♦	Small shop Bunatober
32.7	←	At T-junction
39.9	←	At crossroads
41.7	←	'N84' in Headford
	♦ ATM	
42.1	↑♦	'Ross Errilly Friary'
43.3	⇨	Ross Errilly Friary 1.5km return
45.2	→	First turn past ruined church
46.9	↑	At crossroads
47.2	☆	Cross Owen river
52.5	↑	At crossroads

Stage 1 Galway to Cong		
55.1	←	'R334 Ballinrobe'
57.5	♦	Cross has supermarket
	←	'R334 Cong'
61.1	⇐ ▲	Cong hostel, campsite and caravan park 400m
61.5	←	Gates of Ashford Castle; alternative route to Cong straight on
62.8	→	Turn right before bridge to castle
62.9	→	After 20m
63.5	☆	Pass Cong Abbey
63.6		Arrive – tourist information across road

Stage 2 Cong to Westport		
0.0		Cong visitor information centre, head downhill (one-way)
0.1	WC	
0.3	←♦ ATM	'An Fhar', shop opposite
0.4	→	After river bridge
0.9	←	Just past Dry Canal bridge
4.6	→	At T-junction
5.0	←	'Caherrobert' on wall
6.6	→	At T-junction
7.2	⇐	Inishmaine Abbey 5km return, track rough near end. Turn right through gate at 9.4km then right again
11.6	←	'R334 Ballinrobe'
12.0	←⇨ ♦ ATM	'Castlebar/Westport'. Turn right then left at bottom of Ballinrobe market place for supermarket and ATM
	♦ ATM	In service station
12.5	↑	'Claremorris Knock', at crossroads
12.6	↖	'Connaught Signs'
12.8	☆	Ballinrobe Abbey
15.0	←	Unsigned road
15.4	→	At T-junction
18.2	←	'Brownstown'
21.0	←	At T-junction
24.6	←	'Burriscarra Abbey'
25.4	☆WC	Car park for Moore Hall; Hall is about 1km return walk

Stage 2 Cong to Westport		
26.0	→	'Burriscarra Abbey'
28.8	☆	Burriscarra Abbey and Church
29.3	←	'Castlebar'
30.8	←	Unsigned road opposite iron gates
33.6	↑	Care – give way to right
33.8	☆WC	Ballintubber Abbey
35.3	↑ATM	'Killavalley' (cross N84), shop across road
38.5	→	Information point about mill on corner
42.0	←	At T-junction
43.5	→	'Westport'
51.9	☆	Westport railway station
52.1	◆	Tesco supermarket
52.5	↑O	Unsigned
52.9	↗	Follow one-way system at clocktower
53.0		Arrive Westport, St Patrick's statue. Turn right for tourist information and hostel

Stage 3 Westport to Roonagh Quay		
0.0		Westport opposite St Patrick's statue, take Louisburg (R335) direction
0.7	△	From low summit, views of Croagh Patrick and Clew Bay
1.4	◆	Small supermarket
1.6	⇨	To Westport House
4.9	→	'Murrisk'
5.4	◆	Service station and shop
8.7	→	'L5878 Murrisk Pier' (can continue straight on on R335 for more direct route)
8.9	☆	Murrisk Fisherman's Monument
9.5	↑☆	Murrisk pier has picnic tables, views. Keep following road
9.8	↑	Road joins from left
10.0	←	At T-junction
10.4	☆	View of priory
10.7	→	'R335 Louisburgh'
10.9	☆	Croagh Patrick car park – bike racks
12.9	⇨	Bertra Strand
14.8	▲	Croagh Patrick Caravan Park
19.7	▲⇨	L1827 Old Head – to Old Head Forest camping about 0.5km

Stage 3 Westport to Roonagh Quay		
22.9	◆	Louisburgh has shops – open early
23.2	→	'L5885 Carrowmore' (if not going to Clare Island could take left R335 Leenaun)
23.9	→	'Carrowmore' or if rushing for ferry, continue straight on R378
24.7	☆	Beach and sand cliffs
24.9	↑	At crossroads
25.4	→	At T-junction
27.9	↖	Ignore right fork
29.2	↑	
30.0	→	At crossroads – continue straight on if not going to island and continue from 1.4km mark, Stage 5
31.4	☆	Ticket office
31.5		Roonagh Quay

Stage 4 Tour of Clare Island		
0.0		Clare Island, by gates of Granuille Castle, head towards village
0.2	→	Follow road along back of beach
0.3	▲→	Head right at camping area
0.4	◆ WC	Community centre on left serves food 9am–9pm and has toilets
2.3	→	At T-junction
4.3	↑	'Lighthouse'
6.2	↑↓	Arrive lighthouse
8.1	↗	'Ballytoughey Bay'
11.1	☆	Clare Abbey
11.2	◆	Small shop and PO
11.3	→	'Napoleonic tower'
14.4	↗	At fork
15.3	↑↓	At 'Site 19' sign
19.1	⇨	Road leads to rocky shore 0.5km return
21.7	↑	Unsigned
21.9		Arrive back at Granuille's Castle

Stage 5 Roonah Quay to Tully		
0.0		Ticket offices, Roonah Quay, head away from quay
1.4	→	At crossroads
1.8	←	Unsigned

Stage 5 Roonah Quay to Tully

2.9	←	At T-junction
3.0	←	At T-junction
4.4	←	At T-junction
5.0	→	At crossroads
6.1	←	At crossroads
11.1	→	'R335 Leenaun 25'
12.7	☆	National School – 1945
18.0	☆	Doo Lough Memorial
21.7	⇐	Turn to Drummin
23.1	☆	Delphi Lodge (private, behind trees)
24.3	▲	Delphi Mountain Resort
27.0	☆	Views across water as road skirts Killary Harbour
32.2	☆	Gate to Aasleagh Falls – few hundred metres to falls
32.8	→	'N59 Clifden'
33.5	☆	'Coyne's First Pub in Connemara'
36.1	♦	Leenaun (Leenane) has shops – note road layout may change, follow N59 Clifden
38.9	☆	Quay for Killary Cruises
41.5	▲⇨	To Sleepzone Connemarra 1km
41.6	▲	K2 Killary
42.7	△(77)	Surrounded by mountains
43.4	→	'Tully Cross'
48.2	▲⇨	To Harbour House Hostel at Rossroe Pier
51.1	⇨	Side-trip to nice beach 2km return, signed Scuba Dive West
51.8	♦	Shops
52.6	▲	Connemara Caravan and Camping Park
57.8	→	'Tully' – need to give way at second part of junction
58.9	♦	Service station at Tully
59.1		End at Teach Ceoil Renvyle ('house of music') – has picnic tables

Stage 6 Tully to Clifden

0.0		From main road in front of Teach Ceoil Renvyle – head uphill
0.9	▲	Renvyle Beach Caravan and Camping Park
1.3	⇨	Beach access

Stage 6 Tully to Clifden

1.7	↖	At Renvyle House Hotel
4.1	←	Tower-house in front
4.3	←	'Connemara loop'
7.6	→	At T-junction
9.8	↑	Continue on road, right leads to Ballynakill quay
11.1	→	At T-junction
13.8	→ ⇐ ▲⇧	'N59 Clifden', at Letterfrack crossroads. Side-trip to Kylemore Abbey 9km return. Old Monastery Hostel is 200m through crossroads
13.8	♦ ATM	Fresh food shop
14.1	⇐	National park visitor centre
17.8	♦	Small shop in service station
18.2	→	'Cleggan' (note this is second of two turns close together)
20.4	→	At T-junction
20.8	↖	Road bears left
23.4	⇨	Road leads to beautiful, idyllic beach 3km return
26.1	→	'Cleggan'
26.7	♦ ⇨	Shop in Cleggan. Side trip to Cleggan pier for Inishboffin ferry
27.4	⇨	Beach access
29.3	⇐	Short-cut – saves about 8km
30.3	→	Unsigned
32.3	⇨	Beach access
33.8	←	At T-junction, right goes to Aughrus Head, which you can walk to
34.3	→	At T-junction
36.4	♦	Small shop and bar
36.5	♦	Service station and shop – short cut rejoins from left
37.0	↗	Road bears right
37.7	⇨	Side trip to Omey Island and beach. 1km return to beach
39.3	▲	Actons Beachside Caravan and Camping Park
45.6	→	'N59 Clifden'
47.4	⇐ ▲	Shanaheever Camping and Caravan Park
49.1	→	At T-junction
49.2	←	Follow one -way
49.4	→	'Sky Road'
49.7		Arrive Clifden central square

Stage 7 Tour of Inishbofin

0.0		Landward end of Inishbofin quay, head right
0.3	↰	Bear left at fork
1.0	⇦ ▲	Hostel and Dolphin Hotel 100m
2.1	⇨	To beautiful sandy beach – about 400m
2.4	←	At T-junction
2.8	→	Turn onto track at rear of beach
3.3	←	At end of beach turn onto road up hill
3.5	→	Through gate onto grass track
4.6	↑↓	Small bridge here is about as far as you can go
5.8	→	Back at gate turn right
6.6	→	'To pier'
7.2	⇦	Takes you back to hostel
7.7	⇦	Takes you back to quay
7.9	↗	'Doonmore Hotel'
9.1	→	'Doonmore Hotel'
9.5	▲	Doonmore Hotel
9.6	→	Unsigned
10.4	☆	Fine shingle spit
10.9	↑	Through gate
12.0	↑↓	Track peters out near small cove
15.0	↑	At Emerald Cottage B&B
15.6	⇦ ◆	Road to community centre. Shop on corner.
15.7		Back at pier

Stage 8 Clifden to Kilkieran

0.0		Clifden, from the bike racks outside Foyle Hotel head down Main Street (one-way)
0.1	→	One-way
0.3	↑	'Roundstone'
0.5	→	'Roundstone'
3.5	←⇧	Just before a bridge – easy to miss. Carry straight on for Alcock and Brown site and Marconi station
13.3	←	'Cashel'
15.0	⇧ →	'Cashel', straight on for Ballynahinch Castle 8km return
23.0	→	'Glinsk'
23.6	⇦	Alternative route/short-cut to Kilkieran Bay

Stage 8 Clifden to Kilkieran

30.9	⇨	Alternative by coast road
36.3	◆ ⇨	Turn right for shop at Carna, 1.2km
36.7	◆ ATM	Service station has shop
39.1	⇨	To beach 600m
39.6	⇨	To pier
40.5	◆	Shop
45.0		Arrive Kilkeiran 'Quickpick' shop

Stage 9 Kilkieran to Galway

0.0		Kilkieran 'Quickpick' shop
1.0	◆	Another shop
4.2	▲	Hillside House B&B
12.4	⇨	Side-trip to Pearse's Cottage 0.5km return
12.9	☆	At Glenoch Village
17.5	→	'Casla'
29.1	←	'Gallimh'.
	⇨	400m to shops at Casla.
	◆ ATM	
30.8	⇨	Turn here for Aran ferries from Rossavcel approx 2km
35.4	◆	Small shop
41.5	▲	Seaview Lodge Holiday Hostel
45.1	◆	Shop
49.3	WC	At Spiddal
49.4	◆	Shop at service station
49.8	☆	Beach, Burren views
54.9	☆	Beach
55.8	◆	Medium-sized shop at service station
59.6	◆	Barna has range of shops
63.2	→	'Salthill'
63.6	▲	Bayview Holiday Park
	▲	Salthill Caravan Park
63.7	▲	O'Hallorans Caravan Park
63.9	◆	Shop in service station
64.9	☆ WC	Beach – can be busy!
65.6	○↗	'R336 via Claddagh'
66.3	→	'Grattan Road'
68.0	→	Turn right and cross bridge into Galway city
68.1		Pull over safely to pedestrian area

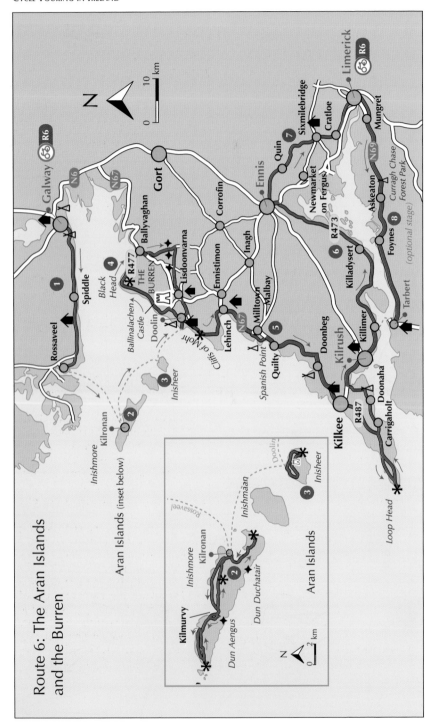

Route 6: The Aran Islands
and the Burren

ROUTE 6

THE ARAN ISLANDS AND THE BURREN – MUSIC AND ROCK

Stage		Terrain	Distance (km)	Summit (distance from start/height)
1	Galway to Inishmore	Flat, busy road	39.0	29km/30m
2	Tour of Inishmore	A few very short steep sections	37.6	25km/80m
3	Tour of Inisheer	Gentle coastal terrain	10.4	5km/50m
4	Round the Burren	Hilly	63.7	49km/190m
5	Doolin to Kilrush	A few coastal hills	130.6	6km/180m
6	Kilrush to Ennis	Short sharp hills	60.1	30km/60m
7	Ennis to Limerick	A few gentle hills	39.8	19km/50m
8	Limerick to Tarbert (optional)	Main roads, mostly flat	59.4	41km/50m
		Total	**440.6**	

This tour takes you from the granite lands around Galway, through the limestone karst of the Aran Islands and the Burren, and on to the sandstone plains of County Clare, before a sweep up the Shannon estuary to Limerick.

Day-trippers swarm to the Aran Islands, renting bikes to zip around the sights in an afternoon. But a more relaxed itinerary allows you to enjoy the islands in the peace of long summer evenings, with just the sound of the wind for company. There are three islands – Inishmore to the west, Inishmaan in the middle and Inisheer towards the Clare coast. The big island, Inishmore – often just called Aran – is the best set up for visitors, with regular ferries, plenty of accommodation and some fantastic sites to visit. The other less visited islands are, however, exceptionally beautiful and, at least to the outsider, seem to maintain a more traditional society.

The tour outlined here stays two nights on Inishmore and one on Inisheer before heading to Doolin on the Clare coast. This is a simple itinerary to manage as far as the ferries and accommodation goes. One disappointing aspect of the islands is that there is little opportunity to learn about their rich cultural history once you are there – so read up beforehand.

Doolin might not be for the purists, but it is a fun place to enjoy traditional music, and a good base for exploring the Burren and the nearby Cliffs of Mohr. The wildflower-encrusted limestone pavements of the Burren are one of the great landscapes of Europe, and the dark sandstone and shale cliffs of the Clare coast are justifiably one of Ireland's top tourist draws.

Further on, the north shore of the Shannon estuary is off the main tourist routes and has a pleasant, backcountry feel. East of Kilrush the drumlins make a reappearance to slow down progress a little, but all in all it is a pleasant run, via the historic town of Ennis, to Limerick.

Options

The Aran Islands are discussed above, but if skipping the islands the coastal route from Galway to Ballyvaughan is a scenic ride, although it can be busy as far as Kilcolgan. From Ballyvaughan there is the choice of climbing over the Burren (second part of Stage 4) or continuing along the coast (first part of Stage 4 in reverse).

If the planned direct ferry service from Galway to Inishmore starts, this would cut out Stage 1 to Rossaveel and a rather busy stretch of the R336. See Stage 1 for more on this.

If heading south into Kerry, the Shannon ferry from Killimer (Stage 6), 9km east of Kilrush, allows you to join Route 8 at Tarbert, saving a whopping 150km or more of cycling via Ennis and Limerick.

Getting to the Start

For Galway connections see Route 5.

When to Go

Galway town is very busy for the two weeks of the Galway Arts Festival from mid-July and the following week of the Galway Races. The wildflowers of the Burren are impressive through spring and summer, with different species dominating different times, but fine spring weather here is hard to beat.

Accommodation

The north side of the Shannon and Limerick itself are the problem areas for budget accommodation on this route. There are no hostels between Kilrush at the start of Stage 6 and Sixmilebridge (close to Limerick at the end of Stage 7) and this might be another factor pushing you towards the Shannon ferry to Tarbert and Route 8.

There are plenty of camping options around Doolin, but only one site (Green Acres) between Loop Head and Limerick.

Maps

The Ordnance Survey Ireland West sheet covers the route at 1:250 000. At 1:50 000 the following Discovery series sheets are required: 45 Galway, 51 Clare Galway (covers Aran Islands), 57 Clare, 63 Clare Kerry, 64 Clare Kerry Limerick, 65 Clare Limerick Tipperary and 58 Clare Limerick Tipperary. If heading south via the Shannon ferry, sheets 58 and 65 are not

required. The best maps of the Burren and the Aran Islands are the hand-drawn Tim Robinson folding landscapes series. They have more detail than the 1:50 000 maps, and should be considered if otherwise relying on the 1:250 000 maps. The Aran map is at 1:28160 scale (ISBN 09-530509-0-4) and the Burren at 1:31680 scale (ISBN 09-530509-1-2).

Onwards

Route 8 connects at Tarbert, which can also be reached by ferry from Killimer. For something different, you could try Route 7 in reverse and head to Dublin along the Shannon and the Grand Canal.

STAGE 1
GALWAY TO INISHMORE

39km Flat, busy road

This is a brief description of the route west from Galway to the Rossaveel ferry port for the Aran Islands. This is a pretty coast, with sandy beaches and views across Galway Bay to the Burren and the Aran Islands. Spiddle (an Spiddal) (19km) was once a refined seaside resort where the Connemara gentry would escape from the summer heat. The coast is still popular, and this contributes to the at times unpleasant traffic on the R336. This fast, narrow and busy road is by far the worst cycling in the whole of this guidebook – but unfortunately, at the time of writing there are no alternatives (although see Options, below – this may change). So try to pick a quiet time, wear bright colours and take care. Mid-morning and mid-week seem relatively quiet, while fine sunny weekends and public holidays are awful.

At the start of the route keep an eye out for the Claddagh Piscatory School (0.2km), which is a reminder that the west bank of the River Corrib was once home to a fishing village distinct from the city across the river. The school was established by Dominican brothers to educate the children of fishermen.

The ferry lands at the Kilronan quay on Inishmore. The next stage starts from the Ridgeway and Blyth commemoration by the quay, opposite the tourist information centre.

Bike-hire rush hour on Inishmore

On the Road

The most relaxed approach to planning this stage is to book outward travel to Inishmore, then arrange onward travel via Inisheer, and possibly Inishmaan, to Doolin at the start of Stage 5 while on the islands. The Doolin services run on quite small boats and are the most likely to be cancelled due to weather. Inishmaan has fewer ferries and some careful juggling of the schedules is needed to get there. The tourist office on the quay at Kilronan will help you with onward plans (099 61263).

For the outward leg, buy your ferry tickets in one of the Galway offices. There are two companies operating from Rossaveel – Aran Direct (091 566535, www.arandirect.com) and Aran Island Ferries (091 568903, www.aranislandferries.com) – both with city centre offices on Forester Street. Note that not all the connecting bus services to the Rossaveel ferries take bikes. Check when you book.

To follow the suggested itinerary in this book, take a 1pm ferry from Rossaveel to Inishmore with either Aran Direct or Aran Island Ferries, stay two nights, then take the 11.30am Aran Doolin Ferries (065 7074 455, www.doolinferries.com) service, which stops at Inisheer, stay a night and pick up the same ferry the next day to Doolin.

There are plenty of shops for snacks en route, and Kilronan on Inishmore has an excellent shop with plenty of fresh food and an ATM, so there is no need to haul a huge amount on the road.

This stage is Route 5, Stage 9 in reverse as far as the turn at 33.3km.

Accommodation

Inishmore has a selection of independent hostels. The biggest is a lively affair in the heart of Kilronan (Kilronan Hostel, 099 61255, www.kilronanhostel.com). The Killeany Lodge Pilgrim Hostel is in a peaceful hilltop location overlooking the bay a couple of kilometres from town; they also allow camping (099 61393, www.aislinglodge.com). Turn left after the Aran sweater shop, after 2.3km turn right and the hostel is near the top of the hill. The other camping option is a small site to the west of Kilronan, which has no showers but is in a quiet spot looking across Galway Bay towards the Connemara mountains (see Stage 2, 1.9km).

For a mid-stage overnight stop between Galway and Rossaveel, there are three campsites close to each other at Salthill (4.4km–4.5km). These are Bayview Caravan Park (091 523316), O'Halloran's Caravan Park (091 590576) and Salthill Caravan Park (091 523972, www.salthillcaravanpark.com).

Options

Aran Direct (contact details above) has been planning a direct Galway city to Inishmore ferry

Dun Aengus Fort's position is dramatic

service. If this happens, it will be an excellent way of avoiding the R336 out to Rossaveel.

STAGE 2
TOUR OF INISHMORE

37.6km A few very short steep sections

The basic structure of the three main Aran Islands is the same. They are the remnants of a limestone escarpment, with the strata dipping very gently to the southwest. The southwestern shore is generally the steep, cliff-bound one, while the northeast shore is more gentle. The layers of limestone are interleaved with narrow bands of clays and shales, and as a result the islands have weathered into a series of terraces separated by short sharp rises. These climbs slow down cycling a little, and it might take longer than expected to get around.

Writer JM Synge's one-act Aran play *Riders to the Sea* is perhaps his best work, while *The Aran Islands* (1907) portrays an island life very different to that seen today.

A good general plan for Inishmore is to head out to the west on the coast road and come back on the more exposed road along the spine of the island. This puts the wind at your back for the return trip and means the best views are in front.

The highlight of the day is the Bronze Age ring fort of Dun Aengus (8km), which some say is the most magnificent ancient monument in Europe. The vertiginous cliff-top location is spectacular and there are views down the island. One of the most tranquil spots on the islands is the diminutive Teampall Bheanáin. Set on a bare limestone pavement high above

Transatlantic rowers John Ridgway and Chay Blyth landed on Inishmore on 3 September 1966 after 91 days at sea. They accepted help from the Aran lifeboat, which was called out when the emptying of a toilet bucket was mistaken for emergency bailing.

Killeany, it is particularly beautiful around sunset (turn at 30.5km). The Black Fort, or Dun Duchatair, doesn't have the intriguing geometry of Dun Aengus, and the cliffs aren't quite so high, but the promontory location, massively undercut shoreline and the lack of visitors make it the equal of its more famous sibling (turn at 29.2km).

The very steep climb to the old lighthouse and nearby Dun Eochla (turn at 25.2km) leads to the island's highest point. The ride out to the western end of the island takes you to an exposed storm beach, while at the eastern point, grey water surges down the channel separating Inishmore and Inishmaan. Kilmurvy (7km) is the most popular choice for a swimming beach.

The island is littered with other prehistoric and early Christian sites. The free maps handed out around the landing point are a good start, or see the maps section above if you plan to explore further.

On the Road
There are a few spots to get snacks around the island, mostly around Dun Aengus (8km), but the best option is to stock up at the Kilronan supermarket.

Accommodation
Listed in Stage 1.

Options
Now is a good time to arrange onward ferry connections or bookings on the other islands – the tourist office is by the quay at Kilronan (099 61263).

STAGE 3
TOUR OF INISHEER

10.4km Gentle and coastal

At under 3km² and with fewer than 250 inhabitants, Inisheer is tiny. There are a few concessions to tourism – a hostel, campsite, bike hire and the odd pony trap for hire – but this is far removed from the tourist-processing facilities on Inishmore. The island is lower and flatter than the larger islands, but has the same characteristic limestone landscape.

Inisheer, and the *Plassy* wreck, shot to fame by featuring as Craggy Island in the opening sequence of the comedy TV show *Father Ted*.

These directions go to the *Plassy* wreck (2km) on the rocky pavement of the east shore and out to the eerie west shore. Along the way there is a ride along a grassy lane, a castle, and a fine beach near the pier.

On the Road

There is a shop on the island – from the pier turn left, then when you see the track to the beach on your left, follow a road up the hill to your right for about 200m. There are three pubs that serve food, and a café too.

Accommodation

The campsite (099 75008) behind the beach (600m) has basic facilities, but be aware that the shower/toilet block was locked quite early when we stayed. The hostel (Bru Radharc Na Mara, 099 75024) is close to the pier – just turn right. For other accommodation, the island cooperative website is a good place to start – www.inisoirr-island.com.

Connections

Confirm your departure time with the boat's crew when you arrive. Sailings are subject to change. The ferry from Inisheer to the Clare coast lands at Doolin pier, the start of Stage 4.

STAGE 4
ROUND THE BURREN

63.7km Hilly

The limestone slab of the Burren is similar geologically to the Aran Islands, but the extra altitude of this corner of northwest Clare provides added dramatic perspective. There are dozens of different routes through the Burren, and on a mountain bike, many more following the traditional 'green road' routes that are found inland. But it is the climb from the small fishing town of Ballyvaughan (32km) into the high Burren that makes the route described here the pick of the bunch.

Before reaching Ballyvaughan, however, there is some coastal scenery to enjoy beyond Doolin. The castle at Ballinalacken (6.8km) guards the southern approaches to the Burren, and as the road swings along the coast it passes

One of Cromwell's men famously said of the Burren that there was neither wood to hang a man, water to drown him or earth to bury him.

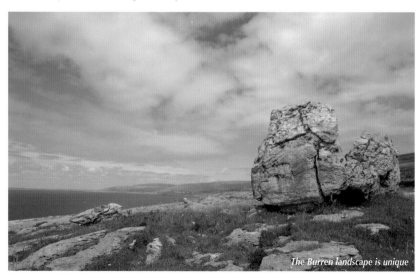
The Burren landscape is unique

BREHON LAW

Before the imposition of English rule, Ireland had an indigenous system of law dating from Celtic times. The law was administered by Brehons, and is hence known as Brehon Law. The Brehons' task was to preserve and interpret the laws that had been handed down orally through the generations, and which were only written down for the first time in the seventh century. English common law slowly encroached on Brehon Law from the Norman invasion of 1169, but away from the areas of strongest English influence Irish law survived well into the 17th century. Cahermacnaghten was the core of the estate of the Uí Dhábhoireann (O'Davoren) hereditary legal family from about 1300 to 1700, and the law school here was probably at its peak in the mid-16th century.

through a land of wide white limestone pavements lapped by the deep-blue water of Galway Bay. The bare escarpments stack up to the north, but before climbing away from the coast, it is worth taking a short walk either along one of the pavements, or straight up Black Head (22km) from behind the lighthouse. Just gaining a 100m or so in height opens up a view along the edge of the limestone plateau and also gives a close-up view of the wildflowers.

Back on the road, Ballyvaughan, set in woodlands and with lush coastal vegetation, feels a little removed from the Burren itself, but this creates a wonderful change in the landscape climbing out of the town – the trees and hedges slowly fade away, then the soil and pasture become thinner, and within a few kilometres is a land of wind and rock. Adding drama to this wild landscape is the Poulnabrone Dolmen (41km) – a Neolithic portal tomb dating from about 4200BC to 2900BC. Nearby Caherconnell stone ring fort is similar to those on the Aran Islands. In the same area is the less impressive but culturally important Cahermacnaghten (turn at 48.1km), at one time a school of Brehon Law.

The way back to Doolin follows the southern edge of the Burren through Lisdoonvarna (55km), site of the famous wedding fair in September (www.matchmakerireland.com), and along the narrow slash of the Aille valley to the coast.

Doolin's development as a hot spot for Irish music began in the 1960s, pretty much on the back of flute player and tin whistler extraordinaire the late Micho Russell.

On the Road
There are a handful of shops on the early part of the ride, but Ballyvaughan (32km) has the best choice of food for lunch – either to eat there or take into the high Burren. There is a farmers' market at the village hall on Saturday mornings from May to October. There are no ATMs in this area – the nearest to Doolin is at the Cliffs of Mohr visitor centre, 6km into Stage 5.

Accommodation
Doolin seems to have monopolised the hostel supply in northwest Clare, so budget accommodation is a little sparse on this stage. With the climbing involved, it is much better exploring without luggage, but there is a hostel at Kilfenora a few kilometres off-route – Kilfenora Hostel (065 7088908, www.kilfenorahostel. com). Lisdoonvarna (55km) has an An Óige hostel – Sleepzone the Burren (01 8304555 for bookings, www.anoige.ie).

Options
There is a maze of small roads across the Burren to explore.

STAGE 5
DOOLIN TO KILRUSH

130.6km A few coastal hills

This stage was made ridiculously long by an obsession to get to the lighthouse at the end of the Loop Head peninsula. The cliff scenery to the west of Kilkee is very fine, but realistically it is better to either split this stage in two, or skip the trip out to the lighthouse.

Lahinch is one of the prettiest spots in County Clare

Kilrush is a heritage estate town and port that was developed extensively in the 18th century by the Vandeleur family, prominent landlords in West Clare. The town retains many buildings from this period, and nowadays is the spot from which to take the boat to the early Christian sites on Scattery Island.

The first point of interest is the Cliffs of Mohr (62km) – 200m high and 8km long. Following this a beautiful, if less spectacular, low coast with some fine beaches and sand dunes continues to the resort town of Kilkee (60km).

West of here the cliff scenery returns, and this stretch of coast, with its dark, folded rock, stacks and arches, is as beautiful as the more visited cliffs to the north. Loop Head itself (89km) can be a little disappointing, especially if tired from – almost certainly – pushing against a westerly wind. But the enticing views across the mouth of the Shannon to the Kerry coast are filled with the promise of mountains unclimbed, while the narrowing silver line of the Shannon estuary points the way towards the bright lights of Limerick.

The dark Cliffs of Mohr being pounded by Atlantic breakers is one of the great coastal sights in Ireland. The new underground visitor centre here cost €31.5 million to build.

The French sailing ship *Leon XIII* wrecked near Quilty in 1907. The heroic rescue of the crew by local fisherman made news around the world.

On the Road
Any of the small towns along this stage are pleasant places for a break. Quilty (35km) has a fine open aspect and benches near the information panel about the *Leon* wreck. The Victorian resort town of Kilkee (60.2km) has the pick of the many beaches, and this might be enough to tempt you to stay nearby and skip the long trip out to Loop Head.

Accommodation
This corner of Clare is a holiday coast, and so well provided with accommodation. There are hostels at Lehinch (17km) – Lahinch Hostel (065 7081040, www.visitlahinch.com) – Kilkee (60.2km) – Kilkee Hostel (065 9056209) – and Kilrush (130km) – Katie O'Connor's (065 9051133).

For camping, Lahinch has Ocean View Caravan Park (18km), Spanish Point (28km) has Egan Camping and Caravan Park (neither list telephone numbers) and Lahiffes (065 7084006), Doonbeg (49km) has Strand Camping (065 9055345, www.strandcampingdoonbeg.com), and Doonaha (112km) has Greenacres (065 9057011) overlooking the Shannon.

Options

There are several short-cuts to Kilrush. Continuing straight on at 60.3km in Kilkee and following the N67 to Kilrush gives a total distance of approximately 73km. A quieter option is to turn at 49.2km at Doonbeg. From here it is 12km to Kilrush, giving a total distance from Doolin to Kilrush of 61km.

**STAGE 6
KILRUSH TO ENNIS**

60.1km Short sharp hills

The strip of land along the Shannon between Kilrush and Ennis reveals as false the reputation of southwest Clare for being rather dreary countryside. While the underlying sandstones do tend to produce rather drab boglands, the more fertile soils of the drumlin swarms make

> *The Colleen Bawn* is a 19th century melodrama by Dion Boucicault based on the shocking murder of a beautiful Irish farmer's daughter, Ellen Hanley, by her husband John Scanlan. There is a statue of the Colleen Bawn at Killimer.

The Colleen Bawn is remembered at Killimer

THE COLLEEN BAWN

picturesque rolling farmlands, with hedge-lined hay meadows and small pockets of woodland.

The road here alternates between high sections with fine views over the shining Shannon, and low crossings of inlets by small fishing harbours. The drumlins do tend to make the going slow however, and it is also further to Limerick than might be expected, thanks to the detour north made necessary by the broad estuary of the River Fergus.

Ennis is a historic market town that grew up around the site of a Franciscan friary. The Clare Museum is worthy of a visit, as are the ruins of the friary.

The roads and small towns are peaceful along here, but all in all this is an enjoyable day's cycling rather than a spectacular one, and there is always the temptation to cut out about 150km of cycling by taking the Shannon ferry across to Tarbert and County Kerry (9km), linking with Route 8.

On the Road

Killadysert (36km) and Ballynacally (43km) have shops and are pleasant places to take a break.

Accommodation

Ennis has no budget accommodation. The closest camping/hostel is 15km in the wrong direction (to the north), at the Corofin Hostel and Camping Park (065 6837683, www.corofincamping.com). A better bet is to continue towards Limerick on Stage 7, where there is the excellent Jamaica Inn (061 369 220, www.jamaicainn.ie) at Sixmilebridge (22km), or even push on to the end of Stage 7 (39km).

Options

The main choice on this stage, if heading further on into Kerry, is whether to take the ferry across the Shannon, or cycle the long way round via Ennis and Limerick (Stages 7 and 8). ShannonFerry (065 9053124, www.shannonferries.com) operates the service from Killimer (on the north bank) to Tarbert, every hour, on the hour, and in the reverse direction every hour, on the half hour. The first service is at 7am, 9am on Sundays, and the last one at 9.30pm in summer and 7.30pm in winter. From May to September the service is upgraded to half hourly in each direction, with an extra ferry running from 10.30am (from Killimer) to 6pm (from Tarbert). It is €5 one way, pay on board.

STAGE 7
ENNIS TO LIMERICK

39.8km A few gentle hills

The run into Limerick from Ennis is short and sweet, with no major hills and little traffic away from the main road. The countryside is pleasant and, judging by the number of castles, was at one time of strategic importance. Some of the fortifications, such as Knappogue (13km), have been developed, while others lie as rather romantic roadside ruins.

Also of interest, to the east of Ennis, is the 15th-century Franciscan foundation of Quin Abbey (10km), which sits on a small rise in the water meadows near the Rine river.

The south-flowing rivers and streams draining the Clare plains into the Shannon estuary are a natural source of water power, and there have been several mill developments in the area. Sixmilebridge (23km), in particular, retains many of the features of a 17th- to18th-century mill town.

'The Miller Returns' statue at Sixmilebridge recalls the town's industrial past

The approach to Limerick from the west continues through woods and farms until 4–5km from the heart of the city. The Normans built a still largely intact walled town and castle on King John's Island, and the old town is interesting to wander around. The main part of the city has fine wide streets and busy shops. From a cycling point of view it is also easy to get into and out of, although like most Irish cities the traffic is congested.

Limerick was founded by the Vikings at the lowest crossing point of the Shannon.

On the Road
There is a new shopping centre being built close to the tourist office in Ennis, so be aware that the directions might change in this area. On this short stage, the best places to stop are at Quin (9km) and Sixmilebridge (23km), both of which have shops. There is an ATM on the way into Limerick (36km), which saves you hunting around the town centre, as well as a couple of shops if you are pressing on through the city.

Accommodation
Hostels seem to have passed Limerick by. Courtbrack Accommodation (061 302500, www.courtbrackaccom.com) is student accommodation, available on a hostel basis from late May to mid-August, about 2km south of the city centre. The best nearby choice is the Jamaica Inn, early in the stage (061 369 220, www.jamaicainn.ie) at Sixmilebridge, about 16km from the city centre. If you are pushing on southwards into Kerry, the next hostel is the Ferry House Hostel (068 36555, www.ferry-hostel.com) at Tarbert – see Stage 8, 59km.

Options
If you are flying into or out of Shannon Airport, the roads from the Sixmilebridge area are quieter than some – it's about 12km from the village to the airport. In fact if you stay at the Jamaica Inn you'll meet many travellers who have chosen the hostel for their first or last nights in Ireland.

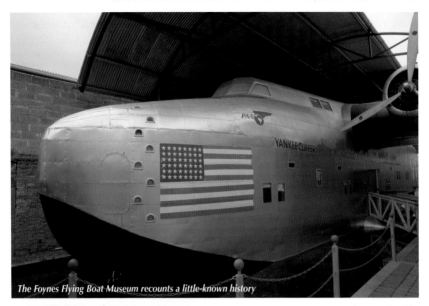

The Foynes Flying Boat Museum recounts a little-known history

STAGE 8
LIMERICK TO TARBERT (OPTIONAL)

59.4km Main roads, mostly flat

This stage is included primarily to provide a link from Limerick to the main loop of Route 8, but the south side of the Shannon is pleasant enough for cycling, and the fertile limestone plains have grown some fine houses.

The castellated Gothic towers of Dromore Castle (17km) are an impressive sight from the road, but further on is somewhere you can visit. Curraghchase (20km) Forest Park hides a fine neoclassical house, Askeaton, which with its castle, friary and 15th-century bridge is a piece of medieval Ireland bypassed by the main roads (27km).

> Curragh Chase was once the family home of 19th-century poet Aubrey de Vere.

One of the less well known aspects of the history of the Shannon is told at the Foynes Flying Boat Museum (38km), open daily March to November, 10am–6pm (4pm in November) (069 65416, www.flyingboatmuseum.com). For a brief few years Foynes was the most important commercial airport in the world. The first direct commercial transatlantic passenger flight landed on the Shannon here in July 1939. During the Second World War, Ireland's neutrality meant the airlines kept operating here, and many luminaries and celebrities passed through, including Ernest Hemingway and Eleanor Roosevelt. The last flight was in 1945.

The east-facing escarpment at Foynes marks the end of the Carboniferous limestone of the central lowlands and the start of the hillier Namurian sandstones.

Tarbert is a small, quiet town, best known as the jumping-off point for the Shannon ferry. Tarbert Island prospered as a port in the 18th and 19th centuries, and the town, with its wide main street and neat buildings, still shows signs of its glory days. There are a couple of things to see around town, including the 19th-century gaol – the Tarbert Bridewell (068 36500).

On the Road
At the time of writing, a new road junction was being built where this route leaves Limerick between the 2km and 3km mark, so watch the directions. This stage has long sections on the N29 that can't be avoided. The road is mostly wide, with broad hard shoulders, and the only unpleasant stretch is a narrower bumpy section

between the alumina plant at Aughinish Island (33km) and Foynes.

Get any bike-related or camping supplies in Limerick before you leave. The local shops at 4.7km are a good place to re-supply with food. Kildimo (15km) also has a shop and ATM. Medieval Askeaton (27km) has shops and is interesting to look around. At the end of the day, Tarbert has shops and an ATM.

Accommodation
Tarbert has a hostel – the Ferry House Hostel (068 36555, www.ferryhousehostel.com). There is camping leaving Limerick (20km) at Curraghchase Caravan and Camping Park (061 396349, www.coillte.ie), which is open from early May to early September.

Options
It is possible to get off the main road by taking to the hills before Foynes, at 36.6km, at the turn signed Knockpatrick Gardens, but there are some steep climbs. The Tarbert ferry (065 9053124, www.shannonferries.com) links this stage to or from Stage 7, and is signed in the town. Route 8 starts where the road from the ferry meets the N69 (about 2.5km from the ferry). For the ferry timetable, see Stage 6, Options.

ROUTE 6
THE ARAN ISLANDS AND THE BURREN

Stage 1 Galway to Inishmore

0.0		Galway, west end of Wolf Tone Bridge, join traffic when safe!
0.1	←	'Salthill via coast road'
0.2	☆	Claddagh Piscatory School
1.7	←	At T-junction, can join shared cycleway here but road is easier
2.2	☆	National Aquarium
2.4	←O	'R336 an Spiddal'
3.2	WC	Beach as well
3.7	↑O	'an Spiddal'
3.8	WC	
4.4	▲	O'Halloran's Caravan Park
4.5	▲	Salthill Caravan Park
4.5	▲	Bayview Caravan Park

Stage 1 Galway to Inishmore

4.9	←	'an Spiddal'
6.4	♦	Shop at service station
8.3	↑♦	At lights, Barna has shops and pharmacy
13.3	☆	Beach
18.9	♦ ☆ WC	Shop in garage, picnic area opposite and beach close by
19.2	♦ ATM	An Spiddal Spar shop has ATM
23.2	♦	Supermarket in service station
24.3	♦	Small shop
27.0	▲	Seaview Lodge Holiday Hostel
33.1	♦	Small shop
33.3	↑	Where R336 turns right, continue straight ahead
38.5	←	'R372 ferries'
39.0		Arrive ticket office at quay

Stage 2 Tour of Inishmore

0.0		Kilronan, Inishmore, by Ridgway and Blyth commemoration, head away from ferries
0.1	WC	
0.2	↘	Road swings round to right
0.3	♦ ATM	Supermarket and ATM down lane to right
0.5	☆	Ionad Aran (cultural centre) – currently closed
	☆	Bank
0.8	→	At Joe Watty's Pub
1.9	▲	Campsite in field on left
2.4	⇦☆	Teampall Chiaráin 260m return
3.1	⇦☆	Teampall Asurnaí 900m return
4.5	☆	Seal colony on right, telescope
7.1	←	Beach at Kilmurvy on right
	→	After 50m
7.5	WC	
	↖	'Dun Aengus'
7.9	♦	Souvenir shop
8.1	↑↓	Dun Aengus car park – bike racks
8.2	←	At shops
9.2	←	At T-junction
10.0	⇦☆	'Dun Eoghanachta'
10.9	☆→	Na Seacht dTeampaill – on the corner
11.3	←	Along shore

Kilmurvy Beach is one of Inishmore's best swimming spots

Stage 2 Tour of Inishmore

14.8	→	At T-junction
15.2	↑↓	End of the island
21.9	↗	Veer right
25.2	☆⇨	To lighthouse and Dun Eochla – views 800m return
26.7	▲	Mainstir House Hostel
28.1	→	Just before Aran Sweater Market
29.2	☆⇨	Turn here for the Black Fort, turn right after 300m
30.5	▲☆⇨	Turn to Killeany Lodge and Teampall Bheanáin
30.6	⇦	Turn to small harbour
31.0	☆	Monument to lost at sea
31.1	⇦	Turn to airfield and access to beach
31.8	↖	Bear left at fork
32.8	↑↓	Beach – views to Inishmaan
37.4	→	Back towards quay
37.6		Arrive back, Ridgway and Blyth commemoration

Stage 3 Tour of Inisheer

0.0		From head of Inisheer pier, head to the left
0.2	☆	Beach on the left
0.4	←	Just past Bronze Age tumulus Cnoc Raithní

Stage 3 Tour of Inisheer

0.6	▲	Camp ground on left
1.0	☆	Ionad Seirbhisi Teanga (I bought a book about the island here)
1.4	←	Unsigned
2.4	⇦☆	To Plassy wreck
2.8	→	Straight on is rough track along foreshore
3.8	←	At T-junction
3.9	←	At T-junction
4.2	→	Turn down gravel track, turns to firm grass
4.6	←	At T-junction (go right for castle)
4.7	☆	Pass signal tower
5.0	→	Down grassy track
5.2	→	At T-junction
5.5	→	At T-junction
	←	At T-junction
5.6	→	At T-junction
5.7	←	At T-junction past church
5.9	←	At T-junction
6.1	←	Road swings left
7.3	→	'Burren Way', grassy lane
7.5	←	Join tarmac
7.6	☆	St Enda's Well
7.8	→	On to rocky track

		Stage 3 Tour of Inisheer
8.9	↗	Bear right at fork
9.6	←	At T-junction
9.8	→	At T-junction
10.1	←	At T-junction
10.2	←	Unsigned
10.4		Arrive back at quay

		Stage 4 Round the Burren
0.0		Doolin Pier
0.2	WC ▲	Toliets in car park and access to Nagles Caravan and Camping
1.5	◆	Small shop
1.6	←	Turn left just over bridge
	▲	Doolin Hostel
2.2	⇦▲	Aille River Hostel & O'Connors Riverside Camping about 200m
2.9	▲	Rainbow Hostel
3.2	▲	Flannagan's Hostel
6.7	←	'Fanore'; Ballinalacken Castle across road
9.6	☆	Great rock terraces
14.5	◆	Small café
16.3	◆	Small shop
18.5	⇦☆ WC	Fanore beach, 150m
21.2	☆	Rock pavements
22.9	☆	Pass Black Head lighthouse; can stop here and walk up into the Burren
31.6	☆	Picnic area on way into Ballyvaughan followed by small harbour
32.4	↑	'N67 Lisdoonvarna', at centre of Ballyvaughan, shops to left
34.1	←	'R480 Ennis'
35.5	☆	Aillwee Caves
36.5	☆	Limestone pavements start to appear
39.8	△(187)	Now surrounded by limestone pavements
41.7	☆	Limestone depression
41.9	☆	Car park for Poulnabrone Dolmen
42.5	☆	Caherconnell – stone fort
43.3	→	'L5094'
47.4	→	At T-junction

		Stage 4 Round the Burren
48.1	←⇨	Turn right for Cahermacnaghten Cathair Mhic Neachtain 1.2km return
49.1	→	Unsigned
51.2	←	Unsigned
53.3	←	At T-junction
54.0	→	Just at end of pine wood
55.8	← ◆ ▲	At Lisdoonvarna, shops to left, Sleepzone
56.2	→	'R478 Enystmon', at T-junction
56.5	◆	Small shop
57.6	↑	'Doolin', at crossroads
61.2	◆ →	'R479 Doolin', service station shop
63.1	←	Doolin crossroads
63.7	▲	Arrive, Doolin Hostel

		Stage 5 Doolin to Kilrush
0.0		At bus stop opposite Doolin Hostel, head right – towards bridge
0.1	↖	Head uphill
1.1	↗	Road joins from left
1.2	→	Signed 'Clare Jam Shop'
3.4	→	At T-junction
6.2	☆ ATM	Cliffs of Mohr
8.5	☆	Conelius O'Brien memorial pillar
9.6	☆	Story of Liscannor Stone
11.5	◆	Liscannor, service station and shop
15.1	☆	O'Brien's Bridge and ruined castle
16.8	→	At T-junction
16.9	☆	Tourist information at Lahinch
	◆	Shop
17.1	◆ ▲	Shop on left, centre of Lahinch, hostel across road
18.1	▲	Ocean View Caravan Park
27.3	→	'R482 Spanish Point'
28.6	▲	Egan Camping and Caravan Park
29.1	◆	Convenience store
30.7	☆	Cliff-top car park
30.9	→	'R285 Quilty'
31.0	☆	Beach
31.2	◆	Small shop

Stage 5 Doolin to Kilrush

Dist	Symbol	Note
31.9	→	'Kilrush'
35.0	☆	Quilty – *Leon* wreck information
36.0	♦	Shop in service station
38.8	→	'Kilkee'
49.0	♦ ☆	Doonbeg has shop and beaches
49.2	⇐	'Kilrush 12'
49.5	♦	Bigger shop
49.6	▲	Strand Camping
60.2	↖	Entering Kilkee, road veers left. Turn right for 'Waterworld' and beach
60.3	♦ →	Just in front of Neville's and past shop on the left – carry straight on for direct route to Kilrush 13.5km
60.5	→	At main road, tourist information is behind you before the turn
60.7	ATM	Bank of Ireland
	▲	Kilkee Hostel
60.9	○↗	'Coast road'
61.1	WC ♦	Mace store on corner
61.4	←	'Loop Drive'
69.5	→	At T-junction
71.8	→	'Loop Head'
74.6	→	'R487 Loop Head'
76.8	♦	Cross has small shop
80.2	→	'L2000 Ross'
83.3	⇨	Bridges of Ross 0.5km return plus 1km return walk
84.2	→	'Loop Head Lighthouse'
87.5	→	'Loop Head'
89.9	↑↓	Arrive lighthouse
94.2	☆	Kilbaha memorial – Fenian Rising 1867
103.9	↑	'L2006 Doonaha'
107.0	☆	Beach
112.0	▲⇨	Greenacres camp site 0.9km
116.0	←	'Kilrush', at crossroads
118.9	↗	Road joins from left
121.1	→	At T-junction
125.1	⇐ ☆	West Clare Railway Company
130.1	○↑	Unsigned
130.3	☆♦	Cycle Centre
130.4	○→	'R473'
130.6	▲	Hostel and tourist information, Kilrush

Stage 6 Kilrush to Ennis

Dist	Symbol	Note
0.0		Kilrush, tourist information and hostel building, head away from the Shannon
0.1	○↗	'N67 Killimer'
0.4	→	'N67 Killimer'
1.2	☆	Vandeleur Walled Garden
9.1	☆ ♦⇨	Turn to Shannon ferry 300m – shop in service station and memorial to Colleen Bawn
12.8	☆	Track to small beach
	☆	Steep hills in this section
15.7	→	'R473 Killadysert'
16.9	♦	Small shop
23.4	←	'R473'
30.3	☆	View across Shannon to Namurian sandstone escarpment near Foynes
36.4	↗ ♦ ATM	'R473 Ennis'; Killadysert has shop, ATM
43.1	☆	Ballynacally has benches and grass area
43.3	♦	Shop
49.7	♦	Medium-sized supermarket
57.1	←	At T-junction
57.3	○↑	'Ennis'
57.4	○↑	'Ennis'
58.3	○↑	'Town centre'
58.7	→	'Town centre', at lights
59.3	○↑	Unsigned
59.7	←	'Tourist centre'
59.8	○↑	'Tourist centre'
60.1		Ennis tourist centre and Clare Museum straight ahead through car park; bike racks

Stage 7 Ennis to Limerick

Dist	Symbol	Note
0.0		From bike racks at Ennis tourist centre and Clare Museum, head through car park
0.3	○↑	Unsigned
0.4	→	At T-junction
0.8	←○	'Quin R469'
	☆	Pass bus and train station
1.7	♦	Medium-sized shop in service station

143

Stage 7 Ennis to Limerick		
9.7	⇦	Turn for view of Quin Abbey and picnic area
9.8	◆	Medium-sized shop
	◆	Shops in Quin town centre
	←	'Quin Abbey, Limerick'
10.1	☆	Quin Abbey
13.9	☆	Knappogue Castle
17.9	→	'Shannon Airport'
22.8	⇦▲	Jamaica Inn – 50m on left
23.1	↑	Sixmilebridge crossroads at centre of village
28.3	⇦	To Cratloe Woods 7km
28.6	←	Opposite Woodcross restaurant
28.7	◆	Shop
31.2	↗	Cross level crossing
34.9	☆	Limerick city limits
36.2	◆ ATM	At shop
37.0	◆	Supermarket
37.3	○↑	'City centre'
37.8	☆	Pass GAA stadium
37.9	↑	At lights
38.8	☆→	Just past square-towered church, before river, Treaty Stone on this corner
39.4	←	Turn left over bridge
39.6	←	'Liddy Street'
39.7	→	At lights
39.8		Arrive Limerick tourist information

Stage 8 Limerick to Tarbert (optional)		
0.0		Limerick, O'Connell Street, corner with Cruises' Street, outside McDonald's, head down street (oneway)
0.7	☆	Daniel O'Connell statue
0.9	◆	The Bike Shop
1.8	↑	At lights – need to be in right-hand lane
2.0	↑	'N69 Foynes'
3.1	○↗	'R526 (N69) Patrickswell' – cycleway starts
3.6	○→	Unsigned
3.9	◆	Medium-sized shop
4.8	◆	Local shopping centre, pharmacy, convenience store
4.9	○↑	'Mungret College Office Park'

Stage 8 Limerick to Tarbert (optional)		
5.3	☆	Pass former Jesuit college
6.6	←	'N69 Tralee', now at Mungret
9.3	○↑	At Clarina
15.2	ATM ◆	At service station – Kildimo
17.1	☆	Gothic towers of Dromore Castle on right
19.6	☆	Celtic Theme Park and Garden (061 394243)
20.6	⇦▲	Curraghchase Forest Park approx. 3.5km, closest camping to Limerick
26.1	←	'Askeaton'
27.3	ATM ◆	Service station has large shop and ATM
27.6	☆	Askeaton East Square has tourist information. View of castle through square
28.7	←	'N69 Tralee'
33.3	☆	Entry to Aughinish Alumina
36.6	⇦	Knockpatrick Gardens, approx 2km
38.1	◆	Service station has large shop
38.8	◆	Supermarket
38.9	☆	Foynes Flying Boat Museum
46.4	☆	Rest area has views of Shannon
52.7	ATM ◆	Service station has shop
52.9	☆	Picnic area
53.5	☆	Pass Glin Castle
58.2	☆	Enter Kerry
58.6	☆	Picnic area, power stations ahead
59.3	▲◆	At Tarbert crossroads, hostel on left
59.4	ATM ◆	Shops and ATM
		Finish at turn to ferry (to right)

ROUTE 7
DUBLIN TO LIMERICK – THE GUINNESS ROUTE

Stage		Terrain	Distance (km)	Summit (distance from start/height)
1	Dublin to Edenderry	Gravel and grass towpaths	68.6	47km/90m
2	Edenderry to Shannon Harbour	Mostly grass towpaths	71.6	0km/80m
2a	Edenderry to Shannon Harbour	Mostly grass towpaths (extended route via Clonmacnoise)	(104.5)	
3	Shannon Harbour to Mountshannon	A few gentle hills heading south	62.4	59km/50m
4	Mountshannon to Limerick	A few steep hills near Killaloe	49.0	14km/190m
		Total	**251.6**	

The histories of the Grand Canal and Guinness are inextricably intertwined. Canal construction started in 1756, three years before Arthur Guinness signed the lease on the St James's Gate brewery site in Dublin, and until its closure the canal remained important for Guinness distribution – the lack of vibration ensuring casks arrived in prime condition. The last official cargo on the canal was a bargeload of Guinness that departed James' Street Harbour on 27 May 1960, but the association didn't stop then, as Guinness continued to be made from canal water until the mid-1980s.

As well as being a worthy tribute to the great drink, this ride is also a chance to address two misconceptions about Ireland. Firstly, Ireland's history is often presented as primarily rural, so many visitors remain unaware of the country's industrial heritage. Secondly, the Midlands (usually said as two distinct syllables – mid-lands) are generally regarded as a boggy wasteland through which to drive as fast as possible to somewhere more interesting. Historically, the bogs were some of the poorest places in the country. But times and sensibilities change – to the city-jaded eye, the network of bogs, streams, rivers and floodplains is both beautiful and a tranquil retreat, while the increasingly bypassed small towns retain a much more traditional atmosphere than their more popular counterparts in the tourist regions.

Options

On arriving in Ireland, it is a great temptation to take a train out of Dublin to the west coast, but do consider this alternative cross-country route. There are some highlights – the Shannon-side monastic site at Clonmacnoise on Stage 2 and Portumna Castle on Stage 3 – and the glassy calm of Lough Derg, while watching the sun rise over the Grand Canal in the silence of the bog, is unforgettable.

Even after very wet weather the towpaths are firm enough for a normal road bike. The conditions are better than described in John Dunne's 2005 book *Towpath Tours: A Guide to Cycling Ireland's Waterways*, which suggests things are generally improving. Average speeds will probably be some 5–6km/h slower than on sealed roads, and riding is also more tiring because the rolling resistance is higher. Also slowing progress is a number of locked gates with narrow pinches, especially in the Edenderry area. Pannier bags might have to be taken off to pass, making some sort of quick-release system almost a necessity. Because of

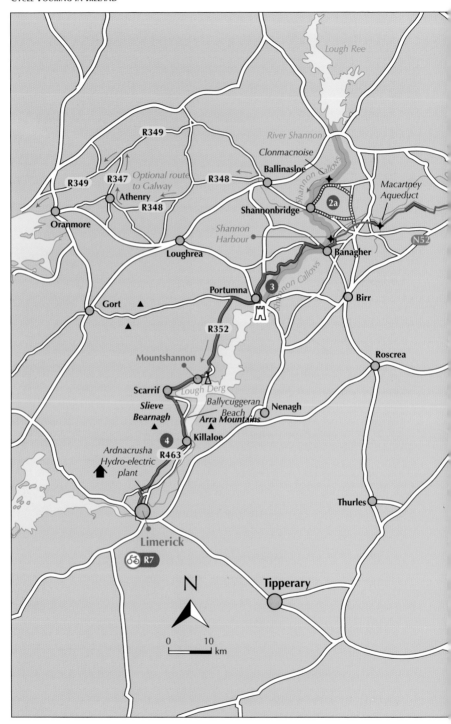

Lough Ree

R349

River Shannon

Clonmacnoise

Ballinasloe

R349   R347   Optional route   R348   Shannon Callows
                to Galway

Athenry   Shannonbridge   2a   Macartney
R348   Aqueduct

Oranmore   Shannon
                        Harbour   Banagher   N52

Loughrea

Portumna   3   Shannon Callows

Gort ▲   Birr

▲   R352   Roscrea

Mountshannon

Scarrif   Lough Derg

Slieve   Ballycuggeran
Bearnagh ▲   Beach   Nenagh
                    Arra Mountains ▲

                    4   Killaloe

Ardnacrusha   R463
Hydro-electric ↑
plant
                                     Thurles

Limerick

🚲 R7

N

Tipperary

0   10
━━━━━━ km

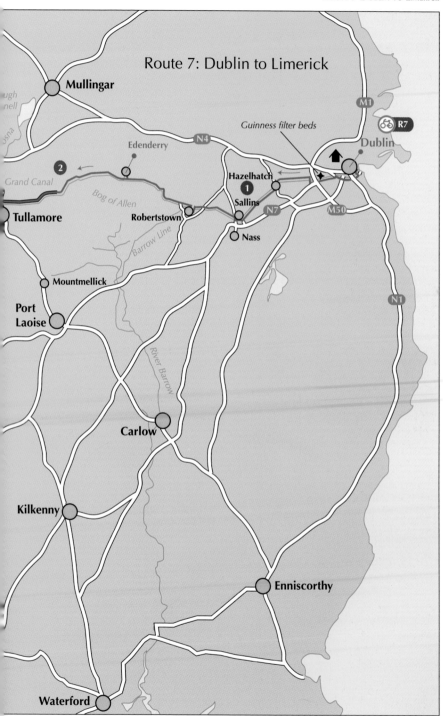

Route 7: Dublin to Limerick

these and other gates, taking a tandem is not recommended.

If the towpaths get too much, there is always the option of switching to the roads. Stay off the N roads though – they are frightening.

Stage 2 divides close to Shannon Harbour, where a loop to visit Clonmacnoise (see route card 2a) adds an extra 33km to the direct Edenderry to Shannon Harbour route.

At the Shannon this route heads southwestwards towards Limerick, but Galway is also close, to the west. Galway city is approximately 77km west of the Shannon – giving a total Dublin–Galway distance of 232km; Ballyvaughan and the Burren (Route 6, Stage 4) are a similar distance west of Portumna, giving a total Dublin–Ballyvaughan distance of just over 240km. For more details on these routes, see Options for Stages 2 and 3.

Getting to the Start
As Dublin is the major port of entry for the Republic of Ireland, most of the information on getting there is included in the introduction to this guidebook. The Grand Canal Docks is not too hard to find – just cross to the south side of the Liffey and head as far east as you can, then turn right. One of the best ways to do this trip is to arrive at Dublin Docks on the overnight ferry, ride through a slowly wakening city, and by the afternoon be in the middle of the bog.

When to Go
It's quiet at any time, making this an ideal route to try at the busiest times of year – mid-July to August.

Accommodation
There are no hostels at all on this route, so get hold of some bed and breakfast numbers before setting out. The canal section of the route is a bit thin on accommodation generally, although this picks up at the Shannon. It used to be possible to camp the whole way, with one night's wild camping near the canal, but the campsite near Clonmacnoise was closed at the time of writing (see Stage 2).

Maps
At 1:250 000 both the West and East sheets of the Ordnance Survey Ireland series are required. The West sheet starts just west of the Shannon. At 1:50 000 the following sheets are needed: 50 Dublin Kildare Meath Wicklow, 48 Offaly Westmeath, 47 Galway Offaly Roscommon Westmeath, 53 Clare Galway Offaly Tipperary, 59 Clare Offaly Tipperary and 65 Clare Limerick Tipperary from the OSI Discovery series. The main route only has about 7km on a corner of sheet 47, although it does cover the Clonmacnoise area. Likewise there is only 2km on sheet 59. Limerick city is just on the north edge of sheet 65, so this sheet could be skipped if you are ending your trip at Limerick itself.

Towpath Tours: A Guide to Cycling Ireland's Waterways by John Dunne (Collins, 2005) is a valuable companion on this route.

Onwards
Limerick is well connected to other routes in the book. One option is to head northwest by bike or bus, joining Route 6 around the Burren, then crossing the Shannon to Tarbert to continue with Route 8 into Kerry. (Route 6, Stage 8 links to Route 8 at Tarbert.)

STAGE 1
DUBLIN TO EDENDERRY

68.8km Gravel and grass towpaths; some road

This stage takes you from the heart of Dublin to the heart of nowhere in the Bog of Allen. The scenery is not spectacular, but 50km of traffic-free riding can't be bad, and there is a beauty and serenity about this canalside adventure that puts it in the top rank of Irish cycle trips.

The starting point, the Grand Canal Docks, is rather an odd mix of the brand new, the beautifully restored and the abandoned. Because of pedestrians it is best to stay off the towpaths until after the light-rail Luas station at Suir Road (6km), but from there this stage is almost entirely towpaths, with a few strips of canalside road. In this early section you can see one of the original Grand Canal Company hotels – now the Portobello Institute – as well as the Cathal Brugha Barracks, which was built

Grand Canal at Robertstown

by the British between 1810 and 1815 as the Portobello Barracks.

Where the route crosses the Luas tracks and joins the canal, the tram tracks to the right follow what was the James Street Branch, which took the canal to the terminus at James's Street Harbour, and the key connection for the Guinness Brewery. This section was filled in in the 1970s.

From the 11th lock onwards fields start to appear on the north bank, and the sounds of birdsong and rushing water slowly take over from the hum of traffic. A rather scruffy

The filter beds on the north side of the canal at 11.1km provided water for brewing Guinness until the mid-1980s. The water is still used at the brewery, but not in the beer.

marina and colourful, if neglected, boats herald Hazelhatch (21km), and from here there is little to do except enjoy the peace and quiet of the canal.

Sallins (34km) flies by, and the first view of the Midlands Bog is the Bog of Moods, on the approach to the rather appealing canalside village of Robertstown (47km). This summit section of the canal is marked by another canal company hotel – the Grand Hotel, opened in 1801 – which is sadly not in use. The canal now enters an embanked section along the Bog of Allen. Historic Edenderry is reached via a short branch canal.

On the Road
This route is easy to follow as it clings to the canal. Some sections of the canal have a choice of towpath, but the side described in here is generally the better surfaced, with fewer accessibility issues (gates, etc).

Clonmacnoise High Cross and Round Tower

The early part of the route is on road or sealed towpath. The first grass is at 14km, and from here there is a mixture of gravel and grass, apart from the few road sections.

Sallins (34km) is a pleasant spot to take a break by the canal and has a shop. If this is your first visit to Ireland, remember that public toilets are as rare as leprechauns. Robertstown (47km) and Edenderry at the end of the day also have shops. The latter also has an ATM at the Ulster Bank branch. There are a couple of awkward gates en route, mainly intended to check trail bike riders, the one at Hazelhatch is tandem proof (21km, and there is no simple alternative route), and the two at lock 20 (60km) required the removal of panniers to squeeze through.

Accommodation
There are no hostels or campsites on this route. There is a bed and breakfast in Edenderry – see both www.offaly.ie and www.kildare.ie, as Edenderry is close to the border. It would be a good idea to have a booking or at least some phone numbers before you leave Dublin.

Wild camping is possible by quiet sections of the canal, and watching the sun rising over the Bog of Allen is wonderful.

Options
None.

STAGE 2
EDENDERRY TO SHANNON HARBOUR

71.6km Grass towpath;
couple of muddy sections

With the traffic of Dublin just a distant memory, this section plunges into some of the least spoiled countryside in Ireland. The Bog of Allen continues for a while, and the only town of any note is the Offaly county town of Tullamore (34km). The Charleville Demesne and castle here are worth a visit (turn at 34.4km), but the castle – probably Ireland's best Gothic building – may be closed, so best check with the Tullamore tourist office (057 9352617) before going 3km (return). The tourist office is in the canalside Tullamore Dew Heritage Centre (www.tullamoredew.com). The distillery here closed in 1959, but while it operated the Grand Canal was an important transport link for sending the whiskey to markets in Ireland and overseas.

Passenger traffic continued on the Grand Canal until 1852, and many Irish emigrants passed through here on their way to Limerick and Cobh.

Shannon Harbour was once a bustling port

West of Tullamore is a forgotten bit of Ireland. In the summer of 2008, the River Brosna and the Shannon beyond flooded in summer, turning wide areas of the lowlands into silver sheets, and providing a reminder of why this area is so undeveloped. Shannon Harbour, with its grand layout and fine, if crumbling, stone buildings seems to encapsulate the feeling of an area slowly being reclaimed by the bog.

> The Bog of Allen took 10,000 years to form, but during the last 400 years, more than 90 per cent has been lost to drainage and peat mining.

Fences block the way past the 36th lock to the Shannon, but the best view of Ireland's longest river is to the north at Clonmacnoise, one of Ireland's most important early Christian sites (along the longer alternative Stage 2a). Saint Ciaran founded a monastery here in AD545 at a point where an ancient route across Ireland – the Esker Road, or Esker Riada – crossed the Shannon. The road followed a series of glacial ridges – or eskers – all the way from Dublin to Galway.

Also on this loop is the Clonmacnoise and West Offaly Railway, where you can bump around the bog on the light railway and learn all about peat.

> In the ninth century a wooden bridge some 120m long was built across the Shannon at Clonmacnoise; the vertical posts can be seen at low water.

On the Road

This stage is slightly heavier going than Stage 1, and contains the only (short) section that was difficult to ride on the whole route – from 40.5km to 41.6km – but this was after heavy rain and widespread flooding. There has been an outbreak of locked gates with narrow 'pinches' to the west of Edenderry and again approaching Shannon Harbour. These hinder progress, as luggage may have to be removed to squeeze through.

Tullamore (34km) has the best range of shops, probably in the whole county, and there are ATMs here too, and a camping store – Midlands Leisure and Camping (057 9341047). By the canal, near the heritage centre, is Buckley Cycles (057 9352240, www.buckleycycles.ie). Daingean (19km) is also a pleasant canalside stop.

Accommodation

There are no hostels in this area – in fact there are none in County Offaly. The Harbour Master's House at Shannon Harbour is a Georgian building and offers bed and breakfast (050 951532) and there are a number of bed and breakfasts around Clonmacnoise – see www.offaly.ie for a list. There is also a campsite near Clonmacnoise – the excellent Glebe Caravan and Camping Park, but at the time of writing this was closed.

Options

At Belmont Bridge (65.3km) there is a choice of routes. The Stage 2 route card continues direct to Shannon Harbour, while the alternative Stage 2a route card adds an extra 32.9km with a loop out to Clonmacnoise, returning to Belmont Bridge, from where the remaining 6.3km can be followed from the Stage 2 route card. The total distance for Edenderry to Shannon Harbour via Clonmacnoise is 104.5km. See below for accommodation options to split what would be a tiring day's riding.

Clonmacnoise is wonderful, especially early in the morning before the crowds arrive (it opens at 9am from mid-May to mid-September – see www.heritageireland.ie). An early visit would mean staying the night in the area. Taking the loop up to Clonmacnoise and then continuing on to Shannon Harbour would make a very long day (over 104.6km), and as much of it is on grass, a tiring one too. Tullamore (34.4km) is the obvious place to split the stage.

If continuing to Galway rather than Limerick, the best route is to cross the Shannon at Shannonbridge (leave Stage 2a at 86km), then follow the R357 to Ballinasloe and then the R348 to Athenry. From there it is possible to get most of the way to Galway, without using the busy N roads, by heading northwest to the R339 and following this to the city fringe. The total distance, Shannonbridge to Galway, is approximately 77km, giving a total Dublin–Galway distance of 232km.

STAGE 3
SHANNON HARBOUR TO
MOUNTSHANNON

62.4km A few gentle hills heading south

This is an idyllic day following the Shannon southwards to Portumna, where the river swells into sinuous Lough Derg. The stage then follows the western shore of the lake. After a couple of days on grass and towpath, the going is much faster, and the riding along the quiet back roads of the Shannon valley is easy.

At Banagher (5km) the Shannon – some 200m wide in spate – is an impressive sight, and Fort Falkland and a Martello tower guard this important river crossing. The town grew

Novelist Anthony Trollope lived in Banagher from 1841–5, when he worked for the Post Office. He travelled here from Dublin via the Grand Canal, landing at Shannon Harbour on 16 September 1841.

up on slightly raised ground at a point where the Shannon could be forded. Crossing the river here the route follows an esker road for about 5km west.

Most of the roads along the Shannon keep a respectable flood-free distance away, but there is a chance to get close to the river at Merrick Quay (14km), and later on down a small lane through the Shannon Callows (turn at 23.4km). This floodplain of the river, between Athlone and Portumna, turns into a 40km-long shallow lake in most winters (and some summers). Largely free from artificial fertilisers, and subject to the whims of Europe's last great undrained river (the Shannon has not been artificially widened, deepened, or forced into manmade channels to contain its flood-waters), the callows are home to a rich variety of grasses and wildflowers. The birdlife is also impressive – this is one of the few places in Europe where the corncrake is still found.

Lough Derg is one of the most beautiful of all the Shannon lakes, and sitting near its head is Portumna (33km). The de Burgos, a Norman family, crossed the Shannon here in the 13th century and went on to conquer most

The corncrake is the only bird whose call is the same as its Latin name – *Crex crex.*

Lough Derg at Mountshannon

of Connacht. They moved their seat of power to Portumna in the early 17th century. The castle (open 10am–6pm daily in summer, www.heritageireland.ie) was gutted by fire in 1826, but has been conserved rather than restored – making it one of Ireland's most interesting heritage buildings. The ornamental gardens are also fascinating.

South of Portumna there are occasional glimpses of the lake. A small climb heading into Mountshannon opens up the view, with the lake narrowing as the Arra Mountains encroach from the east and Slieve Bearnagh from the west. Mountshannon is a pretty village set high above the lake.

On the Road

Banagher (5km) has a supermarket and ATM, and is the best place to stock up a little for the two days to Limerick. Merrick Quay (14km) is pleasant for a break by the river. Save some time for Portumna Castle if possible. Mountshannon only has a small shop, so pick up any overnight supplies at Portumna (33km).

Accommodation

Unfortunately there are no hostels in the area. The Lakeside Holiday Park at Mountshannon (061 927225, www.lakesideireland.com) is well set up for touring campers and is in a pretty spot – take midge repellent though. Mountshannon is a popular getaway from Limerick, so there are plenty of bed and breakfasts – see www.clare.ie for an up-to-date list. If Portumna appeals there are also plenty of bed and breakfasts here – see www.portumna.net. The tourist office on Abbey Street (090 9759092) is open from 9.30am to 5pm, June to September)

Options

As this is a relatively fast day on the road, consider staying near Clonmacnoise and tacking a section of Stage 2a onto this one – this would add about 26km to this day's riding. To connect with Route 6, Stage 4 and the Burren, pick up the R353 at Ballyshrule, west of Portumna (33.9km), and cross the Slieve Aughty mountains to Gort (a further 39km). From Gort it is approximately 30km to Ballyvaughan on the coast via some quiet roads on the east side of the Burren and the N67 (links to Route 6, Stage 4 at 32.4km). The Ireland West 1:250 000 map

is sufficient to pick out a good route. The total approximate distance Dublin to Ballyvaughan is about 243km.

The prettiest scenery comes early in the day around Mountshannon, so at least take a spin down to the lake and back. It might also be possible to squeeze in a visit to Holy Island out on the lake.

For boat trips to Holy Island and its 25m round tower, contact East Clare Heritage Centre (061 921351, www.eastclareheritage.com).

While Mountshannon exudes aesthetic appeal, nearby Scarriff (8km) is a more practical town, complete with shops and banks. There is a small, semi-derelict Art Deco cinema on the main street, which may be of interest. Further on, the East Clare Heritage Centre (061 921351, www.eastclareheritage.com), in a 10th-century church at Tuamgraney (10km), might also appeal. For a change of scene the route then takes a climb across a spur of Slieve Bernagh. This opens up the views over the lake and, from late summer, wild blackberries can be eaten from the roadside.

Killaloe (23km), a pleasant town at the end of the lake, is the birthplace of 10th-century Irish High King Brian Boru. There is a heritage centre in town and the route passes Boru's fort to the north of the town. The hills crowd in towards the lake here, and leaving the town there are a few short sharp climbs to negotiate.

Patrick Sarsfield crossed the Shannon just north of here on his famous mission against the Limerick-bound Williamite siege train in 1690. This stage follows some of his route to the southwest of town, where, after days of lowland scenery, the hilltop views and the tall oak, sycamore and beech woodlands make a refreshing change.

The Ardnacrusha hydro-electric scheme (41km) is on the approach to Limerick,

Limerick Castle

Ardnacrusha was the largest hydro-electric generating station in the world for a while. When it opened in 1929 it supplied more than 95 per cent of Ireland's electricity.

although there is little to see from the road. The entrance to Limerick from the north is easy enough, meeting the Shannon again across from Limerick Castle, before crossing the last, or first, lock on the navigation – Sarsfield Lock – on the Sarsfield Bridge.

On the Road
Scarriff (8km), Killaloe (23km) and Ardnacrusha (40km) all have decent shops. Killaloe is the best place to stop, although the one-way system leads up and down a steep hill. Ballycuggeran (19.7km) is a lake bathing beach. Treacy's Service Station (8.8km) just south of Scarriff does some cycle repairs (061 921014).

Accommodation
Limerick has limited budget accommodation, see Route 6, Stage 7 for more information.

Options
None.

ROUTE 7 DUBLIN TO LIMERICK

Stage 1 Dublin to Edenderry			
0.0			Dublin, Grand Canal Basin, by Westmoreland Lock (1761), follow side of basin
0.4	♦		Small supermarket – open early
0.5	←		At end of basin, into Grand Canal Quay
0.7	↑		Cross road (use crossing to right if busy)
0.8	☆		Waterways Ireland visitors centre
1.2	←		At T-junction
	→		At lights, Clanwilliam Place
1.9	☆		Baggot Street
2.4	←		At T-junction, go over bridge, cross at lights and follow road on left side of canal
3.4	☆		Grand building on right was one of original Grand Canal Company hotels
3.9	☆		Cathal Brugha Barracks
5.4	♦ ATM		At service station
6.4	↖		Veer left at lights
	→		Cross at lights, join cycleway between Luas track and canal
8.0	↑		Pick up path across road through gate

Stage 1 Dublin to Edenderry		
10.1	↑	Pass under bridge
11.2	☆	Filter beds for Guinness!
12.8	→	Cross bridge and continue on north side of canal
13.7	☆	Lock 11
14.2	☆	Grass towpath starts – still firm
15.9	↑	Join canalside road
16.8	↑	At crossroads, Lock 12 on left
18.2	↗	Slight veer to cross bridge approach, continue along canal
19.9	☆	Original Thomas Omer canalside house in ruins
21.5	↗	Go through gate, head towards exit of pub car park (not possible for a tandem)
21.6	←	Turn left out of pub car park
	→	Turn right after Hazelhatch Bridge (careful – bad visibility), now on south towpath
23.7	☆	Aylmer Bridge
24.8	☆	Lock 13
25.8	↑	Canalside road starts after Henry Bridge
28.4	↑	At Ponsonby Bridge, road ends, now gravel
29.1	☆	Grassy section starts – bit slow and wet
30.8	☆	Devonshire Bridge
31.0	☆	Lock 14 and cottage
31.6	☆	Lock 15 and falling-down cottage
33.8	☆	Under rail bridge
33.9	↖	Join muddy track leading uphill, slightly away from canal
34.1	↑	Through gate and join road
34.9	↖	Road goes left
	→	Turn right onto road and cross canal bridge at Sallins
35.0	←♦	After bridge turn and join road on north side of canal, shop straight ahead
36.8	☆	Leinster Aqueduct over River Liffey
39.1	←	At Digby Bridge join road – canal side is too wet
	→	First right after bridge
39.2	→	After 100m

Stage 1 Dublin to Edenderry		
39.9	☆	Towpath joins road – now on south side of canal
40.3	☆	Landenstown Bridge and Lock 17 (continue on road as it crosses canal – now north side)
41.5	←	Turn onto towpath
41.7	☆	Lock 18 – wet section follows but rideable
43.0	☆	Cock Bridge
44.9	←	Cross Bonynge Bridge and continue south on towpath – this is Bog of Moods
47.1	↑	Through gate and join canalside road
	☆	Grand Hotel – Robertstown
	♦	Shop and pub
47.2	☆	Canalside benches
47.4	♦ →	Turn right and cross bridge – shop on corner
47.5	↖	Follow road along canal – now on north side
48.6	☆	Lock 19 – note that this is a descent lock, we are past the summit section
	↑	On to gravel road
48.8	☆	Note Barrow Line of Grand Canal off to left
49.1	☆	Small aqueduct, gravel surface still OK
50.6	↑	Go under Bond Bridge
52.0	←	Cross bridge on road which slowly leaves canalside – signed 'Lullymore'
52.8	→	Road takes you alongside canal – now on south side
54.4	☆	Lifting bridge for peat railway
55.9	→	Cross canal at Hamilton Bridge
	←	Follow road along north side of canal
56.1	↑	Follow road along canal – gravel, tar and potholes!
57.4	↑	Road joins from right – better surface
59.4	↑	At Hartley Bridge continue on same side of canal (Ticknevin Bridge on maps)
60.4	↑	Lock 20 – gates to pass through
65.3	☆	Blundell Aqueduct
67.0	→	At car park follow Edenderry Branch towpath into town

Stage 1 Dublin to Edenderry		
68.6		Arrive gate at Edenderry Harbour

Stage 2 Edenderry to Shannon Harbour		
0.0		Edenderry, by canal basin at gate to towpath and entrance to Blundell Wood
1.6	→	Over Downshire Bridge (on north side of canal)
2.1	☆	Bad gate
2.5	☆	Bridge
3.2	☆	Lock and Rathmore Bridge – grassy towpath from here
4.7	☆	Bad gate, better gravel road after bridge
6.7	☆	Trimblestown Bridge
11.4	☆	Bad gate before and after bridge
11.9	☆	Swans along this section
12.4	↗	At Toberdaly Bridge, bear right and then join road parallel to canal
12.6	↖	Rejoin towpath through gate
14.3	☆	Bord na Mona lifting bridge – commercial peat extraction on south side
16.3	↑	Road joins
17.2	☆	Kilkeen Bridge, then bad gate
19.3	↑	Through gate on to road
19.8	◆ ↑	Daingean crossroads, shops in town to left and picnic area
25.5	↑	Crossroads at Cambells Bridge
25.9	☆	Kilbeggan Branch of canal to right (filled in)
26.0	☆	Lock 21 and transmitter mast
27.2	☆	Bridge and Lock 22
27.9	☆	Lock 23, Offaly Rowing Club after
31.0	☆	Lock 24
31.7	☆	Digby Bridge and Lock 25
32.6	☆	Bad gate
	☆	Bolands Lock (Lock 26) – lock house museum open 12noon – 2pm July – August
32.7	☆	Gate a tight fit
33.2	☆	Bitumen starts – marina on the left
34.1	↑	Join road

Stage 2 Edenderry to Shannon Harbour		
34.4	◆ ↑	At Tullamore crossroads, shops in town to left, Tullamore Dew Heritage Centre on far bank; turn right for castle (approx. 3km return), but check for access arrangements at heritage centre
34.8	↖	Turn through car park by canal
34.9	☆	Lock 27
	↑	At crossroads
35.1	↑	Follow road by canal
35.3	☆	Lock 28
35.7	☆	Sra Castle
37.7	↗	Veer right (can go straight on but difficult gate)
	←	Turn onto road
38.2	☆	St Brigid's Church (ruins)
38.5	☆	Road rejoins canal
38.9	↑	Crossroads at Lock 29
39.2	☆	Ballycowan Castle (private)
39.3	☆	Aqueduct
40.5	☆	Section very muddy from cattle movements
41.7	☆	Back to bumpy, coarse gravel road
43.2	←	Cross canal at Corcoran's Bridge
43.3	→	Join gravel path on south side of canal
43.6	☆	Grass starts
44.3	↑	Rahan Bridge – go under
45.3	↑	Join canalside road
46.1	☆	Lock 30 and bridge
47.1	☆	Lock 31 and bridge
50.8	↑	At Plunkett Bridge, don't cross canal – continue on south bank
54.0	↑	Road joins from left
54.1	↑	Follow towpath – now light gravel
54.7	☆	Light railway bridge – extensive peat extraction in this area
56.0	☆	Derry Bridge
57.2	↑	Through gate (OK for a bike) – wet section starts, rideable
57.9	☆	Macartney Aqueduct over Silver River

157

Stage 2 Edenderry to Shannon Harbour

58.1	↑	Join sealed road
61.1	→	Onto road
	←	Follow gravel track along canal (still south bank)
61.7	↑	Crossroads with N3
62.6	↑	Lock 32 and bridge, onto grass towpath again
62.7	☆	Awful gate
64.3	☆	Bridge leads to ruined Ballyshiel House on right
65.3	↑	Awkward gate
	↑⇨	At Belmont Bridge (and Lock 33); for detour to Clonmacnoise, turn right
65.6	☆	Gate – broken – dry and fast grass
67.4	↑	Onto tarmac through gate
67.9	↑	Lestrange Bridge and onto gravel
69.1	☆	Lock 34 and Clonony Bridge
70.5	↖	Alongside picnic area
70.6	↑	At crossroads
70.7	☆	Grand Canal Hotel (ruins) at Shannon Harbour
70.9	↑☆	Central diamond – fine house to left – keep straight on
71.0	☆	Lock 35
71.6		Lock 36 – you may be able to get a little further if it is dry

Stage 2a Edenderry to Shannon Harbour via Clonmacnoise (extended route)

65.3	→	At Belmont Bridge
65.7	☆	Belmont Mill
66.5	↑♦	At crossroads – small shop on right
70.2	↑	'Clonmacnoise', at crossroads
71.0	←	'Clonmacnoise'
73.7	←	'Clonmacnoise' – road swings left
74.5	▲	Glebe Caravan and Camping Park – see note in Accommodation
75.5	☆	From low hill, views to Esker Road to north
75.9	←	'Clonmacnoise'
79.2	→	Turn into Clonmacnoise car park
79.4	↑↓	Turn around
79.6	→	Turn right out of car park

Stage 2a Edenderry to Shannon Harbour via Clonmacnoise (extended route)

86.0	←	'R357 Tullamore' (Shannonbridge to right)
89.5	⇦	Clonmacnoise and West Offaly Railway about 1km
91.6	←⇧	'Belmont 4', straight on will take you to Lestrange Bridge (approx 4.5km)
97.1	→	'Grand Canal'
98.2		Arrive back at Belmont Bridge

Stage 3 Shannon Harbour to Mountshannon

0.0		Shannon Harbour, at exit from docks area, turn right
2.3	→	'Banagher'
5.0	♦ ATM →	For shop and ATM (200m) turn left, now in Banagher
5.1	♦	Supermarket
5.2	☆	Tourist office
5.4	☆	Fort Falkland
5.7	☆	Martello tower, over Shannon Bridge
7.0	⇨	Side-trip to Clonfert approx. 14km return
10.7	←	'Meelick Church'
12.0	←	Road veers left
14.1	☆	Merrick Quay by the Shannon – battery across river
14.7	←	Road veers left
15.4	⇦→	At T-junction, Merrick Church on left – 100m
16.1	☆	Plaque on house remembers champion Galway hurler Pat Madden
16.5	←	Pump on corner
17.4	←	Road veers left
19.8	←	At crossroads
23.4	⇦	Side-trip to river – follow road on through gate for about 2km and return
25.4	←	'Portumna'
25.8	♦	Shop
26.2	←	'R355 Portumna'
32.8	←	Portumna Workhouse (1852) on left
33.6	☆	St Joseph's Convent
	♦ ATM →	'St Brendan's Street' – at crossroads (ATM on left)
33.9	⇦ WC ☆	To castle (200m), park with WC, and tourist information (turn left at castle gates)

Stage 3 Shannon Harbour to Mountshannon		
	↑	'R352 Scarriff'
40.0	↖	At Ballyshrule, continue on R352 which swings south, straight on for Galway
54.5	♦	Small shop at service station
55.2	☆	Cross border into Co Clare
57.8	↑	'L4036 Mountshannon', as R352 swings left, continue straight on local road
60.9	→	At T-junction
61.8	⇦▲	Lakeside Camping Caravan and Watersports Park
62.4		Mountshannon central crossroads

Stage 4 Mountshannon to Limerick		
0.0		Mountshannon crossroads
0.1	♦	Small shop
0.5	⇦ WC ☆	Leads to quay, memorial to St Colum (Colmcille) on corner
2.5	⇦	To quay close to Holy Island, 1.5km return
7.9	→	'L4028' (to centre of Scarriff)
8.1	←	At T-junction
8.2	♦	Square has shops
8.3	↑	Road joins from right
8.5	ATM	Bank of Ireland
	→	Back on R352
8.8	♦	Treacy's Service Station services bikes, also shop
9.4	♦	Larger shop at service station
9.8	←	'R463 Killaloe', park/benches on corner
10.0	☆	East Clare Heritage Centre on right
12.0	→	Down small road – can continue on R463 if you wish
14.6	△(193)	Summit, views of lake on ascent and descent – some 13% sections
18.2	→	Back on R463
19.7	☆	Access to lake at Ballycuggeran Beach
19.9	WC	At south end of car park
21.9	☆	Brian Boru'–s fort on left
23.0	→	Turn up hill about 50m before service station on right
23.8	♦ →	In diamond at top of Killaloe, supermarket on left
23.9	←	At end of diamond

Stage 4 Mountshannon to Limerick		
24.1	→	'Lough Derg Way'
25.7	↗	Bear right at fork
29.7	↗	Road swings right
32.0	☆	Bridgetown has picnic tables and a pretty green
32.2	→	At T-junction
32.3	↖	Turn left up hill
36.5	←	At T-junction
36.9	↑	At crossroads
40.4	→	At T-junction
40.6	←	At T-junction
40.7	ATM ♦ →	Shop and ATM at this crossroad about 20m after turn at 40.6km
41.6	☆	Entrance to Ardnacrusha hydro-electric station
43.4	←	At T-junction
44.9	→	On to R464
45.7	☆	Limerick city limits
46.5	♦	Supermarket
47.1	←	At crossroads, new stadium on right
47.3	ATM ♦	Convenience store
48.1	→	At river
48.4	☆	Benches by the river
48.6	←	Over Sarsfield Bridge
48.9	←	'Liddy Street' (first turn after bridge)
49.0	→	At lights
		Arrive Limerick tourist information centre

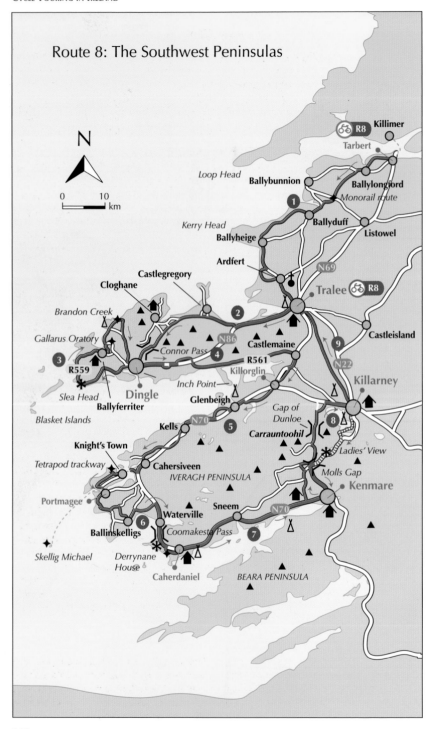

Route 8: The Southwest Peninsulas

N

0   10
km

Killimer
R8
Tarbert

Loop Head   Ballybunnion   Ballylongford
1   Monorail route
Kerry Head   Ballyduff
Listowel
Ballyheige
Ardfert

N69
Tralee   R8

Castlegregory
Cloghane   2
Brandon Creek   Castleisland
Gallarus Oratory   N86   9
3   4   Castlemaine   N22
R559   Connor Pass   R561
Dingle   Killorglin   Killarney
Slea Head   Inch Point
Ballyferriter   Glenbeigh
Blasket Islands   Gap of
Kells   N70   5   Dunloe   8
Knight's Town   Carrauntoohil   Ladies' View
Tetrapod trackway   Cahersiveen   Molls Gap
IVERAGH PENINSULA   Kenmare
Portmagee   Sneem
Waterville   N70
Ballinskelligs   6   7
Coomakesta Pass
Skellig Michael   Derrynane
House
Caherdaniel   BEARA PENINSULA

ROUTE 8

THE SOUTHWEST PENINSULAS – RINGING THE CHANGES

Stage		Terrain	Distance (km)	Summit (distance from start/height)
1	Tarbert to Tralee	A few climbs	69.7	17km/110m
2	Tralee to Dingle	Long climb	48.5	41km/410m
3	Tour of the Dingle Peninsula	Hilly	57.1	50km/120m
4	Dingle to Killorglin	Fast stage	54.9	13km/100m
5	Killorglin to Portmagee	Hill	65.8	17km/140m
6	Portmagee to Caherdaniel	Two stiff climbs	45.5	5km/250m
7	Caherdaniel to Kenmare	Rolling coastal hills	48.2	15km/130m
8	Kenmare to Killarney	Long climbs	47.7	29km/240m
8a	Alternative via Ladies View	Long climbs	(36.3)	26km/260m
9	Killarney to Tralee	One steady hill climb	30.4	22km/175m
		Total	**467.8**	

The combination of mountains, beaches, lakes and forests makes the Kerry landscape enduringly appealing to visitors. And, although beauty is very much in the eye of the beholder, it would be hard to dispute that, in terms of the sheer number of beautiful places in one county, Kerry deserves its status as Ireland's top tourist destination.

Each of the Kerry peninsulas has its own distinct character, but the landscape also varies within each of them. Unsurprisingly, the scenery becomes wilder, with less tree cover and more rock, as you head west. Perhaps less expected is the difference between the north and south sides of the same peninsula – with the south sides tending to have gentler slopes and more settlements than the north sides. On the southwestern tips of these outcrops the warm waters of the Gulf Stream have created a microclimate that verges on the subtropical.

It is almost churlish to pick highlights, but the early Christian monastery on Skellig Michael, the lakes and forests around Killarney, and the tetrapod trackway on Valentia Island spring to mind. The finest piece of coastal road is the section around Slea Head on the Dingle peninsula. Of the towns, Kenmare and Tralee are the pleasantest places to stay, while Killarney must have more beautiful scenery within a few miles than any town this side of the Rockies.

The Ring of Kerry is a popular driving and coach tour route – but plenty of the route described here is off the main roads. Where it is necessary to use the busier roads, however, the visitor traffic has ensured that the surfacing has been improved over the years and the roads are well maintained.

Options

This is a circular route with a link from Route 6 at the Tarbert ferry crossing of the Shannon. If you are looking for a circuit, it is of course possible to start/finish anywhere on the circle.

Popular Killarney, with its mountain backdrop, is a good starting point, but also consider Tralee – it doesn't have the tourist clamour of Killarney, but as the county town of Kerry has all the shops/services you could expect.

Ladies View has fine views of Killarney National Park

There is an official Ring of Kerry cycle route that the route described here follows for the most part, although the signposting is a little sporadic. At the time of writing the map of the route was out of print, but you might be able to pick up a guide at tourist information in Killarney.

Getting to the Start

The route starts at the T-junction where the road from the Tarbert ferry meets the main road. Getting to Limerick is also included below, as many riders will want to start the route in Limerick, taking Stage 8 of Route 6 as the first day.

By Air

The closest airport is Shannon (www.shannon airport.com), about 30km out of Limerick. The suggested route into Limerick is via Sixmilebridge – see Route 6, Stage 7 for more details. Shannon has the best international connections of any of the Irish airports outside Dublin – there are flights to the US, Europe, including eastern Europe, and the UK.

By Sea

No direct connections. If you sailing into Dublin, consider the four-day Grand Canal/ Shannon trip (Route 7) to get to Limerick.

By Rail/Bus

Limerick has Bus Eireann services to Tralee, Killarney and Kenmare, but you are unlikely to get your bike on a bus during peak times, particularly Friday afternoons or evenings and on Sundays.

When to Go

April and September are obviously quieter, but Kerry seems to cope with visitor numbers well, so travelling in mid-summer is fine. The Killarney area is particularly attractive in early September, when there is just a touch of autumn in the air. The Rose of Tralee festival (late August) and the Puck Fair at Killorglin in the second week of August can make things busy in those towns.

Accommodation

Kerry is well set up for visitors, and finding accommodation is generally not a problem. Camping and hostel accommodation is plentiful and mostly of a very high standard, making this county one of the easiest places to organise a tour in Ireland.

Maps

The OSI Ireland South 1: 250 000 sheet covers the whole route. At 1:50 000 you will need the following sheets from the Discovery series: 64 Clare Kerry Limerick, 63 Clare Kerry (these first two only if doing Tarbert to Tralee), 70 Kerry, 71 Kerry, 78 Kerry, 83 Kerry, 84 Cork Kerry (only for a 19km stretch to the west of Kenmare) and 85 Cork Kerry (only for a 1km stretch between Templenoe and Kenmare). If starting from Limerick, sheet 64 Clare Kerry Limerick is also needed.

Onwards

For more of the Kerry coast, Route 9 beckons. An alternative route to Cork is to follow Route 10 from Killarney in reverse, down the Blackwater Valley to Youghal.

STAGE 1
TARBERT TO TRALEE

69.7km A few climbs

This is a day that leaves the lowlands of the Shannon far behind and starts to come to grips with the mountains of County Kerry. The real 'wow' moment on this ride is the low summit just north of Ballyheige (42km), from which the view suddenly opens up along the wide sweep of Banna Strand and out to the mountain wall of the Dingle Peninsula.

This northwest corner of Kerry is probably the only part of the county passed over by tourism, and the villages and roads are

> The world's first motorised passenger monorail service ran through Lisselton Cross Roads for 36 years. A small plaque gives a few details of the remarkably successful line, which opened in 1888.

blissfully quiet. Close to the Shannon, the red-brick-framed windows of Ballylongford's grey stone warehouse (8km) stare out forlornly, awaiting coastal trade that will never come again, while Lisselton Cross Roads (19km), where once a rather peculiar monorail ran to Ballybunnion, is little more than a shop and a few scattered houses.

It was at Banna Strand (50km) that Roger Casement landed from a German submarine on Good Friday 1916 in the lead up to the Easter Rising. There is a monument near the beach.

> Roger Casement landed on Banna Strand on Good Friday 1916 from a German U-boat as part of an ill-fated expedition to provide arms for the Nationalist cause. He was quickly caught, tried and hanged for high treason.

The final settlement before Tralee is Ardfert (60km), where the ruined cathedral, founded by St Brendan in the sixth century, is worthy of a walk around.

Ballyheige Bay with the Dingle Peninsula in the background

The Rose of Tralee festival, which draws thousands of visitors at the end of August, is inspired by a song. 'Roses' from around the world compete for the title.

Tralee is the best town in Kerry for the visitor – it is more practical than the over-popular Killarney, and much less manic. On a long trip, Tralee is an excellent spot to rest tired legs for a couple of days, fix a few bike problems, do a few tourist things, re-supply and generally prepare for the rigours ahead.

On the Road
The section out towards Kerry Head, from the turn onto the coast road at 27.4km, is quite remote, so pick up supplies by Lisselton Cross Roads (19km) at the latest. The junction here is rather odd, but at least it is signed – take the Ballyduff road. The roads and tracks behind Banna Strand are also a bit of a mess, and there are no stand-out places to have a break. If you want to swim, the beaches at Banna (52km) and Ballyheige (44km) are patrolled in season.

Accommodation
There is precious little between Tarbert and Tralee. The hostel at Meenogahane, marked on some maps, has disappeared. Tralee has a hostel in the heart of town, on the street leading to the Kerry Museum – Finnegans Hostel (066 7127610). Woodlands Touring Caravan and Camping Park (066 7121235, www.kingdom camping.com) is one of the best in Ireland. It is in a quiet riverside spot within walking distance of town. The easiest way to find the site is to head south from the town centre on the R556, Princes Quay, towards the Aquadome, the railway and the windmill (all signed). When you hit the Aquadome roundabout on the ring road, turn left and the site is signed a few hundred metres on the right. The alternative for camping is Sir Roger's Caravan and Camping Park at Banna Strand (066 7134730, www.sirrogerscaravanpark.com).

Options
Depending on your forward itinerary, consider pushing ahead onto the north side of the Dingle Peninsula (Stage 3). There are good Bus Eireann services out of Tralee, but you are unlikely to get your bike on a bus during peak times.

STAGE 2
TRALEE TO DINGLE
48.5km Long climb

Blennerville Windmill (2km) – the largest working mill in Ireland – marks the northern entry to the Dingle Peninsula. From here the road continues level along the north side of the peninsula as the mountains slowly close in from the left.

Blennerville Windmill is at the entrance to the Dingle Peninsula

Looking north from the Connor Pass

The highlight of the day is the ascent of Ireland's second highest road pass – the 400m Connor Pass. The challenge is, of course, to do it without stopping. The early stages of the 10km climb are not too steep – in fact the road has been improved so much lately it lacks some of its old drama. The final kilometre though is magic – a single-lane road hangs on to a rock ledge cut into overhanging cliffs. Water is usually dripping down the rocks, and at one stage riders pass under a mini waterfall. The descent towards Dingle is not as steep as the climb, and while it makes sense not to get up too much speed, the road is excellent.

For better or worse, Dingle town has grown from being a small fishing and farming town into the tourist hotspot of the peninsula. On the plus side there is plenty of accommodation and good shops, but it can also be crowded. It is much more relaxing in during off-peak times.

Note Equipment failure meant having to re-calibrate the cycle-computer here, so there may be a slight variation in the measurements for stages after Tralee.

On the Road
It is far cheaper to stock up in one of Tralee's supermarkets than on the Dingle Peninsula, but decide whether it's worth carrying the weight over the Connor Pass. At least take some snacks for the pass from Tralee, or Blennerville (3km). Dingle has shops and ATMs.

Accommodation
The hostel situation in Dingle town is a little fluid. The Rainbow Hostel (1km along Stage 3, 066 915 1044, www.rainbowhosteldingle. com) has the advantage of being a couple of kilometres out of town, so it's quiet, and camping is also allowed. The Grapevine Hostel (066 915 1434, www.grapevinedingle.com) is on Dykegate in the heart of town. For camping it's either the Rainbow Hostel or, on the north side of the peninsula, the Anchor Caravan Park (066 713 9157, www.caravanparksireland.net) near Castlegregory (21km). Also on the north side, Cloghane has a hostel – Mount Brandon Hostel (066 7138299, www.mountbrandonhostel. com) – follow signs for Brandon Point from the 30.4km mark, and the hostel is a further 6km.

Options
This is a short stage, so it is possible to push on after Dingle. The road ahead around Slea Head is hilly, however, and also spectacular – so don't rush in. If on a more relaxed itinerary, consider staying at Cloghane or Brandon

on the north side of the peninsula (about 40km from Tralee). There is no through-road route here, so a backtrack will be necessary, but this is the best area for a day or two of walking.

STAGE 3
TOUR OF THE DINGLE PENINSULA

57.1km Hilly

The coastal scenery west of Dingle, with its rolling meadows, fuchsia hedges and fluffy white sheep, is pretty enough, but just a little further on is one of Ireland's best coastal roads. A steady climb leads to a rock ledge about 50m above the Atlantic. As the road hairpins along the coast, the drop steepens from impossibly precarious fields to sheer, dark-grey cliffs. Around Slea Head itself

> St Brendan's voyages were of Homeric proportions, and included a close encounter with a giant sea-cat, riding on the back of a whale, and meeting Judas Escariot on a temporary release from Hell.

> For David Lean's 1970 film *Ryan's Daughter*, a village was built, and later dismantled, on Cruach Mharthain above Clogher.

(16km), seabirds wheel in the updrafts from Atlantic winds hitting the cliffs, and the air is heavy with salt. Waves break silently on the rocks far below, and there is only a knee-high wall protecting the drop.

Around the head the coast flattens out considerably, though it remains just as attractive. The Blasket Islands stand proudly to the west, and there is a cliff-foot sandy cove at Coumeenoole Bay (18km), which was used as a location for the film *Ryan's Daughter*.

The scenery is not quite so spectacular after Clogher Head, but recovers well with lovely mountain-encircled Smerwick Harbour (28km). The early-Christian Gallarus Oratory (34km) is a popular place to visit, and an interesting example of mortarless building. A short side-trip takes in Brandon Creek – the site from which St Brendan set off on his epic voyage to the promised land – possibly the Americas. The stage returns to Dingle with a climb along the side of Mount Brandon.

The Dingle Peninsula with the Blasket Islands in the background

On the Road

Apart from a small shop at Ventry (10km) it is thin pickings until another small shop at Ballyferriter (29km) – which is a lifesaver if staying out here – so it's best to take your days supplies from Dingle. Carry some cash, as there are no ATMs.

Accommodation

There is a good campsite right next to the Gallarus Oratory (34km) – Oratory House Camping (066 9155143) – while Ballyferriter (29km) has the Black Cat Hostel (066 9156286). The Dún Chaoin (Dunquin) An Óige hostel (22km) is the westernmost hostel in Europe (066 9156121, www.anoige.ie).

Options

The short-cut back to Ventry from Ballyferriter (30.7km) looks like an interesting climb – on the map.

STAGE 4
DINGLE TO KILLORGLIN

54.9km Fast stage

After a great couple of days, it can be a wrench to leave the Dingle Peninsula, especially with the fine views over Dingle Harbour heading east out of town. But across the bay the wall of mountains of the Iveragh Peninisula and the Ring of Kerry are calling.

The N72 can be followed all the way to Annascaul (17km), but the route described here takes a couple of deviations from the main road where this is practical. When the R561 takes over at Annascaul the traffic quietens down, and this becomes a very scenic road as it follows a rock ledge high above the bay.

Inch (24km) is a popular bathing beach on a low peninsula that almost touches the Iveragh Peninsula near Glenbeigh (Stage 5).

In Annascaul a fine bronze statue commemorates Tom Crean, a veteran of three epic Antarctic expeditions, including Robert Falcon Scott's ill-fated Terra Nova Expedition of 1910–13.

Continuing east, Dingle Bay becomes a protected lowland estuary with broad tidal flats. A 4km section of the N70 follows Castlemaine (44km), but at Milton a very scenic road leads over the hilltops with stunning views of the shining Laune river at Killorglin, and beyond to the mountains of Dingle and Iveragh.

Killorglin is a traditionally laid out Irish town, with its central diamond set high above the river. The town is best known for its Puck Fair. Held on 10, 11 and 12 August, this is one of Ireland's oldest and oddest fairs. A wild goat is captured, crowned King Puck, and kept in a cage on a high stand in the middle of town to look down on three days of revelry.

On the Road

This is a quick stage, with the flat section from Inch to Castlemaine particularly fast. It is possible to follow main roads all the way to Killorglin, but best to get off the N72 at Lispole (8km) and out of the traffic, despite the steep climb. Inch (24.4km), with its long beach, makes a good stop. Castlemaine (44km) has a shop and a stone bench close by. At the end of this stage, Killorglin has a decent-sized supermarket and an ATM in its central diamond.

Accommodation

Killorglin has a hostel that also offers camping. The Laune Valley Farm Hostel (066 9761488) is signed from the N70 a couple of kilometres out of town (53km). The other camping option is Wests Caravan and Camping Park (066 9761240), also signed on the way into town (54km). Campers should consider pushing on to the excellent site at Glenbeigh (13km) along Stage 6.

Options

None.

STAGE 5
KILLORGLIN TO PORTMAGEE

65.8km Hilly

West of Killorglin the scenery changes quickly and dramatically. Mountains loom up on three sides, and patches of bog and dense pockets of woodland emphasise that upland landscapes

Cahersiveen Royal Irish Constabulary Barracks is now a heritage centre

are more dominant on the Iveragh Peninsula than neighbouring Dingle.

The valley-foot town of Glenbeigh (13km) has a distinctly Scottish feel. The scenery remains grand from here, but by Cahersiveen (there are many spellings) the landscape has to take second place to history and prehistory.

The first site of interest is the former Caheersiveen Royal Irish Constabulary Barracks (42km), which towers over the entrance to the town. Now a heritage centre (www.theold barracks.com, open Monday to Friday 10am– 4.30pm, Saturday 11am–4.30pm and Sunday 1pm–5pm), it is a goldmine for local history. The fortress-like barracks, built between 1870 and 1875, show the strategic importance of the nearby Valentia Island telegraph station, and just how worried the British were about security in the aftermath of the 1867 uprising. Here you can also find out more about Daniel 'the Liberator' O'Connell, who was born nearby, and Monsignor Hugh O'Flaherty – the Scarlet Pimpernel of the Vatican – who is buried in Caheersiveen.

The way to Valentia Island is via a short ferry hop from Reenard Point (47km) to Knight's Town – the ferry trip is the best place from which to appreciate the grand design of

Transatlantic telegraph cables operated from Valentia Island from 1866, until Western Union International terminated its cable operations in 1966.

Knight's Town. The street layout was planned by Scottish engineer Alexander Nimmo in 1830, and the village was developed in the 1840s. The cable station building, one of more than 50 protected structures in the village, was designed in 1868 by the 19th century Cork architect Thomas Deane. For more on the history of the transatlantic cables, visit the Valentia Island Heritage Centre (48km). Out near the coastal radio station on the island's northern tip are the fossil tracks of a tetrapod (52km) – probably a salamander-like creature about a metre long. Also on the island you can see the slate quarries that produced Queen Victoria's billiard table, and which are now home to a rather eerie grotto.

The 385-million-year-old fossilised trackway on Valentia Island is the earliest known record of an amphibious creature walking on the land.

But pride of place for this stage has to go to the Unesco World Heritage Site of Skellig Michael. Unfortunately you can't cycle there – it's 15km offshore – but Portmagee is the place to pick up a boat trip. This sixth-century Christian monastery perched on a rock face a couple of hundred metres above the Atlantic defies belief. The island looks more like a fairytale impregnable fortress than a likely landfall. From a small jetty, stone steps cut into solid rock lead to the small clutch of stone beehive huts clinging to a cliff. There are a handful of boat operators going to the Skelligs. Try the *Sea Quest* (066 9476214, www.skelligsrock.com), which leaves at 10.30am from Portmagee – although there are others. Booking is a good idea and sailings are subject to weather.

On the Road

This stage takes every opportunity to get away from the Ring of Kerry N70. This creates a couple of steep sections, especially leaving Rossbeigh (16km) and around Kells (28km). On the main roads it is not safe to stop except in parking areas, but there are plenty of these. Rossbeigh beach is a pleasant place for a break, or there are some viewing areas from the 21km to 25km mark. The climb along the spine of Valentia Island takes you up to 120m and the climb back from the fossil trackway is about 15 per cent.

Take some cash with you – athough there are ATMs at Cahersiveen, they are thin on the ground after that. The Valentia Island ferry operates continuously from April to September from 8.30am to 10.30pm. At the crossroads at the 50.9km mark on Valentia Island you can go right to the tetrapod tracks, straight on to the quarry, or left to follow the road down the island. The directions assume you do all three in that order.

Accommodation

Portmagee Hostel (066 9480018, www.port mageehostel.com) is a modern hostel just through the village. Earlier in the day the Glenross Caravan and Camping Park (066 976 8451, www.killarneycamping.com) at Glenbeigh (13km) has excellent facilities for touring campers. Caitin's Hostel is on the main Ring of Kerry at 25.7km (066 9477601).

Cahersiveen (42km) has the Sive Hostel (066 9472717, www.sivehostel.ie) and the Mannix Point Camping and Caravan Park (066 9472806, www.campinginkerry.com).

Options

There is an alternative flatter route across Valentia Island through Chapeltown on the R565 – bear left at the church (48.1km).

STAGE 6
PORTMAGEE TO CAHERDANIEL

45.5km Two stiff climbs

This stage includes the prettiest section of the main Ring of Kerry route – the climb over the Coomakesta (Coomakista) Pass (38km) and round the coast to Caherdaniel – as well as a fine hilly section on quieter roads heading out of Portmagee. The view from the pass over the crescent-shaped sandy beaches and low rocky isles of Derrynane Bay is one of Ireland's most photographed. Early in the day the views across Valentia Island, St Finan's Bay and Ballinskelligs Bay are also outstanding.

It was from St Finan's Bay that the monks went to and from Skellig Michael, and when the saw-tooth-shaped rock was abandoned in the 12th century the monks set up a coastal priory at Ballinskelligs.

Further on, Waterville (30km) is a bright and breezy seaside town with a wide, open bay and a sandy, though slightly stony, beach. Silent film star Charlie Chaplin liked to take his holidays here and there is a statue of him on the front.

The lush woodland around Caherdaniel is almost tropical, and in this sheltered spot it is hard to resist a swim at the beach. Daniel O'Connell's ancestral home, Derrynane House, is open to the public – opening hours vary (066 9475113, www.heritageireland.ie). The nearby village Caherdaniel has been named after 'the Liberator' – there are few historical figures as revered in Ireland as Daniel O'Connell. The Catholic Association that O'Connell helped establish in 1823 was at the forefront of radical

Skellig Michael monastery is a testament to the power of faith

populism in Europe. Pressure for Catholic civil rights came to a head when O'Connell himself was elected as Member of Parliament for Clare in 1828 – but as a Catholic was not allowed to take his seat. The following year the Emancipation Act removed anti-Catholic oaths from MPs. O'Connell took his seat in 1830.

On the Road
The steep climb out of Portmagee gets the heart started first thing in the day. Waterville (30km) and the Coomakesta Pass (38.5km) are the choice places to stop. The latter can be busy with Ring of Kerry tour buses, although they only tend to stop for 10 minutes or less. The climb up the Coomakesta is a steady four per cent. The service station approaching Waterville is the first decent-sized shop of the day, and there is also a very handy ATM in the village (30km). At the end of the day there is a small shop in Caherdaniel at Freddie's Pub, and also one at the Wave Crest Caravan and Camping Park through the village. The best place for a swim is Derrynane beach (42km).

Accommodation
The Traveller's Rest hostel (066 9475175, www.caherdanielhostel.com) is a few metres from the crossroads – just turn left at the end of the stage. The Skellig Hostel (066 9479942,

www.skellighostel.com) is at Ballinskelligs (14km). For camping there is a site just through Caherdaniel at the start of Stage 7 – this is the Wave Crest Caravan and Camping Park (066 9475188, www.wavecrestcamping.com).

Options
Despite the two climbs, this is a relatively fast stage, so consider doubling up with the next stage to Kenmare.

STAGE 7
CAHERDANIEL TO KENMARE
48.2km Rolling coastal hills

The shoreline on the south side of the Iveragh Peninsula is mostly well wooded, and in places almost tropical. The warm waters of the Gulf Stream kiss this coast, and it is noticeably warmer than on the north side of the peninsula.

Of note along this section are the Victorian resort hotel at Parknasilla (24km), which was much loved by George Bernard Shaw, among others, and the grounds of Dromore Castle (39km), which are popular with walkers. Sneem is oddly schizophrenic – quiet and reserved on the west side of the river, bustling with coaches, tourists and blaring Irish music on the other. Fortunately the grassy diamond and the memorial to former French president General de Gaulle, who was a visitor here, are in the quiet half (21km).

Kenmare is one of the finest Irish small towns. Laid out in the late 17th century, it retains many Georgian town houses. Big enough to have good shops and small enough to be quiet, it is one of the pleasantest towns in the southwest.

On the Road

The road surface to the east of Sneem for about 10km is rough for an N road. The first part of Sneem (21km), at the diamond, has benches and a shop nearby, and is a practical and quiet place to stop. Kenmare, at the end of the day, has a decent-sized supermarket (turn left at the central diamond).

Accommodation

If you want to camp, the next place is the Peacock (064 6684287, www.bearacamping. com), which is 13km along the N71 – see Route 9, Stage 1. Kenmare has several hostels. The Failte Hostel (064 6642333) is in a sympathetically adapted Georgian house – just head up Main Street, turn right at Shelbourne Street

and it's 200m on your left. On the way you will pass Kenmare Lodge Hostel (064 6640662), which is mid-way up the main street. The Greenwood Hostel (064 6689247, www. greenwoodhostel.com) is about 7km west of Kenmare on the N70 at Templenoe. Ask for directions if you are staying here – the turn is easy to miss.

Options

From Kenmare you have the choice of heading south on Route 9, or turning north towards Killarney and Tralee to close the loop of Route 8.

At Sneem it is possible to head straight for Killarney (46km) via Molls Gap – a total of 67km from Caherdaniel – the turn is at 21.4km.

If you want to see Killarney, but aren't continuing northwards, you can do it as a long, day-trip loop from Kenmare – see Stage 8.

STAGES 8 AND 8A   **KENMARE TO KILLARNEY**
47.7km (or 36.3km) Long climbs

There are two excellent cycling routes from Kenmare to Killarney – either via the Gap of

Dromore Castle has a fine Gothic Revival gate lodge

Dunloe (Stage 8), or along the main N71 and through Killarney National Park, taking in Ladies View (Stage 8a). If the plan is to continue southwards, but you would like to see Killarney, these two routes combined make a pleasant, lightly loaded, return day trip from Kenmare. Killarney can be busy, so a day trip means enjoying the scenery surrounding the town and avoiding some of the central bustle.

Either route can be done in either direction, the only hitch being the one-way system operating for bikes in the national park from Muckross House (5.6km) to the Meeting of the Waters (11.9km). This makes the national park/ N71 route (Stage 8a) work better if coming from Killarney to Kenmare, so route cards are included for Kenmare to Killarney via the Gap of Dunloe (Stage 8) and Killarney to Kenmare via Ladies View (Stage 8a).

This national park/main road route has fantastic views over the Killarney lakes, including the famous Ladies View. The lakeside cycleway through the national park is also delightful, and

> Killarney National Park is one of the few places in Ireland to have been continuously wooded since the end of the last glaciation.

> Pony trap rides are popular over the Gap of Dunloe – look out for pony droppings, as these are very skiddy in the rain.

there is a chance to visit a couple of historic buildings – Muckross Abbey is a 15th-century Franciscan foundation, while nearby Muckross House is one of Ireland's leading stately homes. The only way to visit the Victorian pile itself is by an hour-long guided tour, but its spectacular position at the head of the lake and the well-tended gardens make it worth just wandering around the outside if time is limited.

The woodlands around Killarney are its greatest treasure, and never look better than in the early autumn, with the still-lush trees punctuated with the bright-red berries of mountain ash, the purple heather still flowering and the bracken turning the surrounding hills brown.

On the other route, the Gap of Dunloe (29km) is a classic notch-through-a-mountain pass, while the wild Black Valley to the south of the pass has some of the grandest mountain scenery in Kerry. The steady climb, followed by a descent along the hairpin road past a string of small lakes, makes this one of the most enjoyable passes in Ireland (in either direction). It

Gap of Dunloe

really is impossible to choose between these two routes from Kenmare to Killarney – do them both!

On the Road

The N71 is fine for cycling. There are enough bends and enough sightseers to keep the speeds sensible and the traffic is not excessive. The one-way system for cycles in the national park goes anticlockwise around Muckross Lake. Both routes are shop-free apart from cafés at Ladies View (20km) and the northern end of the Gap of Dunloe (35km). There is a large supermarket opposite the tourist information centre in Killarney. The central car park here also has a public toilet – right over in the far corner. O'Sullivan's Cycles (064 66927) is on New Street, across from Killarney cathedral.

Accommodation

Accommodation is plentiful in and around Killarney. The Killarney International Hostel (064 6631240, www.anoige.ie) is an An Óige hostel about 5km out of town towards the Gap of Dunloe – look for the R563 turn to Dingle off the N72, and the hostel is a few hundred metres down there. Close by is the Fossa Holiday Hostel (41km, 064 6631497, www.camping-holidaysireland.com), which is also a campsite. For centre-of-town options, try one of the many independent hostels, such as the Killarney Railway Hostel (064 6635299, www.killarneyhostel.com). The Flesk Caravan and Camping Park (064 6631704) has good facilities and is close to the town centre on the N71 – handy for the national park – see Stage 8a, 2km.

Options

There are good Bus Eireann services, but you are unlikely to get your bike on a bus during peak times.

STAGE 9
KILLARNEY TO TRALEE

30.4km A steady hill climb

After the rigours of southwest Kerry, the run back to Tralee from Killarney is a breeze. The trip is also a very pleasant one, with some fine views from the climb over the hills to the north of Ballyfinnane.

> The Ballyfinnane Hill Climb of 1903 was won by the Honourable Charles Stewart Rolls, of Rolls-Royce fame. There is a memorial by the road.

On the way out of Killarney there is a final chance to gaze back over the lakes and woods from Agadhoe Heights (2km), with its remains of a round tower and castle.

The climb to the north of Ballyfinnane, along the flank of the Slieve Mish mountains, is not too taxing, giving you time to soak up the pretty landscape of rushing streams, purple and red fuchsia hedges, and road margins thick with wildflowers. Devonian rocks make a brief re-appearance on the summit plateau (21km), and with them bog, gorse and heather also emerge briefly, before a descent to the green crescent of fertile pastures surrounding Tralee.

On the Road

There is just a very short section on the main N22 north out of Killarney – after that the roads are very quiet. There are no shops at all on this stage until Tralee.

Accommodation

See Stage 1 for accommodation options for Tralee.

Options

For public transport at Tralee, see Stage 1.

ROUTE 8 THE SOUTHWEST PENINSULAS

Stage 1 Tarbert to Tralee

0.0		Tarbert, at turn to ferry (small parking area next to shop if required), continue straight on R551 Ballybunion
0.1	→	'Coastal Drive'
	☆	Shannon drowning memorial
4.8	☆	Krugers
7.3	⇨	Lislaughin Abbey 0.4km return
8.7	→	At Ballylongford crossroads, follow R551 Ballybunion
8.9	ATM ♦	Medium-sized shop
11.1	←	'Lissellton'
13.9	△(90)	3–4% climb
14.6	↑	At crossroads
16.8	△(115)	Views to coast
18.3	←	At T-junction
19.9	♦ →	Shops on right at Lisselton Crossroads – see note in text
20.0	→	'R553 Ballybunion'
20.1	←	'Ballyduff'
23.6	←	'R551 Tralee'
27.4	→	'Coast road'
30.5	⇨	To Kilmore Strand 2km
35.6	♦	Small shop
42.4	←	At crossroads
42.7	△(85)	'Wow' moment as view opens up along strand
43.4	→	'Ballyheige' (at crossroads)
44.4	⇨ ☆ ♦ WC	To Ballyheige village and beach, 1.5km return
50.8	→	'Banna Strand' (can continue straight on)
52.2	▲	Sir Rogers Caravan Park
	↑	Carry straight on to beach
52.6	WC	
52.8	↑ ↓	Turn around at car park, short walk to beach
53.3	→	Back at junction
53.6	↗	Bear right at fork
54.3	↗	Bear right at fork, Casement memorial is on left
56.4	☆	Pass castle at Rahoneen – may have been Bishop of Ardfert's residence
59.2	←	At T-junction
59.8	☆	Church and IRA memorial

Stage 1 Tarbert to Tralee

60.0	←	At Ardfert – have to turn, one-way
60.2	→	'Ardfert Cathedral'
60.3	☆	'Ardfert Cathedral'
	→	Just after cathedral
60.4	↑	'R551 Tralee'
67.1	O ↑ ♦	Grocery store on corner
68.0	♦	Shop
68.8	↑	'Town centre', at lights
69.0	→	'Town centre', at lights
69.1	←	One way – Kirby's Brouge Inn opposite
69.2	←	On to the Mall
69.4	→	'Denny Street', in front of AIB Bank
69.6	WC	In park on left
	←	At Kerry Musem
69.7		Arrive tourist information (round side of museum)

Stage 2 Tralee to Dingle

0.0	↶	Outside Tralee tourist information centre, follow one-way
0.2	←	One-way
0.4	←	'(N86) An Daingean'
0.7	O →	'N86 An Daingean'
2.7	←	Road swings left across bridge
2.8	↑ ⇨	Blennerville Windmill on right
3.2	ATM ♦	Service station has good shop
11.7	☆ ⇨	Derrymore Strand 600m
15.2	⇦	Alternative route to Dingle via N81 (34.5km)
21.0	♦	Anchor Caravan Park, food store on left
	▲ ⇨	
23.4	⇨	Castlegregory 2km
27.1	☆ ⇨	Stradbally Strand
28.6	☆ ⇨	Gowlane Strand
30.4	▲ ⇨	'Brandon Point'; turn here for hostel at Cloghane
35.6	⇨	Brandon Point, here is start of pass (73m)
40.9	△(413)	Connor Pass summit
47.9	↑	Now in Dingle, first crossroads (slightly staggered)
48.2	O ↑	'Slea Head Drive'

Stage 2 Tralee to Dingle

48.4	← WC	'Slea Head Drive', WC on left
48.5	←	Turn into quayside area by Dingle tourist information

Stage 3 Tour of the Dingle Peninsula

0.0	←	From car park exit on Dingle quay, next to tourist information, turn left
1.0	←○ ▲⇧	'Slea Head Drive'. Rainbow Hostel, straight on in a few hundred metres
1.3	ATM ◆	Good shop in service station
7.4	⇦ ☆ WC	Ventry Strand 100m
10.1	◆	Small shop
11.2	☆	Celtic and prehistoric museum
12.2	△(50)	Steady climb, don't forget to look back
13.0	☆	Dunbeg Fort
	☆	Famine cottages
13.9	☆	Beehive Huts, also photo opportunity down coast
15.1	☆	Parking
15.4	☆	Parking
16.4	☆	Now rounding Slea Head. Parking and information board about birdlife
16.7	☆	Cliff-side section of road ends, views of Blaskets ahead
17.5	☆	Parking
18.5	⇦ ☆	Swimming beach – Coumeenoole Strand, where *Ryan's Daughter* was partly filmed
20.2	⇦ ↑	At crossroads, left goes to Dunquin pier
22.7	⇦ ☆	To Krugers – westernmost pub in Europe (100m)
22.3	↑▲	At crossroads, Dunquin Hostel on right
28.6	⇦	To beach at Smerwick Harbour – approx 3km
28.8	▲◆	Small shop and Black Cat Hostel
29.3	☆	Ballyferriter – couple of places offer food
29.7	☆	Local history museum
30.8	↖	'R559 An Daingean' (right goes to Ventry – Ceann Trá)
31.3	⇦ ☆	To Wine Strand

Stage 3 Tour of the Dingle Peninsula

	◆	Pub has small shop and serves food
33.3	←	'Gallarus, Slea Head Drive'
34.5	▲ ☆⇨	Gallarus campsite on corner, Gallarus visitor centre 50m on right
36.1	←☆	'An Fheothanach', access to beach just before turn
37.0	◆	Shop
37.1	⇦ →	At T-junction, left leads to pretty harbour and beach at Ballynagall (100m)
37.6	☆	Radio Gaeltach
39.2	←	T-junction
40.2	⇦	Road leads to small quay
41.1	←	'Slea Head Drive'
45.1	⇦ →	'An Daingean', left leads to Brandon Creek (2km return)
48.4	←	'Slea Head Drive'
49.9	△(115)	Fine views on ascent
56.1	○↑	Back on outskirts of Dingle
57.1		Back at Dingle tourist information

Stage 4 Dingle to Killorglin

0.0	→	From car park entrance, by quay, next to tourist information centre, turn right
0.1	→	First junction
0.3	○→	'N86 Tralee'
8.8	→	Leave main road. Just past bridge at Lispole – take care – steep climb follows
10.9	↑	Road joins from left
	↑	Carry straight on when road swings left
11.1	→	Rejoin main road – poor visibility, take great care
13.1	←	At crossroads, steep climb after
13.2	↗	Take right fork
14.3	↑	Odd crossroads – just keep in a straight-on direction
17.4	→	At T-junction in Annascaul
17.5	←	At N86
17.5	◆ →	Small shop
17.6	☆	Tom Crean Memorial Gardens on right
18.7	←	'R561'
24.3	☆	Views of Inch Island from car park

Stage 4 Dingle to Killorglin

24.4	☆	Access to Inch beach and takeaway, fast section beside water follows
34.3	♦	Shop in service station
44.7	♦ →	'N70 Killorglin', shop on corner, at Castlemaine
45.3	→	'N70 Killorglin'
48.0	←	At Milltown, follow N70, swings left
48.0	♦	Shop
48.0	⇧ →	'Killorglin N70', straight on to Killarney 18km
48.1	♦	Shop
48.6	←	'Knockavota', opposite cemetery
50.6	☆	Views down Dingle Bay to Inch
52.5	←	At T-junction, rejoining N70
53.2	⇦ ▲	Laune Valley Farm Hostel
54.5	O →	'Ring of Kerry'
54.5	⇧ ▲	Wests Caravan Site has some touring pitches (approx. 1km)
54.7	☆	O Shea's Cycle Centre
54.8	↑	'Town centre', at crossroads, note Bianconi Inn opposite
54.9	ATM	Arrive Killorglin diamond

Stage 5 Killorglin to Portmagee

0.0		Killorglin 'The Square' – take Langford St (upper left corner by Fish Shop)
0.8	→	'Glenbeigh'
8.4	☆	Fine view of mountains ahead
9.2	↑	At crossroads with N70
10.3	←	At T-junction
10.7	→	'Glenbeigh (back on N70)'
13.1	▲	Glenross Caravan and Camping Park
13.7	♦	Shop at Glenbeigh
13.9	♦	Supermarket in service station
14.1	→	'Rossbeigh'
14.4	→	'R564 Rossbeigh'
14.7	☆	Small rest area on left
16.5	☆WC	Rossbeigh beach
16.8	↖	At fork
17.9	△(145)	Steep Climb to here
18.3	↑	At cross roads

Stage 5 Killorglin to Portmagee

19.3	♦ →	'Cahersiveen' – on N70, shop on corner
21.7	☆	Viewing area on cliffs
22.2	☆	Viewing area on cliffs
22.8	☆	Rail tunnel on cliff to left
24.0	☆	On-road cycleway for 1km
24.2	☆	Viewing area
25.0	☆	Gleensk viaduct on left
25.7	▲	Caitins Hostel and Bar
26.8	→	'Kells'
28.5	↗	Take right fork, left signed 'Kells PO'
31.0	→	At T-junction (N70)
31.1	←	Continue on small road parallel to N70
34.3	→	Unsigned, but 'Rock Walk' is signed to left
34.9	↑	'Dooneen', at crossroads
38.3	→	At T-junction
38.8	↖	Left fork
41.3	☆	Fabulous chalet – Arts and Crafts-style house – in poor repair
41.4	←	At T-junction
42.1	☆	Cross bridge – note old rail bridge to left
42.4	☆	The Old Barracks Heritage Centre at Cahersiveen
42.5	WC	
42.6	→ ⇦ ▲☆	At crossroads, tourist information on right. Sive Hostel 100m to left, O'Connell birthplace 1.5km
42.7	♦ ATM	Shops and pharmacy down main street
43.5	☆	Casey's Cycles
43.6	ATM ♦	Large supermarket
44.2	▲	Mannix Point Camping and Caravan Park, turn just before observatory
44.8	→	'Valentia Island ferry'
47.6	↑	Arrive ferry quay at Reenard Point
47.7	⇦ →	On leaving ferry at Knight's Town, turn right at T-junction in front, go left to transatlantic cable station – 400m
47.8	←	At clock
47.9	♦	Small food shop

Stage 5 Killorglin to Portmagee

48.1	→	Just before Church of Ireland church, bear left for lowland route by R565
48.3	☆	Valentia Island Heritage Centre
48.9	↑⇨	At crossroads, Glanleam House to right
50.9	→	'Dohilla', at crossroads, tetrapod tracks
52.6	↑↓	Turn around at tetrapod car park, 200m walk to tracks
54.7	→	Back at crossroads, turn right to slate quarry
56.0	↑↓	Turn at quarry and grotto
57.3	→	Back at crossroads turn right
57.4	→	Unsigned
59.1	☆	Geokaun Mountain and Fogher Cliffs – entry fee
60.2	↑	At crossroads
63.0	←☆	Memorial to landing of first transatlantic cable is in field on right
64.7	→	'Portmagee '
65.0	☆	Skellig Experience Centre
65.6	→	'Skellig Ring', WC on corner
65.8		Arrive Portskellig quay, Lost at Sea memorial

Stage 6 Portmagee to Caherdaniel

0.0		Portmagee car park at Lost at Sea memorial and telephone box. Head away from bridge
0.0	←	Road swings left
0.4	▲	Portmagee Hostel
2.6	☆	Coffee shop and walk to 'most beautiful cliffs in Kerry'
4.5	△(250)	Views over Finan's Bay and to Skelligs
7.6	↖	Road swings left
8.4	↖	'Cahersiveen', road swings left
8.5	◆	Small shop
10.7	△(110)	
10.8	→	Unsigned road
14.0	▲	Skellig Hostel
16.1	↑	'Strand'
16.4	▲	An Óige hostel
16.6	←	'R556 Baile an Scellig', straight on to beach and WC, right to priory
17.1	◆	Ballinsbelligs post office has internet access

Stage 6 Portmagee to Caherdaniel

17.9	→	Just before gallery with thatched roof
18.3	↑	At crossroads, main road swings left, but keep heading straight on
20.5	→	At crossroads
21.2	⇨	To beach 500m
25.8	→	'N70 Kenmare'
27.6	◆	Medium-sized shop in service station
	↗	N70 swings right. Straight on is good alternative but closed at time of writing
30.4	WC	
	⇦◆	Waterville tourist information and WC here, shops up street on left
30.6	☆	Charlie Chaplin statue
31.5	→	'Kerry Way'
33.6	←	Gentle climb back to main road
34.3	→	Onto N70 – careful, poor visibility, start of climb to Coonmakesta Pass
38.5	△(210) →	Turn into car park at top of pass, fantastic view
38.6	→	Turn around and leave car park, continue towards Caherdaniel
41.3	→	'Ring of Kerry Cycleway'
41.9	☆	Enter Derrynane Historic Park
42.6	←⇧	Turn left – straight on would take you to beach
43.4	← ☆⇨	Turn left – right takes you to Derrynane House (600m return)
43.6	☆	Ogham stone by road
45.5	◆	Arrive Caherdaniel crossroads, Freddie's on right has food and shop

Stage 7 Caherdaniel to Kenmare

0.0	→	Caherdaniel crossroads, turn right, 'Sneem'
1.6	▲◆	Wave Crest Caravan and Camping Park has shop
2.5	⇨	To beach
6.2	⇦	Staigue Fort (approx 4km and 150m climb)
6.6	◆	Small shop in service station at Castle Cove

Stage 7 Caherdaniel to Kenmare

14.9	△(130)	3–4% climb
21.0	☆♦	Sneem central diamond/green – note General de Gaulle memorial, also shop
21.4	⇦↑ ATM	'N70 Kenmare', Mace shop has ATM, left here will take you to Killarney approx. 45km
24.5	☆	Parknasilla resort
30.2	☆	Lake has rather folorn picnic table
32.9	☆	Fine section along water starts
35.3	☆	Cross river gorge (Blackwater river)
39.6	☆⇨	Dromore Castle
40.5	⇨	Turn to Coss Strand
41.0	☆	Pat Spillane's Bar, Templenoe
47.5	→	'Town Centre', at T-junction, Kenmare
47.6	♦	Supermarket in service station
48.2		Arrive Kenmare central park, tourist information on right

Stage 8 Kenmare to Killarney

0.0	←	Kenmare, from outside heritage centre/tourist office, turn left
0.6	←	'N70 Cahersiveen'
5.8	→	'Rossacoosane'
10.3	△(200)	Climb levels out onto open moor
12.6	→	'Killarney'
14.1	☆	Barfinnhy Lake has picnic table
14.9	←	'Black Valley Hostel', carry straight on for a few metres for fine view
17.6	→	'Hillcrest Farmhouse'
22.2	☆	Pass rapids on Owenreagh River
25.2	⇨	To Lord Brandon's Cottage, approx. 1km
26.4	▲	Black Valley Hostel
27.0	→	First turn past hostel
29.1	△(240)	Head of the Gap of Dunloe
35.2	▲	Kate Kearney's Cottage Café
36.8	→	'Killarney'
40.7	→	'N72 Killarney'
41.3	▲	Fossa Caravan and Camping Site and Hostel

Stage 8 Kenmare to Killarney

41.6	▲	Beech Grove Caravan and Camping Park
44.0	♦	Good shop in Esso station
45.8	O→	'Town centre'
46.9	↑	'Town centre parking' (left also goes into town)
47.6	←	'Tourist office'
47.7	← WC	Turn into car park by tourist office

Stage 8a Alternative via Ladies View

0.0		Killarney tourist office, Beech Road, turn right out of car park
0.1	←	'N71 Kenmare', at T-junction
0.3	O→	'N71 Kenmare' – big roundabout
0.5	O↑	Mini-roundabout
0.6	☆⇨	Ross Castle – approx. 3km
1.0	♦	Shop in service station
	⇦ ▲↑	At lights, left leads to White Bridge Caravan and Camping Park – approx. 3km
1.7	→	Cross road, join cycleway parallel to road by phone boxes
2.4	▲	Flesk Caravan and Camping Park (stay on road at 1.7km if going here)
2.6	♦	Shop at service station
3.3	☆	Cycleway enters national park
3.8	↗	Unsigned
4.6	☆↑	'Muckross House', Muckross Abbey on left
5.6	⇧ ☆→	'Meeting of the Waters', Muckross House straight on
9.2	☆	Brickeen Bridge
10.3	☆	Dinnis Cottage and Meeting of the Waters
11.9	→	At car park
	→	Join N71
14.0	☆	Five Mile Bridge – good lake views
15.9	☆	Alongside Upper Lough
16.6	☆	Through rock arch, steady climb follows
19.0	△(110)	Galway's Bridge
19.8	☆	Ruined, turreted lodge
20.1	☆♦	Ladies View Cafe
20.3	☆♦	Real Ladies View

Stage 8a Alternative via Ladies View		
21.6	☆	Best view
26.3	↖	'N71, Kenmare', Avoca café and shop on corner at Moll's Gap
35.7	◆	Shop in Esso station
36.3		Arrive Kenmare central park, tourist information on right

Stage 9 Killarney to Tralee		
0.0	←	Killarney tourist information centre, from car park entrance turn left
0.1	→	At T-junction (New Street)
0.3	←	One-way (High Street)
0.6	↑	'All routes N22 Tralee'
1.4	◆	Supermarket
1.5	O↑	'N22 Tralee'
2.2	←	'Aghadoe'
2.6	⇦	Side-trip to Aghadoe round tower and castle 5km return
7.5	↑	At crossroads
10.1	↑	At crossroads
11.4	↑	At crossroads
14.2	→	'R561 Farranfore'
14.4	←	'Ballyfinnane'

Stage 9 Killarney to Tralee		
18.2	↑	'Tralee', at Ballyfinnane crossroads
19.8	☆	Ballyfinnane Hill Climb memorial
21.9	△	Windy summit plateau
22.1	↑	At crossroads
23.9	←	At T-junction
23.9	→	After 20m
26.6	↑	Cross N70
32.1	↑	At slightly staggered crossroads
28.1	→	At crossroads
28.9	☆	Level crossing
29.1	O↑ ▲⇨	'R551 town centre', turn right here for Woodlands camping
29.5	↑	At lights
29.6	◆	Jim Caball Cycles on right
29.6	↑	'Town centre'
29.8	→	'Killarney N21' (just past orange Brogue Inn)
29.9	←	Into Bridge Street
30.1	→	'Tourist office'
30.3	←	Museum in front
30.4		Arrive tourist information

The Roses of Tralee – in the town park

179

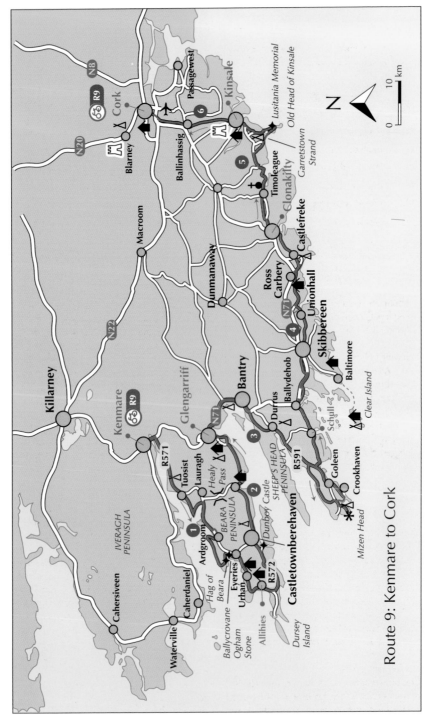

Route 9: Kenmare to Cork

ROUTE 9

KENMARE TO CORK – THE FUCHSIA COAST

Stage		Terrain	Distance (km)	Summit (distance from start/height)
1	Kenmare to Allihies	Tiring, short sharp climbs	76.1	68km/100m
2	Allihies to Glengarriff	A few easy climbs	57.6	46km/130m
3	Glengarriff to Schull	Coastal hills	94.5	24km/160m
4	Schull to Clonakilty	Coastal hills	61.1	45km/100m
5	Clonakilty to Kinsale	Coastal hills	44.8	6km/130m
6	Kinsale to Cork	Undulating with one steep climb	25.2	16km/150m
		Total	**359.3**	

Southwest Ireland's characteristic pattern of narrow bays and long peninsulas continues south of Glengarriff, and the scenery is just as beautiful as the better-known peninsulas to the north. The Beara Peninsula, with its wild rocky western tip and the warm waters of Bantry Bay to the south, is particularly appealing. The Mizen Peninsula has the added attraction of having Ireland's most southwesterly point at Mizen Head.

After the peninsula hopping, it is a relief to get onto a normal section of coastline, and the stretch of South Cork from Schull through to Kinsale is a pleasure to ride. The towns and villages here are, for the most part, well looked after and prosperous, with a number of older buildings in their centres.

Kinsale is one of Cork's most popular visitor towns – and deservedly so. Cork city, although less attractive, still has its fair share of fine buildings. Cork is Ireland's second biggest city (population 120,000 or so), so this is the place to stock up or get any repairs done if heading further around the country.

Options

Short-cuts are possible across all the peninsulas. The route described here skips most of the Sheep's Head Peninsula to keep the distance down. If there is time to spare though, the Sheep's Head is almost deserted, and has fine views towards the Mizen. Stages 5 and 6 can combine into one day. If flying out of Cork, there is no need to head right into Cork city, as Stage 6 passes within 10km of the airport.

Getting to the Start

Below are the options to consider for this route. Kenmare does not have great transport connections, making cycling the easiest way to get to the start of this route. Taking either of the Route 8, Stage 8 options from Killarney to Kenmare (either Stage 8 in reverse – 47.7km, or Stage 8a – 36.3km), adds an attractive day's riding to the start of this route. The routes in the southwest can also be combined into longer tours – for example the Tour of the Southwest (965.5km) from Cork to Cork, see Grand Tours, Appendix 2.

By Air
No direct links.

By Sea
No direct links.

By Rail/Bus

Most Bus Eireann services to Kenmare are via Killarney where there is usually a change of buses.

When to Go

Any time from spring to autumn.

Accommodation

There is a budget accommodation gap between Bantry and Skibbereen, but plenty of bed and breakfasts along the coast. While camping is by no means necessary, this is a good area for tenting.

Maps

The OSI 1:250 000 Ireland South sheet covers the whole of Route 9. For 1:50 000 coverage, the following sheets from the OSI Discovery series are needed: 85 Cork Kerry, 84 Cork Kerry, 88 Cork, 89 Cork, 87 Cork. About 1km of the route leaving Kenmare is on sheet 78 Kerry – but it is barely worth buying this unless required for another route.

Onwards

From Cork, Route 10 takes you further east along the coast to Youghal, then to Waterford via Stage 4, or Stages 1 to 3 follow the Blackwater Valley to Killarney. For a 10- to 12-day route starting from Cork, consider going east to Youghal, then north and west to Killarney via the Blackwater Valley, before picking up this route – Route 9 – at Kenmare. Route 8, Stage 8 describes the link between Kenmare and Killarney.

Pushing west from Cork out towards the Mizen can be very tiring with the prevailing westerlies.

STAGE 1
KENMARE TO ALLIHIES

76.1km Tiring, short sharp climbs

This is a hard day, but a rewarding one. All of the southwestern peninsulas show a marked transition from a relatively protected climate and lush vegetation at their eastern end, towards a rocky, exposed western tip, but it is on the Beara Peninsula that this change is the

most abrupt and dramatic. The last sign of lush woodland is around Lauragh (27km) – where Derreen Gardens (open April to September) is known for its subtropical plants, including bamboos, magnolias and eucalyptus – but to the west is a land of open coasts and small harbours and wave-scoured headlands. It can be a battle against the wind getting out here, and the outcrop of carboniferous slates on the north edge of the peninsula has weathered into a stepped profile that forces the coastal road into a series of short, leg-sapping steep climbs.

The open headlands provide dramatic backdrops for both the Ballycrovane Ogham stone (56km) and the Hag of Beara. The former is the tallest Ogham stone in Europe, while the latter figures in the mythology of the peninsula. On a dull day the bright yellow, pink, red and green houses of Eyeries (59km) glow optimistically in a landscape of grey water and grey rock, while on a sunny day the water sparkles and the small coves invite swimmers.

Ogham is a primitive script that probably dates from the fourth century. The letters of the alphabet are represented by a series of lines, commonly carved along the edge of a rock or stone.

After crossing a col in the lee of Cod's Head (70km), the coast road enters some of the most dramatic scenery in Ireland. Grey stone hills with tortuously folded rocks plunge down into the open Atlantic, while the road clings to a narrow foreshore. Abandoned copper workings dot the mountains here, a reminder that these rocks once produced great wealth for a few, and dangerous underground work for many (for more on the copper mines, see Stage 2).

Allihies, like Eyeries before it, is painted brightly, as if to ward off the sometimes bleak landscape. Here a warm hostel and a fine beach await the weary traveller. There is also a mining museum in a restored non-conformist chapel through the village.

On the Road

The best shop on the stage is at Ardgroom (38km). Take cash with you from Kenmare – there is no ATM until Castletownberehaven,

19km along Stage 2. As noted above, be prepared for this stage to be more tiring than the
relatively small climbs suggest – there are
many 5m to 10m climbs/descents that barely
show up on contours. There is a supermarket in
Allihies at the end of the day.

Accommodation

Allihies Hostel (027 73107, www.allihieshostel.
net) is right in the heart of the village. Between
Eyeries and Allihies is Urhan Hostel (64km, 027
74036). Earlier in the day there is camping and
hostel accommodation at the Peacock (064
6684287, www.bearacamping.com) – take supplies though, there is not much around here
(13.8km). Further on is an An Óige hostel at
Glanmore Lake (064 6683181, www.anoige.ie)
a couple of kilometres off the route (28km), and
Creeveen Lodge Caravan and Camping Park
(064 6683131, www.creveenlodge.com) is in
the same area. See Options for directions.

Options

It is possible to complete Kenmare to
Glengarriff in one day (and save about 71km)
by following the Healy Pass across the peninsula from Lauragh to Adrigole. For this option,
turn left at 27.8km, then right after about 300m
and onto the R574. Creeveen Lodge camping
is a further 1.5km down this road. The pass

summits at about 300m. The distance Lauragh
to Adrigole (Stage 2, 35.6km) is 13km, giving
a total distance for Kenmare to Glengarriff of
about 63km. An earlier route to the Healy Pass
(at 16.5km) saves another 4km, but involves a
climb to about 170m.

STAGE 2
ALLIHIES TO GLENGARRIFF

57.6km A few easy climbs

Eastwards from Allihies the terrain gets easier, but not without a final flourish climbing
over the spine of the peninsula through the
Bealbarnish Gap (4km). There are, however,
fine views here back over Ballydonegan Bay
and Allihies. The turn for Dursey Island is just
over this summit – the island is reached by a
cable car slung over a swirling tidal race.

Approaching the bustling port of
Castletownberehaven there is a chance to visit
Dunboy Castle and Puxley's Mansion (16km).
The castle was the scene of the 1602 Siege of
Dunboy, in which the English broke O'Sullivan
Bere rule over the peninsula. The castle fell
after fearsome artillery bombardment from
forces sent to suppress a rebellion led by Donal
Cam O'Sullivan Bere. Castletownberehaven

Glengarriff nestles at the head of the Beara Peninsula

(19km), now a busy fishing port, was one of the Treaty Ports, not abandoned by the British until 1939.

East of the town a grey rockface starts to loom over the road – this is the Hungry Hill from the Daphne du Maurier novel of the same name. The hill is the highest peak in the spine of the peninsula, and from this point the landscape continues to soften, although it remains mountainous as far as Glengarriff, an attractive town that shows its resort pedigree through the fine 250-year-old Eccles Hotel commanding the mountain-backed bay. Garinish Island, with its Italianate gardens and lush subtropical vegetation, is worth a visit.

In the novel *Hungry Hill* the Puxleys, who grew rich from the Beara copper mines, are called the Brodricks, and Puxley's Mansion is Clonmere.

On the Road

Castletownberehaven (19km) has shops, an ATM and a central square in which to sit down for a break. The small quay near Puxley's Mansion/Dunboy Castle (16km) is also pleasant, although it might become busier when the hotel opens. There is no ATM in Glengarriff.

Accommodation

In Glengarriff there is Murphy's Village Hostel (027 63555, www.murphyshostel.com), or try the Cottage Bar/Hostel (027 63226, www.cottagebar.com). There are two campsites on the way into town (55km) – Dowlings Caravan and Camping Park (027 63154) and O'Shea's (O'Shea's Camping Site, 027 63140). For details of other accommodation, enquire at the tourist office (027 63084).

Early on the stage (11km) is Garranes Hostel (027 73032, www.dzogchenbeara. org). In Castletownberehaven (19km) there is Harbour Lodge (027 71043) behind the supermarket, while Filane Lodge is on through town near the golf course (027 71599), where there is also a campsite – the Berehaven Camper and Amenity Park (23km, 027 71957 www.berehavengolf.com). Adrigole (35km) has the Hungry Hill Lodge Hostel and campsite (027 60228, www.hungryhilllodge.com).

Options

Consider pushing on to Bantry to take some of the sting out of Stage 3.

It is possible to skip the side road at 47.9km and stay on the R572. The trip out to the Dursey Island cable car would add about 16km to the stage. Check locally for the latest timetable information.

STAGE 3
GLENGARRIFF TO SCHULL

94.5km Coastal hills

This stage heads to Ireland's far southwestern tip at Mizen Head, and it is quite common to run into groups of cyclists on the Malin–Mizen (or Mizen–Malin) length-of-Ireland run – usually done in a week or so.

Early in the day the town of Bantry (17km) is a fine traditional market town, with winding narrow streets and an open square by the harbour. Memorials in the square and around town commemorate the French invasion fleets of 1689 and 1796, and there is more about the fleets at nearby Bantry House (open daily 10am to 6pm mid-March to October, 027 50047, www.bantryhouse.com). This fine 18th-century house has some grand authentic interiors and the gardens are also of interest.

During the Second World War years ('the Emergency' in Ireland) the Second Cyclist Squadron of the Irish Army was stationed at Bantry House.

The south side of Dunmanus Bay has a couple of tumbling tower-house castles. Dunmanus Castle (45km) is the best preserved of the O'Mahony castles that dot the Mizen, and it guards a pretty harbour of the same name.

Mizen Head has a visitor centre (028 35115, www.mizenhead.net), and you pay €6 to walk right out to the lighthouse, but it is a spectacular spot (closes at 6pm). After the Mizen there is one of the best beaches hereabouts, at Barley Cove (70km), which is also notable for the fine machair grasslands behind the foreshore.

Mizen Head – Ireland's most southwesterly point

Crookhaven (73km) is a picturesque harbour village in a long, narrow rocky cove, while Schull at the end of the day is the first decent-sized town since Bantry.

On the Road

Bantry (17km) is the biggest town in the area. As well as general stores and ATMs, Nigel's Bicycle Shop (027 52 657) is on the way into town. Wolf Tone Square has benches, and even public toilets nearby. For an out-of-town stop, it is hard to beat pulling over on the climb over the Sheep's Head Peninsula (24km). Durrus (29km) has a fine shop, and the local cheese – Durrus Gold – is an excellent keeper.

Accommodation

This stage is feast and famine when it comes to accommodation. There are no hostels or campsites in the Schull area. Earlier in the day there are a few campsites – Eagle Point Camping (027 50630, www.eaglepointcamping.com) is 6km from Bantry in a beautiful waterside location. At 34km is Dunbeacon Caravan and Camping Park (027 62851). The closest site to Mizen Head (72km) is Barley Cove Holiday Park (028 35302).

Options

There are a few short-cuts across the Mizen to Schull, at 32.3 and 36.2km, giving total distances, Glengarriff to Schull, of approximately 42km and 46.km respectively.

STAGE 4
SCHULL TO CLONAKILTY

61.1km Gentle coastal hills

After the excitement of rounding Mizen Head, the coast immediately to the east of Schull is rather uninspiring, and it is necessary to stay some distance inland at times to keep the distances down. The cycling is nonetheless pleasant, the roads are not too busy, and the interest starts to pick up approaching Skibbereen (23km).

This area was one of the worst affected by the Great Famine of 1845–9. The famine is one of the watersheds in Irish history. Before the famine, Ireland's population was about 8.2 million. By 1851 this had dropped by about 2.25 million, with some 1.5 million people emigrating. Ireland's population (currently about 6.2million) still hasn't recovered to the pre-famine level – find out more at the Skibbereen Heritage Centre (028 40900, www.skibbheritage.com), which is open 9.30am to 6pm daily from mid-May to late September, and slightly less frequently out of season.

185

THE GREAT FAMINE

The potato fungal disease *Phytophthora infestaris* first struck in Ireland in 1845. There had already been warnings that there was an over-dependence on potatoes in what, at the time, was one of Europe's most densely populated countries, but it was when the blight returned in 1846 that the full horror of the Great Famine began to unfold. The disease did not appear in 1847, although by this stage there was a lack of seed potatoes and the crop was low. The blight then returned in 1848 and 1849, and had run its course by 1850. Contemporary political ideas put faith in markets to deal with shortages (so called 'laissez faire') and private charities and landlords to deal with the immediate crisis. It was not until 1847 that the British government changed tack and began actively feeding the population – but by then Ireland was already the scene of harrowing starvation and disease was rampant. Estimates of the total number of deaths vary, but they amounted to at least a million. Some of the accounts recorded at the Skibbereen Heritage Centre are truly shocking, but it is in the silence of the Abbeystrowry famine graveyard, where 8000–10,000 unidentified people are buried, that the true scale of the tragedy can start to be comprehended.

By the slate-roofed waterside village of Unionhall (34km) the coast has settled into a pattern of long sea inlets snaking into low coastal hills. Glandore (37km), with its tiny harbour and beach hemmed by wooded slopes, is straight off a holiday postcard. Just past here, the Drombeg Stone Circle (39km) is a popular megalithic site. Further on, Ross Carbery (44km) – now bypassed by the highway – is a classic hilltop market town.

Ownahinchy – or Ownahincha – (47km) has a bathing beach. The castellated Gothic outline of Castlefreke is in private hands, but nearby Rathbarry is one of the finest estate villages in Ireland. The Sprigging School was established here by Lady Carbery in 1825 to teach lacemaking.

Clonakilty is a bright and bustling market town. Irish patriot Michael Collins was born here, and in the centre of town there is a statue of him overlooking an elegant garden square.

Collins was a charismatic Irish revolutionary who also showed organisational and political skills in his role as minister for finance in

Michael Collins looks out on Clonakilty

Michael Collins was killed in the civil war that followed the Anglo-Irish Treaty. Liam Neeson played the title role in the 1996 film, *Michael Collins*.

the First Dáil of 1919. He was at the forefront of the War of Independence and a member of the team that negotiated the Anglo-Irish Treaty of 1921. Find out more at the Michael Collins Centre (023 8846107, www.michaelcollins centre.com), about 5.5km along Stage 5.

On the Road

The best place to shop before Clonakilty is the supermarket at Schull. Skibbereen also has plenty of shops and ATMs. By the harbour in Unionhall (34km) is a good halfway point for a break. Ownahinchy (47km) is the best beach on the stage.

The roads leading into Clonakilty are a little confusing, but fortunately most of them end up in the town. This stage finishes with a loop through the town centre. And a short detour up the hill into Ross Carbery is also rewarding. Clonakilty has two cycle shops – MTM Cycles is on Ashe Street (023 8833584) and Sidney Perrott's on Connolly Street (023 8833641).

Accommodation

This holiday coast is well provided with campsites, but the hostel situation is not great. Meadow Camping (028 8833280) is close to Glandore (39km). O'Riordan's Caravan Park (023 8848216) is by the beach at Ownahinchy (48km). Clonakilty is one of those towns where hostels seem to appear sporadically, so check for the latest information. The route passes the tourist information office (023 8833226), where opening hours change. The Desert House Caravan and Camping Park (023 8833331) overlooks the bay and is only a couple of kilometres from Clonakilty – carry straight on at 0.4km on Stage 5. The Russagh Mill Hostel (028 22451, www.russaghmill hostel.com), a couple of kilometres outside Skibbereen on the Castletownshend road, also has camping – turn right at 23.5km and follow R596 Castletownshend signs. On the same road is the Hideaway Camping and Caravan Park (028 22254).

Options

From Skibbereen you could head south to Baltimore (13km) – there is a hostel here – Top of the Hill Hostel (028 20094, www.topofthe hillhostel.ie) – and also ferries to Cape Clear Island (028 39153, www.capeclearferry.com). On the island there is an An Óige hostel (028 41968, www.capeclearhostel.com) and seasonal campsite (028 39119).

STAGE 5
CLONAKILTY TO KINSALE

44.8km Gentle coastal hills

The final two stages into Cork pass through unspoilt towns and picturesque countryside right up to the fringes of Cork city. One of the highlights comes early in the day on this stage – a fine airy ridge road leaving Clonakilty with views back as far as the Beara Peninsula. This same road passes the Michael Collins Centre (5.5km, 023 8846107, www.michaelcollinscentre.com). Soon after this is Timoleague (9km), with its 13th-century Franciscan friary set alongside tidal flats at the head of a protected estuary.

> The original monastic settlement at Timoleague was founded by St Mologa in the sixth century. He also brought beekeeping to Ireland.

From Timoleague the road follows the shore along the north side of the estuary – keep an eye out for the crows that have learnt to put shells on the road for passing cars to split open. Garranefeen Strand (18km) has well-developed saltmarsh and dune systems, but after here the stage leaves the shore for a while until the approach to one of the scenic highpoints of the south coast – the Old Head of Kinsale. The

> The Cunard liner RMS *Lusitania* was torpedoed about 13.0km off the Old Head of Kinsale by a German U-boat in May 1915. Of the 1959 passengers and crew, 1198 died.

head itself – a 5km long promontory of slates and grits – is probably most impressive from the fine beach at Garrettstown (27km), but the ride out to the end is worthwhile for the sense of space and the views along the coast. The very tip of the head is a private golf course, but the ruined castle, a signal tower and the *Lusitania* memorial (32km) are all before the gates.

Kinsale is a beautifully situated historic port town that has maintained a traditional core. The estuary here is strategically important – the Battle of Kinsale in 1601 had far-reaching consequences in Irish history, while the 17th-century star-shaped Charles Fort, close to the town, is the most impressive and best preserved of its kind in Ireland. In the historic centre, Desmond Castle is a fine example of an urban tower-house. Built around 1500, it now houses a wine museum.

On the Road
One or other of the beaches at Garrettstown (27km) is a good point to take a break. There is a small shop nearby, but it is better to pick something up at Timoleague (9km), which has a shop at the service station, or even before leaving Clonakilty. There are no shops between Garrettstown and Kinsale. At the end of the day Kinsale has a choice of shops, including a good supermarket in the middle of town. There are also plenty of ATMs here.

Accommodation
Dempsey's Hostel (021 4774111) is on the R600 towards Cork, about 700m from the town centre. You can also pitch a tent in the garden. The nearest campsite to Kinsale is at the Garrettstown Holiday Park (021 4778156, www.garrettstownhouse.com), which is about 14km away. Pad Joe's pub in Timoleague (9km) offers hostel-style accommodation (023 8846125).

Options
Combining this stage with Stage 6 makes it is possible to ride Clonakilty to Cork in a day (70km).

STAGE 6
KINSALE TO CORK

25.2km Undulating with one steep climb

This old route from Kinsale to Cork gives a taste of what many Irish main roads were like until not very long ago. The former highway rollercoasts its way over hill and dale, with the numerous crossroads still marked by black-on-white cast-iron signs showing distances in miles. Trees and hedgerows crowd the road, while beyond a patchwork of green pasture and yellow wheatfields spreads to the low hills on the horizon.

Old Head of Kinsale is an outcrop of slates and grits

Colourful Cork

famous Bells of Shandon at St Anne's Church, and visiting the 19th-century Gothic Cork City Gaol – now a heritage centre.

On the Road

This is a surprisingly hilly route that will take at least three to four hours to ride. The only shop on route is at Ballinhassig (13km). If heading on past Cork, the city is the place to resupply and organise any bike maintenance you might need. There is a choice of cycle shops. Kilgrews Cycle Centre (021 4276255, www.kilgrewscycles.ie) is in the central area of the city – just head north up Grand Parade/Corn Market and look for Kyle Street on the left just before the river. There is any number of outdoor equipment suppliers, including the Outdoor Adventure Store on MacCurtain Street (021 4504389, www.outdooradventurestore.ie). The tourist office (021 4255100), on Grand Parade, is closed on Sundays.

Accommodation

Cork has a five-star An Óige hostel (021 4543289, www.anoige.ie) about 1km to the west of the city centre, near University College Cork. There is an active independent hostel scene – Kinlay House (021 4508966, www.kinlayhousecork.ie) advertises bike storage. For camping, Blarney Caravan and Camping Park (021 4516519, www.blarneycaravan park.com) is about 9km to the northwest of the city. It is possible to get there, avoiding the main roads, by picking up Blarney Road, off Shandon Street, just north of the river, and then following this small road out of the city. Take the right fork at Cloghan crossroads, which is about 500m after the last industrial estate. The campsite is signed from Blarney.

Options

If you are heading straight to Cork airport, it is on the south side of the city. From this stage at Ballinhassig (13.4km) follow the R613 east and then the R600 – it is about 9km.

The chief historical interest of the day is passing through the sites of the English and Irish encampments in the lead up to the Battle of Kinsale in 1601. The English forces were camped on a ridge immediately north of the town (2km). The Irish forces occupied a ridge further towards Cork (6km).

Defeat at the Battle of Kinsale heralded the end of the old Gaelic order in Ireland. Hugh O'Neill – Earl of Tyrone – headed back to Ulster, while 'Red' Hugh O'Donnell left for Spain.

The southern approach to Cork city is guarded by a line of low Old Red Sandstone hills. The climb up from Ballinhassig (13km) is close to 20 per cent, making it one of the steepest in this guidebook, alongside the Torr Head road (Route 1, Stage 2a), but at least it is traffic free. The entry into Cork from this side is through charmless housing estates, but the route is easy to follow into the heart of the city.

Cork itself is not the most appealing of Irish cities, but there are some fine public buildings and the centre of town has elegant shopping streets. Tourist attractions include ringing the

ROUTE 9 KENMARE TO CORK

Stage 1 Kenmare to Allihies		
0.0		Kenmare, the Square, by central park area next to visitor information sign, follow N71 Glengarriff
0.3	→	'N71 all routes', at top of Main Street
0.5	←▲	'Glengarriff 27', Failte Hostel on this corner
1.4	→	'Castletownbere R571', just over bridge
7.6	♦	Small shop
13.8	▲	The Peacock hostel and campsite
13.9	⇦☆	Gleninchaquin Park
16.5	⇧→	'R573 Castletownbere', straight on to the Healy Pass
18.6	☆	Waterfall
22.8	☆	Can get down to stony beach
24.5	☆	Killmakillioge Quay
27.3	☆	Derreen Gardens
27.8	⇦ ▲→	'Castletownbere R571', turn left for Creeveen Lodge Caravan and Camping about 2km
28.8	⇦▲	An Óige Hostel at Glanmore Lake about 2km
31.5	☆	By inlet – rock and water landscape
35.1	☆	Co Cork boundary
36.7	↖	'Beara Way cycle route'
36.8	↗	Bear right at fork
38.7	→	Turn right into Ardgroom village
38.9	←♦	'L4911 Ring of Beara', shop on corner
42.3	←	Road swings left at small harbour
42.7	↗	Road swings right
42.9	↖ ☆⇨	Road swings left, right leads to beach
43.3	△(70)	Few sharp climbs, views along coast
44.1	☆⇨	To Luas pier
44.7	→	'Ring of Beara'
47.0	→	'Ring of Beara', at T-junction
52.8	↑	'Ring of Beara', at crossroads
54.6	☆	Hag of Beara

Stage 1 Kenmare to Allihies		
56.4	☆⇨	Ballycrovane Ogham Stone, about 150m on left, small entry charge
56.8	→	'Ring of Beara'
59.6	♦	Small shop at Eyeries
59.9	♦	Shop and café
60.2	→	'R571 Castletownberehaven'
60.8	→	'R575 Allihies'
64.2	☆⇨	To beach, 100m
64.9	▲	Shop and hostel at Urhan
67.7	←	'R575 Allihies'
68.3	△(100)	Stiff climb – views to Kerry Heads and lonely road along coast
68.7	☆	Mass rock
70.7	△(95)	Views south to Sheep's Head Peninsula
71.7	☆	As far west as we go
73.1	☆	Parking area, benches
73.9	☆	Harbour at foot of massive hills of exposed grey rock
74.2	☆	Massively folded rocks
74.6	☆	Copper workings all around
74.8	←⇧	'Allihies', beach is straight on about 2km
76.1	▲♦ WC	Arrive Allihies, hostel on left, WC on right, supermarket 100m further on

Stage 2 Allihies to Glengarriff		
0.0		From centre of Allihies, by hostel across from WC, head south
0.1	♦	Supermarket
0.4	☆	Allihies Copper Mines Museum
1.1	☆⇨	Turn right for sandy cove, 1.3km return
3.9	☆	Parking area, bench view of coast
4.1	△(110)	Bealbarnish Gap
4.3	☆⇨	Leads to Dursey Island, approx. 8km
11.3	▲	Garranes Hostel
12.1	△(110)	Top of long, gentle climb, views east along coast
16.8	☆⇨	Dunboy Castle and Puxley's Mansion, 2.5km return

Stage 2 Allihies to Glengarriff

19.6	☆	Centre of Castletownberehaven – benches
19.8	▲♦ ATM	Supermarket has ATM, hostel on left
20.1	☆	Timothy Harrington statue
20.9	☆	Anchor in park from French Fleet of 1796
21.9	♦	Shop at service station; Bike n Beara bike shop here
23.9	▲	Berehaven Camper and Amenity Resort – camping
26.6	☆	Hungry Hill looms over road
35.3	▲	Hungry Hill Lodge, hostel and camping – register at pub
35.5	♦	Shop
35.6	⇦	'R574 Healey Pass'
37.0	☆⇨	Road to beach and pier, 500m
39.5	☆⇨	To beach
40.5	☆⇨	To beach
40.8	♦	Small shop in service station
46.4	△(130)	Views over Bantry Bay
48.0	→	'L4926 Seal Harbour' (can continue on main road)
48.4	⇐⇧	Turn left, continue straight on for Seal Harbour (600m) – turn is easy to miss, behind rock!
52.0	☆	View over Garinish Island
53.2	⇐	Road swings left
53.7	→	Rejoin R572
55.1	▲	Two camping parks – O'Shea's and Dowling's
57.3	→	'Bantry' at T-junction in Glengarriff
57.5	▲	Murphy's Village Hostel
57.6	WC ☆	Ferries to Garinish and tourist information

Stage 3 Glenfarriff to Schull

0.0		Glengarriff tourist information office – head east on N71 towards Bantry
0.2	☆	Park with benches
0.5	☆♦	Glengarriff pier – ferries to Garinish Island
0.6	♦	Shop in service station
1.3	☆	Beach
11.0	▲♦	Eagle Point Camping, shop in service station on left

Stage 3 Glenfarriff to Schull

16.0	♦	Shop in service station
17.0	♦	Small shop
17.1	♦	Nigel's Bicycle Shop
17.5	↖ WC	Follow one-way system into Bantry
17.6	☆	Tourist information on left – now in Wolf Tone Square
	→	'N71 Skibbereen'
	☆ ATM ♦	Square has benches, ATM across road, shops back in town
17.8	WC ATM	Shops and ATM on left
18.1	♦	Shop in service station
18.8	☆	Entrance to Bantry House
19.9	→	'Killcrohane' (second of two turns close together)
22.5	⇐	'Sheep's Head Way, Durrus'
22.8	⇐	'Sheep's Head Way, Durrus'
24.4	△(160)	Very steep climb – fine views over Bantry Bay
26.1	⇐	Just after bridge
26.7	➚	Road swings right
26.8	↖	Road swings left
28.9	⇐	At crossroads, over stone bridge
29.9	♦ →	At T-junction in Durrus, store opposite
	↑	'R591 Crookhaven'
32.3	⇦	Shortcut to Ballydehob (8km) or Schull (10km)
34.7	▲	Dunbeacon campsite
35.5	☆	Castle on right
36.2	⇦	Shortcut to Schull (10km)
43.9	→	Unsigned turn by empty farmhouse
45.2	☆	Dunmanus harbour
45.5	☆	Castle
52.5	△(150)	Fine views along coast
57.9	↑	At crossroads
58.9	→	'Mizen Head'
59.4	⇦	To Barley Cove 1km
60.9	⇐	'Mizen Head'
64.8	↑↓	Mizen Head car park, turn around, retrace steps
68.8	→	At T-junction
70.2	→	'Crookhaven'
70.9	☆	Beach access – fine machair behind Barley Cove

Stage 3 Glenfarriff to Schull

72.8	▲	Barley Cove Holiday Cove
73.2	←⇨	'Schull', for Crookhaven turn right (approx 2km)
74.9	☆	Past mineral-loading chutes
79.0	↑♦	'Schull', at crossroads in Goleen, shops and greengrocer
84.0	☆	Lagoon at Toormoor
85.2	♦	Small shop
86.8	☆	Alter Megalithic Tomb
94.3	ATM	On way into Schull
94.4	♦	Supermarket (car park entrance is back near bank)
94.5		Finish by turn to pier

Stage 4 Schull to Clonakilty

0.0		Schull – by turn to pier, continue east on R591
7.6	↑	'N71 Skibbereen', at crossroads, in Ballydehob
7.7	☆	Statue to Danno O'Mahony – 1935 world wrestling champ
7.9	♦	Shop
	WC	Roadside park
8.0	☆	Cross bridge; note fine viaduct on former Schull & Skibbereen rail line
9.2	→	'Skeaghanore West' (take care, poor visibility behind)
10.4	↑	At crossroads
10.7	↑	Continue ahead as road swings right
11.6	↑	At crossroads
12.5	↑	At crossroads
12.6	☆	Ruined church
13.0	↖	After bridge take left fork
14.0	→	Onto N71
14.6	☆	Layby has views to Fastnet and Turk Head
17.1	←	'Letterscanlan'
18.0	△(70)	
19.0	↑	Up hill, signed 'Cycle Route 3'
19.5	△(70)	Views over river
19.9	↗	Take right fork
20.9	←	On to N71
21.7	☆	Abbeystrowry – famine graveyard
21.9	→	'Baltimore'
22.0	↖	Road swings left

Stage 4 Schull to Clonakilty

23.0	☆	Skibbereen Heritage Centre
	↑	'Castletownshend'
23.1	♦	Shop
23.3	↖	Bear left with one-way system
23.4	ATM	
23.5	⇦	North Street, tourist information – turn right here for Castletownshend road
	↑	Pass to left of post office
23.6	↖	At police station take left fork
24.4	↗	Road swings right, ignore turn to left
26.4	→	Signed 'Cycle Route One'
27.2	↑	'Cycle Route One', ignore right fork
28.3	←	At cross roads
28.9	↗	'Unionhall'
30.8	↗	Bear right
31.4	☆	Picnic area
32.1	☆	Ceim Hill Museum
32.6	△(80)	
32.8	←	Road swings left, descend into Unionhall
33.7	⇨	Right goes to Reen pier
33.9	WC	In Unionhall
34.3	♦	Shop
	↑	'Glandore, Leap'
34.5	←	'Glandore, Leap', good view from causeway
34.6	→	'Glandore'
35.6	→	'Glandore', after bridge
37.1	→	Road swings right in Glandore village
37.3	WC	
37.7	☆	Steps to beach
39.0	▲	The Meadow camping
39.9	⇨	Drombeg Stone Circle
40.0	△(100)	At Drombeg
44.0	▲⇨	Carraheen Lodge Hostel, 500m
44.2	⇧→	Clonakilty, Ross Carbery centre is straight on
46.3	♦	Shop in service station
46.6	→	'R598 Ownahinchy'
47.7	☆ WC	Beach
48.0	▲	O'Riordan's Caravan Park

Stage 4 Schull to Clonakilty		
48.2	←	'L8025 Rathbarry', past fine gatehouse, keep an eye out for Castlefreke through trees
50.2	←	'R598 Rathbarry', at T-junction
50.4	→	'Galley Head'
50.5	←	'Sprigging School'
50.7	☆	Small picnic area
	☆	Sprigging School
50.9	☆	Estate church
53.2	↑	'Clonakilty'
54.2	△(70)	
56.5	↑	'Duneen', at crossroads
57.3	←	'Clonakilty', at crossroads
59.6	→	'N71 Cork'
59.8	↗	At Clonakilty town pump bear right
60.0	♦ ATM	Supermarket
	←	Unsigned
60.1	↑	At crossroads
60.2	←	At crossroads, tourist information in front
	♦	MTM Cycles
60.3	↑	Just after small park and memorial
60.5	←	At crossroads
60.6	↑☆	At crossroads, Michael Collins statue on right, followed by park
60.7	←	'N70 Cork', at end of square
60.9	←	Back on main road near pump
61.1		End at corner with Croppy Quay

Stage 5 Clonakilty to Kinsale		
0.0		Clonakilty on N71, at Croppy Quay, past Eurospar, before bus stops, head east
0.4	○→	'Ring'
	←▲⇧	Immediately left, carry straight on for Desert House Camping
2.5	→	At T-junction
3.8	←	'Michael Collins Centre'
4.8	↑	'Michael Collins Centre', at crossroads
5.5	☆	Michael Collins Centre
5.8	△(135)	Last views of hills of Beara Peninsula
8.5	↖	Continue ahead as road swings to right

Stage 5 Clonakilty to Kinsale		
9.0	→	At T-junction, descend into Timoleague
9.7	→	At bottom of hill
	☆	Monument to St Mologa
	←	'Franciscan friary, Abbey Street'
	▲	Pad Joes Hostel on left
9.8	←	'Abbey'
9.9	☆	Timoleague Abbey
	←	Continue past abbey and turn left
10.1	WC	Also has tap for water bottles
10.3	→	'Kinsale R600'
10.5	→	'Kinsale'
14.5	☆	Picnic area
16.9	☆	Picnic area
18.7	☆	Access to Garraneteen Strand
19.9	→	'R600 Ballinspittle'
23.7	→	'L3222 Garrettstown'
24.4	↑	At crossroads
27.3	☆	Views of open ocean to south and west – forever
27.8	⇦ ▲→	'Old Head R604', Garrettstown Holiday Park on left, approx. 1km
27.9	☆	Beach
28.3	WC	
29.0	♦	Small shop
29.3	☆	Beach – careful of sand blown over road
30.0	→	'Old Head L3233'
32.5	☆⇨	To castle and golf club, 200m, *Lusitania* memorial and signal tower on left
34.9	→	'Kinsale'
38.7	→	'L3224 Sandycove'
39.4	↖	Take left fork
41.7	↑	Continue straight on over bridge
42.2	←	At T-junction
	→	'R600 Kinsale'
43.1	→	At end of bridge, road swings right
44.2	→	Follow R600
44.6	☆	Small park
44.7	WC	
44.8		Arrive Kinsale tourist office

Stage 6 Kinsale to Cork		
0.0		Kinsale, opposite tourist office, outside Temperance Hall, turn left down road between Temperance Hall and Methodist church
0.1	←	At crossroads, pass to left side of Market Hall – note fish weathervane on roof
0.2	→	Police station on your left just after turn
0.4	☆	Desmond Castle
1.1	↑	At crossroads
1.3	→	At T-junction join R607
2.0	☆→	'Brownsmills, L3203', English camp was in this area – see sign on right
2.5	☆	Oysterhaven Creek – ships supplied English from here, sign
5.2	△(80)	Look back to Ardmartin Ridge – held by the English
6.1	☆	O'Neill set off west from here to flank the English
8.2	△(115)	Steady climb to this point
8.8	↑	At crossroads
10.7	↗	'Cork'
13.4	→	At T-junction in Ballinhassig
	← ♦ ⇧	Take road immediately to left side of shop, carrying straight on takes you to airport (9km) via R613 and R600

Stage 6 Kinsale to Cork		
14.1	☆	Very steep climb – 20%
16.1	△(150)	Views of Cork, ahead
16.6	→	At T-junction
18.9	△(140)	By TV transmitter climb – 7% in places
21.3	○ ↑♦	'South Ring', shop on left
21.8	↑	At lights
22.3	↑	'The Lough', at lights
23.0	↑	At lights
23.8	↑	'City centre'
23.9	↗	Road swings right
24.0	←	'City centre'
24.1	→	'City centre', at lights
24.2	←	'City centre', at lights, cathedral on corner
	☆	St Finbar's Cathedral on right
24.3	↑	Straight on at lights
24.5	→	'An Lar', now at Wandesford Quay
24.6	←	Cross bridge
24.7	→	At lights, pass in front of court building
25.0	→	At lights, enter Grand Parade
25.2		Arrive Cork tourist office

Castetownberehaven was once a Royal Navy port

ROUTE 10

CORK TO KILLARNEY AND WATERFORD – THE BLACKWATER VALLEY

Stage		Terrain	Distance (km)	Summit (distance from start/height)
1	Cork to Youghal	Flat	68.9	68km/60m
2	Youghal to Fermoy	Flat	66.0	17km/150m
3	Fermoy to Killarney	Undulating – surprisingly tiring	104.7	84km/230m
4	Youghal to Waterford	Coastal hills	(96.8)	31km/190m
		Total	239.6	

A connection between Cork and Waterford, and a route up the Blackwater Valley to Killarney, open up a number of possibilities for longer routes in the south of Ireland, but the stages in Route 10 also offer some exceptional riding in their own right. The Blackwater Valley from Youghal to Fermoy is one of the most enjoyable days on a bike in Ireland, while the coast from Youghal to Waterford is stacked with historic and geological interest. Youghal also deserves special mention as being one of Ireland's premier historic towns.

Options
There are two quite long stages on this route. Both Fermoy to Killarney and Youghal to Waterford can be easily split with a bit of chasing around for accommodation. This route divides at Youghal, where Stages 2 and 3 head north, then west to Killarney. Alternatively Stage 4 heads east to Waterford where it links with Route 11.

Getting to the Start
Below are the options to consider for this route.

By Air
Cork Airport (www.corkairport.com) is on the south side of the city (see Route 9, Stage 6). The budget airlines have piled into Cork in recent years, and there are regular flights to and from Germany, Spain, France, Portugal and Poland, as well as particularly good links to UK regional airports.

By Sea
The Roscoff–Cork ferry service makes sense if you are heading to the southwest from France.

This is an overnight service running on Friday nights from Roscoff to Cork and Saturday nights from Cork (www.brittanyferries.ie). The Swansea–Cork ferry service (www.bringback theswanseacorkferry.com) is set to resume in 2010.

By Rail/Bus
Bus Eireann runs six return services a day from Dublin to Cork – the journey takes about 4½ hours.

When to Go
Any time, spring to autumn.

Accommodation
These are not the most visited areas in Ireland, so budget accommodation is not easy to find. The Blackwater Valley has a dearth of places at the cheaper end of the scale, apart from a lone campsite at Fermoy. Book ahead for Cork and Killarney, especially in peak season and at weekends. Elsewhere it is wise to at least call ahead, as there is often only one hostel in town. Campsites are a bit thin on the ground as well – although they are generally of a very

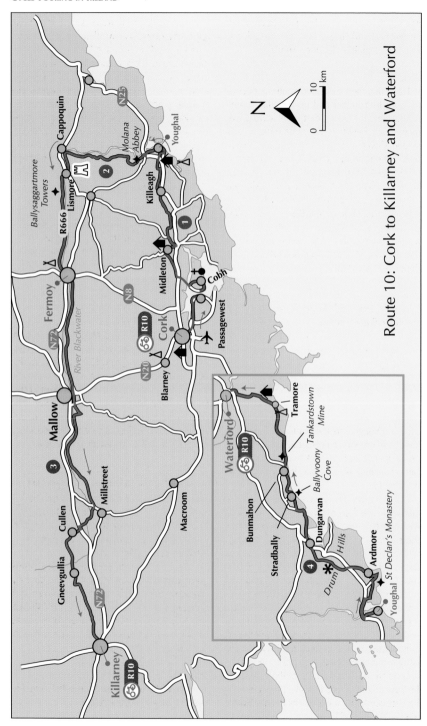

Route 10: Cork to Killarney and Waterford

high standard. Waterford has a tourist office on the quay (051 875823, www.discoverireland. com), although it is closed on Sundays.

Maps

At 1:250 000 the OSI Ireland South sheet covers Cork to Youghal and up the Blackwater to Killarney. If heading east to Waterford the Ireland East sheet from the same series is also needed. Coverage at 1:50 000 requires the following sheets from the OSI Discovery series: 87 Cork, 81 Cork Waterford (these reach as far as Youghal), 82 Waterford and 76 Carlow Kilkenny Waterford Wexford cover the route to Waterford, while for the Blackwater Valley 80 Cork, 79 Cork Kerry and 78 Kerry are needed. There is also a 5km section approaching Fermoy that is on sheet 74 Cork Limerick Tipperary Waterford.

Onwards

This route links with Route 11 at Waterford and Route 9 at Killarney.

STAGE 1
CORK TO YOUGHAL

68.9km Flat

Cobh and Youghal are the highlights of this long day on the road. Also rather fun is a section of the defunct Cork, Blackrock and Passage West Railway, which is now a cycleway alongside the River Lee.

Cobh (pronounced 'cove') (16km) underwent rapid development during the Napoleonic Wars, when it was a key British naval base. The seafront here, with its colourful terraces, park and cathedral towering behind, is the best in Ireland. The Cobh Heritage Centre (021 4813591, www.cobheritage.com) and the nearby museum are also worth visiting. The former is expensive (€7 at the time of writing), but gives a lively and informative account of Cobh's history, including the Irish diaspora and its association with the *Titanic* and *Lusitania*. On the way out of town the stage passes the graveyard where a hundred or so of the victims of the *Lusitania* are buried. Also in this area are the Regency house and gardens of Fota House (23km, 021 4815543, www.fotahouse.com).

Eastwards from here is not the most appealing riding. The Midleton (sic) area was mired in roadworks during 2008 and many of the smaller roads had taken a pounding from trucks – hopefully this situation will improve soon. After Killeagh (53km) things brighten up, and the grand coastline to the south comes into view, approaching historic Youghal (pronounced 'yawl'). Guarding the entrance to the Blackwater River, this medieval walled town is one of Ireland's most interesting. The buildings reflect the town's 18th-century heyday as one of Ireland's premier trading ports.

Sir Walter Raleigh lived at Myrtle Grove in Youghal, and is said to have planted the first potatoes in Ireland here. The town harbour featuerd in the 1956 John Huston film *Moby Dick*, starring Gregory Peck.

On the Road

For most of the day you are never far from a shop. The cross-river ferry to Cobh runs from 7am each morning, and Cobh (16km) is the obvious place to stop for lunch. The one-way system out of the town takes you around the houses a little, but just keep following the Cork signs as far as the main road. Be careful around Midleton (37km), just in case roadworks have changed the traffic circulation or directions.

Accommodation

Midleton has a hostel – An Stor Tourist Hostel (021 4633106 www.anstor.com) is on Drury's Lane – look for the sign on the left about 150m after the Dungourney turn (37.6km). At the end of the day, Youghal has the Evergreen House hostel (024 92877 www.evergreen ireland.com – turn left at 66.1km). If it's camping you're after, there's a site near Youghal, towards Ballymacoda. Clonvilla Caravan and Camping Park is at Clonpriest (024 98288). To get to Clonvilla, turn right at the crossroads at 64.4km then left onto the R633 after 1.4km. It is a further 4km to Clonpriest.

Options

The main N25 to Youghal is an option, but it is fast and dangerous for cycling.

Youghal's clock gate is one of many historic buildings in the town

STAGE 2
YOUGHAL TO FERMOY

66km Flat

The fine houses, castles and ruins are only part of the attraction of this grand day's cycling, as the Blackwater River itself is broad and strong flowing, and scenic for most of its length. The valley immediately to the north of Youghal is the most attractive part, as having flowed west to east for most of its course, the Blackwater makes a right-angled turn to the south at Cappoquin, cutting a picturesque series of wooded valleys and gorges through four sandstone ridges on its way to the sea.

The first of the fine demesnes is at Ballynatray House – a neoclassical pile beautifully set on a bend in the river (6km). The house is private, but on Tuesdays, Wednesdays and Thursdays (9.30am to 4.30pm) from Easter to October you can wander up the drive to the riverside ruins of Molana Abbey. This riverside idyll is followed by a series of oak- and ivy-choked tributary valleys and short climbs over low hills capped with golden fields of wheat. One house you can visit is Tourin House and Gardens (29km, 05 854405, www.tourin-house.ie) approaching Cappoquin, which is open Tuesday to Saturday, 1pm to 5pm, May to September.

Upstream from Cappoquin the Blackwater flows through a limestone-floored vale that is less dramatic, though no less picturesque, than the gorges of the lower valley.

Lismore (38km) is a grand period town with narrow streets and a long, thin central square. St Carthage established a monastery here in the seventh century, which within a century or so was rich enough to attract Viking raids up the Blackwater. The castle, the grandest pile on the river, is the holiday home of the Dukes of Devonshire. The gardens are open 11am to 4.45pm daily from mid-March to the end of September (www.lismorecastle.com). There is also a heritage centre in Lismore (058 54975, www.discoverlismore.com), open daily from May to October and weekdays only during the winter.

Before reaching Fermoy there is still one more architectural treasure to visit – the 19th-century Gothic towers of Ballysaggartmore, grandiose buildings that were meant to set off a fine castle (42km). Arthur Keily began the project at the instigation of his wife, who was jealous of her brother-in-law's castle at Strancally, but the cash ran out and only the gatehouses were built.

> One of the founders of modern chemistry, Robert Boyle, was born at Lismore Castle in 1627. He is best known for 'Boyle's Law', which describes the relationship between pressure and volume in gases.

Ballynatray House sits close to the Blackwater River

Fermoy was once the centre of British military power in Ireland, although much of the military infrastructure was destroyed in the civil war of 1922-3.

The run into Fermoy is marked by several ruined castles, fine houses, and some fine gates and gatehouses. Fermoy is a tidy and pleasant inland town of about 6000 people.

On the Road

Take a few supplies from Youghal, as there is no sign of a shop until Lismore (38km) – the two supermarkets on the way out of Youghal are the cheapest bet. For a place to stop, there is a picnic area by the river at 31km – it's nice enough, but not particularly idyllic. At 26.9km there is a small, falling-down jetty by the water, opposite Dromona Castle – there isn't really anywhere to sit (apart from on the ground), but this is along one of the prettiest gorge sections of the Blackwater.

Fermoy has ATMs and a good selection of shops, including a cycle shop – Hennessy's Cycles (025 30913, www.hennessycycles. com) on Lower Patrick Street. There is also a grand riverside park.

Accommodation

Blackwater Valley Caravan and Camping Park (025 32147) is a well-equipped site next to the town park on the south side of the river – turn right at 65.7km, veer left after 100m, and the site is on the left after a further 400m. Unfortunately there are no hostels nearby, but bed and breakfast accommodation is available.

Options

Fermoy is less than 40km away from Cork city, so a short-cut to here is possible. One possible route is to follow the R614 from Cork, take the R616 at Whites Cross (5km north of the city) then the R639 at Watergrasshill (a further 12km north). The R639 continues all the way to Fermoy – a total of about 35km. This saves about 113km compared to taking Stages 1 and 2.

STAGE 3
FERMOY TO KILLARNEY

104.7km Undulating – surprisingly tiring

The length of this stage is caused by a shortage of accommodation in the upper part of the valley. The day is also tiring, with the road managing to pick out short steep rises and falls without ever gaining much altitude. The first stretch to Mallow is particularly slow – so get an early start.

As far as scenery goes, Ballyhooly (10km), with its ruined castle amongst trees and surrounded by water meadows would sell many a postcard or jigsaw puzzle. Mallow (29km) was once a lively spa town, but shows few signs of its 18th-century resort heyday, although the 19th-century Tudor-revival-style clocktower at the end of the main street gives the town centre a pleasing focus.

The village of Killavullen (19km) has twofold spiritual importance. Nano Nagle – pioneer of Catholic education and founder of the Presentation Sisters – was born near here at Ballygriffin House. For the more Dionysian, Richard Hennessy, of Cognac fame, was from here – the family home was Ballymacmoy House.

Richard Hennessy left Ireland sometime around 1740 to join the Irish Brigades. He was wounded at the Battle of Fontenoy in 1745, settled in Cognac, and founded the distillery that still bears his name.

Nano Nagel was born at a time (1718) when a Roman Catholic education was forbidden, so she was sent to an Irish community in Paris to be educated. At great personal risk, she set up small schools in Cork based on the *petites écoles* she had seen in France. In 1775 she established a congregation of religious sisters with the special vocation of educating the poor, which is now known as the Presentation Sisters of the Blessed Virgin Mary.

After Knocknagree (79km) and the final crossing of the Blackwater the hills begin to close in. The pastures and wheatfields of the middle river seem far behind, as bog,

Back in Kerry

pine forest and sedge take over. There are a few stings in the tail as the route approaches Killarney, with some short, tiring climbs. At the top of one of these, at Gneevgullia (84km), there is a statue to Eamon Kelly, who was born near here. Kelly, who died in 2001, was one of Ireland's greatest storytellers.

For more on Killarney itself, see Route 9, Stage 8.

On the Road

For the start of this stage, turn right at the T-Junction at the end of Stage 2. Newmarket Street is then the first street on the left. This is the easiest place to set the cycle computer and get organised for Stage 3.

Mallow (29km) has a cycle shop – Cremin Cycles (022 42465) on Bridge Street. There is a choice of shops on the main street, and also a big supermarket on the way out of town. Knocknagree (79km) and Gneevgullia (84km) both have shops, and there are no problems finding a shop open late in Killarney.

Accommodation

For Killarney accommodation, see Route 9, Stage 8. There is camping and hostel accommodation near town.

Options

This is a long stage, mainly because there is nowhere between Fermoy and Killarney that really calls out 'stay here'. Millstreet (65km) is the best bet to split the stage; do not approach the town from the R583, which is busy and fast – take the turn at 65.8km.

| **STAGE 4** |
| **YOUGHAL TO WATERFORD** |
| 92.1km Hilly coast |

The coastline east from Youghal is pretty, and also relatively undeveloped for tourism until almost on Waterford's doorstep at Tramore. Outside peak season there are as many beaches as people, and the back roads are almost empty.

If the beach is calling, it is hard to top the sweeping strand at Whiting Bay – turn at 11.4km – while Ardmore (17km), with its round tower and links to St Declan, is one for the history buffs. The holy city of Ardmore was established some time in the fifth century – It could have been as early as AD416 – making this the earliest Christian settlement in Ireland, pre-dating St Patrick.

> Legend has it that St Declan was led to Ardmore by a floating rock.

North of Ardmore a climb over the Drum Hills (32km) gives a fine view along the coast over Dungarvan, guarded by its 13th-century Anglo-Norman castle.

> The Drum Hills extending east to Helvick Head mark the northern limit of the Armorican folding, which has produced the peninsulas of Ireland's southwest.

Dungarvan (39km) has a tourist office (058 41741 www.dungarvantourism.com), just before the bridge leaving town, where you can buy a brochure about the Copper Coast Geopark, which lies ahead. This stretch of coast east of Dungarvan takes its name from the copper mines that once flourished here.

Geological interest aside, the coastal plateau, with its steeply incised streams, produces some entertaining riding, with plenty of gear changes. Stradbally Cove (54km) and Ballyvoony Cove (56.1km) are attractive spots, and though Bunmahon is a little blemished by a caravan outbreak, the Geological Gardens here are fantastic – a timeline of rocks in their stratigraphic order leads the way through the park (63km).

Annestown (71km) has a slightly stony beach, and from here the road leaves the coast for a few kilometres until it approaches the holiday resort at Tramore. Just before the town, keep an eye out for the sharp ridge of the Ballyscanlan Hills, which are formed from volcanic basalt.

The final 13km into Waterford is on the R675. Waterford was founded in 914 by the Vikings and is Ireland's oldest city; during the medieval period it was the second most important. Waterford prosperity during the 18th and 19th centuries was based on trade, along with industries such as shipbuilding and glassmaking, and much of the city's architecture dates from this period.

> The oldest building in Waterford – Reginald's Tower, on the waterfront – was also the first building in Ireland to be built with mortar.

Waterford was once a Viking port

On the Road

This is a long day, and there are enough hills along the coast to make it fairly slow going. Dungarvan with its waterfront park (39km) is the pick of the potential lunch spots, and there is also a choice of shops and ATMs in town. Further on, Stradbally village (54km) is picturesque and has a shop and public toilets, as does Bunmahon (62km). Tramore (82km) is a lively resort town with an impressive beach. Depending on you forward itinerary, consider staying here rather than pushing the final 13km to Waterford – see Accommodation, below.

Accommodation

Waterford has no hostel and no camping nearby. The best option for the budget-conscious is Tramore, where there is the excellent Newtown Cove Caravan and Camping Park (80km, 051 381979, www.newtowncove. com) and also the Beach Haven Hostel – carry straight on at 81.9km (051 390208, www. beachhavenhouse.com).

Options

There is a minor road from Tramore to Waterford parallel to the R675 (it is easy to pick out on the map). If the traffic is bad on the main road, this much hillier route might be tempting, although the main road is wide and not dangerous.

ROUTE 10
CORK TO KILLARNEY AND WATERFORD

Stage 1 Cork to Youghal		
0.0		Cork, Grand Parade outside tourist office, head towards monument
	←	Road swings left
0.1	ATM	Ulster Bank
0.6	→	'South Ring', at lights, cross Parnell Bridge – note fine town hall across river
0.9	↑	'Douglas, Ballinlough', at lights
1.0	↑	At lights
1.2	↑	At lights
1.5	↑	At lights
1.6	↑	At lights
2.0	↑	At lights
2.6	↑	At lights
2.9	♦ ATM	Local shops and ATM
3.1	↑	At lights
3.7	↑	'R610 Douglas'
3.8	↑	At lights
	→	Then right between Tesco and Topaz garage
3.9	ATM	In Douglas
4.0	♦ ↑	At lights
4.3	⬉ ○	'River ferry, Passage West'
5.4	↑	At lights
5.7	↑	'R610 Passage West'
5.9	○↑	'R610 Passage West'
7.3	☆	Old railway building on right
7.4	☆	Platform of old Robertstown Station
8.0	←	'Hop Island Equestrian Centre'
	→	Immediately right onto old rail line
9.6	☆	Passage West Monkstown Railway Trail sign
11.6	→	At site of Passage West station
	←	At child's play area
11.7	→	At car park
	←ATM	Onto road
11.8	↑	At crossroad
	♦	Centra
13.1	←	For ferry to Cobh
13.2	♦ →	'Cobh R624', at top of ferry ramp , shop across road
15.6	→	'Heritage Centre'

Stage 1 Cork to Youghal		
15.7	←	'Cobh Heritage Centre'
16.7	☆	Cobh Heritage Centre
16.8	↑	'Give Way'
16.9	☆	Fine Edwardian park
17.2	◆	Shops in town centre
17.7	←	Just after tall red chimney on right
18.0	↗	Road forks
18.4	→	At cathedral
18.5	←	'Cork' (have to turn)
	→	'Cork'
18.6	→	'Town centre'
18.7	→	'Cork'
18.9	→	(Have to turn)
19.1	←	'Cork'
19.7	◆	Supermarket
20.0	☆	Old Church Cemetery – *Lusitania* memorial
20.2	↑	At crossroads
23.1	→	'Cork', cross bridge
23.4	☆	Fota House
26.4	○→	'Carrigtohill'
26.7	○↗	'Carrigtohill'
28.2	◆ ATM	Supermarket at Carrigtohill
28.6	◆ ATM	Supermarket
28.7	←	First turn after supermarket
34.1	→	'Midleton', at T-junction
36.9	◆	Small supermarket
37.2	◆ ATM	At service station
37.3	○↑	'Youghal R907'. Now in Midleton
37.6	←	'Dungourney' (look for library clocktower on right which is just after turn)
39.6	→	Unsigned road by 4m high estate wall
40.6	→	At crossroads
43.0	←	At T-junction
47.9	←	At T-junction
48.0	☆	Former Mogeely station – dilapidated
48.1	→	'Killeagh'
53.2	←	At T-junction in Killeagh
	◆ ATM	Shop
53.3	↑	'Inch' (go up hill as main road swings right)
53.8	→	First turn off this road

Stage 1 Cork to Youghal		
57.0	↑	At crossroads
	☆	Past old smithy and over bridge
57.3	↖	Take left fork up hill
58.8	→	By yellow building
62.3	←	At T-junction
62.4	○→	'Youghal'
63.0	→	'Youghal Front Strand'
64.4	↑	Youghal Strand, at crossroads – turn right here for camping towards Ballymacoda
64.9	☆	Beach
65.1	WC	
66.0	☆	Old railway station
66.1	▲↗	Road veers right, left to Evergreen Hostel – 100m
66.3	→	'Rosslare'
66.6	☆	Lighthouse
67.0	☆WC	Park
67.1	◆	Supermarket
67.8	☆	Fabulous clocked gate
68.1	◆ ATM	Supermarket
68.2	☆	Castle
	→	First turn past castle
68.4	→	'Cork'
68.9	WC	Arrive visitor centre

Stage 2 Youghal to Fermoy		
0.0		Youghal, main street, by Clock Gate – follow one-way
0.9	◆	Supermarket
1.1	◆	Supermarket
1.2	☆	Park, picnic tables
1.3	○↑	'Rosslare, Waterford'
3.2	○→	'N25 Rosslare' (road OK, wide shoulders)
3.9	←	'Glendine church', just before bridge
6.5	☆⇨	Ruined church and castle, access to river through gate
6.9	☆	Entrance to Ballynatray House/ Molana Abbey
8.9	↘☆	Glendine church 200m
10.5	→	At Glendine view
11.6	←	At crossroads – gate straight ahead
12.9	↗	Take right fork

Stage 2 Youghal to Fermoy		
14.0	↖	'Scenic route'
17.5	△(150)	Steady, long climb
19.5	→	'Scenic route', enter Strancally Demesne
20.7	☆	Fine stone estate buildings
21.3	☆	Views over wheatfields to river
22.2	☆	Fine estate gates
23.0	→	'Lismore'
25.4	☆	Fine section of road at foot of river cliffs
26.9	☆	View of Dromona across river – can get down to river here
27.3	→	'Cappoquin'
29.1	☆	Tourin House and Gardens
29.9	→	At T-junction
31.8	☆	Picnic area, benches
32.5	☆←	Go under old rail bridge and turn just after, before river bridge. Straight on to Cappoquin
34.0	☆	Fine old house
36.0	☆	Motte and bailey castle on right
37.7	☆	Convent
38.1	↑	At crossroads
38.4	☆→	'N72 Waterford, Lismore' heritage centre is on left
38.5	☆	Entry to castle gardens
39.0	←	'R666 Ballyduff'
42.0	☆	Ballysaggartmore – entry
48.1	↑	At crossroads in Ballyduff
59.5	☆	Fine Georgian house over river
65.7	← ▲⇨	'N72 Waterford'. Turn right here for Blackwater Valley Caravan and Camping Park
65.8	☆	Fine riverside park
66.0		Arrive main crossroads in Fermoy, by visitor information sign

Stage 3 Fermoy to Killarney		
0.0		Fermoy town centre, on corner of Newmarket Street and McCurtain Street (main road), head up Newmarket Street
	→	At T-junction, turn into Connolly Street
0.3	←	At T-junction, school in front

Stage 3 Fermoy to Killarney		
0.4	→	At crossroads
0.5	♦	Medium-sized shop
0.6	↑♦ ATM	At lights, shop on corner has ATM
2.1	↗	'Ballyhooly'
4.1	↗	'Ballyhooly'
9.2	→	'Ballyhooly'
10.0	☆	At crossroads, take unsigned road parallel to river. Ballyhooly and castle to the right
13.3	☆	Road runs alongside river
15.0	☆	Grange National School, 1884; Nagles Mountains to south
18.8	△(105)	Descend to Killavullen
19.7	←	'Chapel Street', Killavullen
19.8	↗	Pass to right side of church
29.3	↑ ☆⇨	At lights, turn right to have a look at Mallow
29.9	♦	Big supermarket
31.7	→	'R619 Coachford'
33.7	←	'Glantain' (after Dromhane turn)
36.9	→	A few hundred metres past thatched farm cottage on left
37.9	↑	Manual level crossing
41.9	←	At T-junction
42.0	→	Before crossing railway at Lombardstown
43.4	☆	Section close to river
45.6	←	'Banteer'
51.1	↑	'Rathcoole', at Banteer
51.5	☆	Station
51.7	←	'Millstreet', cross level crossing
51.8	☆	Dr Pat O'Callaghan, Olympic hammer thrower, statue
63.3	→	'Mallow', at T-junction, Millstreet 2.5km to left
63.4	←	Unsigned
64.2	☆	Drishane Castle in trees, 15th-century tower-house in good condition
65.0	↑	Level crossing
66.0	→	At T-junction, Millstreet Station to left
69.1	☆	Cross Blackwater
70.7	←	Before T-junction with N72
70.9	←	On to N72 (limit now 60km/h)

Stage 3 Fermoy to Killarney

71.3	♦ →	At service station in Cullen
72.0	♦	Cullen village has shop
75.8	←	'Knocknagree', at T-junction
76.0	↑	At crossroads
79.9	→♦	'Ballydesmond'. Knocknagree has small shop across central green with seating area
80.0	←	First left
81.2	☆	Cross Blackwater at Lisheen Bridge – now in Co Kerry
81.9	↑	At crossroads
84.6	☆	Eamon Kelly statue
	△(230) ↑♦	Steep climb into Gneevgullia. At crossroads, follow small road straight ahead
86.1	←	At T-junction
87.4	→	At crossroads, watch poor visibility from left
90.2	△(150)	Steep 12–15% climb
92.1	↑	At crossroads, now surrounded by bog
99.8	←	'Killarney', at T-junction
102.1	O→	Unsigned
102.4	O↑	'Town centre'
103.1	O↑♦ ATM	'Town centre', supermarket and ATM on left
103.9	O↑	'Town centre', station on left
104.4	→	'Tralee', Plunkett Street, T-junction
	←	'New Street'
104.5	▲	Neptune's Hostel on right
104.6	←	'Beech Road', tourist information
	♦ ATM	Supermarket
104.7	→	Turn into car park by Killarney tourist office

Stage 4 Youghal to Waterford

0.0		Youghal, by clocktower gate, follow one-way through town
1.3	O↑	'Waterford'
3.1	O→	'N25 Rosslare'
4.3	☆	Nice view back to Youghal, care on bridge – narrow and quite fast
7.9	←	'Whiting Bay'
8.1	←	'Whiting Bay'
9.5	←	'Whiting Bay'
11.4	⇨	Side-trip to Whiting Bay, 1.2km return

St Declan's monastery at Ardmore

Stage 4 Youghal to Waterford

14.8	→	'Ardmore'
17.0	→	'Cliff House Hotel'
17.2	↑↓☆	Turn around at stile – Ardmore Cathedral and roundtower
17.4	↑ ♦ ⇨	Back at crossroads – continue straight on, right for beach and main street
17.5	♦	Small pharmacy
18.9	→	'Dungarvan, South East Coastal Drive (SECD)'
21.6	→	'SECD', at crossroads
22.4	←	At T-junction, right goes to beach
22.9	→	At T-junction
26.7	↑	Two straight-ons at this crossroads – take the one on the right
27.1	↖	Take left fork
28.0	☆	Cross river
28.3	→	Easy to miss this turn
31.4	△(190) ↑	At crossroads, gentle climb to here
32.3	☆	Views over Dungarvan from top of descent
33.6	↑	Ignore right fork

Stage 4 Youghal to Waterford		
34.3	→	Easy to miss this turn, looks as if you are going down a driveway
34.6	→	At T-junction
37.7	O↗	Town centre
38.4	♦	Medium-sized food shop
38.5	↑♦	At lights, fresh fruit and veg shop
39.0	←	At T-junction
39.1	O↑	'View', Dungarvan town centre is to left
39.5	←☆	At seafront, nice park on right
39.7	☆	King John's Castle
40.0	♦	Supermarket through car park
40.1	WC	Pay toilets
	O→	Cross bridge, turn left for tourist office
40.5	♦→	At lights, Eurospar shop on left
40.8	→	'St Augustine's Church'
41.7	←	At crossroads, white house on corner is called Ross-Na-Ree
42.0	→	At T-junction, join R675
43.4	O↑	Unsigned
45.1	O↑ ▲⇨	'R675 Tramore', right to Clonea Strand and Casey's Caravan and Camping, 4km return
50.2	☆	Cross Dalligan river, note steel railbridge on left
50.6	→	'Coomeragh View B&B'
50.8	↑	At Ballyvoyle crossroads
51.4	☆	Standing stone in field on right
54.0	☆⇨	To Stradbally Cove, 200m return
54.2	WC	
54.6	♦→	'Ballyvoony Cove'; Stradbally village straight ahead (150m) has good shop
56.1	☆	Ballyvoony Cove
57.3	→	At T-junction
57.8	↗	Take right fork
61.4	△(55)	View of increasingly rocky coast opens up from low summit
62.5	→	At T-junction
62.6	♦	Small shop at Bunmahon
62.9	WC	
63.0	☆	Access to beach

Stage 4 Youghal to Waterford		
63.2	☆	Memorial to Frank Dwan – *Titanic* victim
63.4	☆	Geological Gardens
63.8	↗	Road swings right
64.4	☆	Mine workings
65.0	☆	Tankardstown Mine
67.2	☆	Kilmurrin Cove
71.5	☆	Access to beach at Annestown – limekilns, etc
73.7	⇦	To Dunhill Castle, about 1km
75.2	☆	Ballyscanlan Hills to left
75.7	↗	'Tramore via coast road', road swings right
80.1	O↑	Unsigned – now entering Tramore
80.2	▲⇨	To Newton Cove Caravan Park 1km
80.7	O↑♦	Shop on right
81.0	↗	Road swings right
81.9	O→	By flower shop on left – straight on to Beach Haven Hostel 500m
82.1	WC	In Tramore town centre
82.2	←O	Unsigned
82.7	↖	Road swings left
83.3	▲	Fitzmaurice's Caravan and Camping Park
83.7	♦	Shop on right
83.9	O→	'R675 Waterford'
84.2	♦	Service station has shop
84.5	O↑	'R675 Waterford'
84.8	♦	Service station has shop
91.0	O→	Join cycleway
92.0	←O	'City centre'
94.3	→	At T-junction
94.4	←O	'City centre'
95.2	←	At lights
95.5	↑	At lights, enter John Street
95.7	←	Straight on is pedestrianised
95.9	→	'City centre'
96.1	→	At small diamond – Spokes Cycles across road
96.2	↑	At lights, Dunnes Store on right – follow one-way to quay
96.4	←	Turn left along waterfront
96.5	☆	Clocktower on quay
96.8		Arrive Waterford tourist office

ROUTE 11

DUBLIN TO WATERFORD – BEYOND THE PALE

Stage		Terrain	Distance (km)	Summit (distance from start/height)
1	Dublin to Donard	A few climbs late in the day	66.0	19km/340m
2	Donard to Kilkenny	Hilly	90.7	12km/360m
3	Kilkenny to Waterford	Gentle climbs	53.6	27km/170m
4	Waterford to Rosslare	Low coastal hills	64.7	33km/50m
5	Rosslare to Courtown	Flat	66.0	47km/70m
6	Courtown to Rathdrum	Surprisingly flat	43.5	43km/140m
7	Rathdrum to Dublin	Big climbs	81.0	39km/520m
		Total	465.5	

This circular route from Dublin covers some of the roads less cycled in Ireland to create a week's riding notable for its variety of landscape and historical interest. Heading southwest from Dublin the route soon crosses the Pale – the medieval limit of English control around Dublin, which in this direction followed the flat land at the foot of the Wicklow Mountains. From here the route skirts the western flank of the Wicklows, crossing the Castlecomber plateau to the historic town of Kilkenny. South of Kilkenny is the lovely southeast coast, with its twin Viking towns of Waterford and Wexford (as well as the ferry port at Rosslare). This is the sunniest and driest corner of Ireland, and home to some of its finest beaches.

Sneaking into Dublin along the coast is not for the true road warrior, so this route heads into the capital across Ireland's highest road pass at Sally Gap (510m), through the Wicklows, before visiting the country's highest waterfall and what is probably its finest country house and gardens at Powerscourt.

Options
It is possible to join the circuit anywhere on the loop. If arriving in Rosslare by ferry, Stages 5, 6 and 7 make an excellent three-day trip to Dublin. Think twice about cycling westwards from Rosslare all the way along the south coast, though, as it can be very exposed in westerly winds. Consider public transport options, or at the very least head up the Blackwater Valley from Youghal (Route 10, Stage 2) to get a break from the coast.

Getting to the Start
Getting to Dublin is covered in Route 7. The starting point for this route is easy to find – it is across the River Liffey from the Customs House on George's Quay.

When to Go
The seaside resorts of the southeast are going to be busy during the peak season (mid-July to mid-August), but there are miles of beaches. Phone ahead, even for campsites, in this period.

Accommodation
If you are hostelling or camping, the problem places are Waterford, Rosslare and Courtown. As alternatives to the first two, Tramore and Wexford have hostels as well as camping. Courtown has camping not too far away, but if staying indoors it will have to be bed and breakfast.

Maps
The OSI 1:250 000 Ireland East sheet covers the entire route. For 1:50 000 coverage

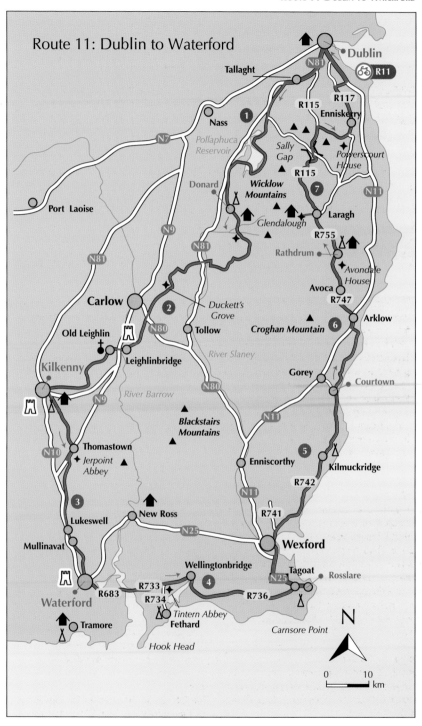

Route 11: Dublin to Waterford

the following sheets are required: 50 Dublin Kildare Meath Wicklow, 56 Wicklow Dublin Kildare, 62 Carlow Wexford Wicklow, 61 Carlow Kildare Kilkenny Laois Wicklow, 67 Kilkenny Tipperary, 76 Carlow Kilkenny Waterford Wexford, 77 Wexford, 69 Wexford and 62 Carlow Wexford Wicklow. Around Dublin the OSI Dublin Street Map at 1:20 000 is handy, as it includes street names.

Onwards

This route connects at Dublin with Route 12 to Belfast and Route 7 to Limerick via the Grand Canal.

STAGE 1
DUBLIN TO DONARD
66km A few climbs late in the day

There are not many capital cities where two hours or so after riding out of the centre, almost entirely on cycleway, you can be in the heart of the countryside. The cycleway isn't perfect – it has a habit of disappearing at junctions, and for the most part is simply paint-brushed onto the main road – but it's cycleway nevertheless.

The cycleway gives an opportunity to devote some attention to the Dublin cityscape.

From the bustle of the quays and the Four Courts, the city core is quickly left behind. There is a brief flirtation with 1930s Art Deco architecture before some modern infill apartment developments. The Grand Canal is crossed by the Emmet Bridge – named after Robert Emmet, nationalist leader in the 1803 rising, who was captured near here – and the route follows a series of older suburbs along the rows of well-built redbrick terraces and villas spreading out along the old tram routes. Terenure (6km) was only incorporated into the city in 1932, but horsedrawn trams began running here from the 1870s.

From 1888, city dwellers could take the Dublin and Blessington Steam Tramway (which this stage closely follows to Tallaght) all the way from Terenure to the Wicklow foothills.

Tallaght (12km) once had a reputation for representing all that was bad about poorly planned city-fringe suburban developments in Europe, but today it is a rather pleasant place to visit, with a thriving town centre and large park.

Soon after Tallaght there is a fast and narrow 800m section of the main N81 (it is hoped

Pollaphuca Reservoir provides some of the prettiest scenery on this stage

that this will be improved soon – the signs are up), before a steep climb away from the main road over Knockannavea. Suddenly the city seems miles behind, birdsong takes over from traffic noise, and horses graze contentedly in tree-studded, hedge-lined paddocks – and that is it for urban cycling until Kilkenny.

This area on the western side of the Wicklow Mountains has a backwoods feel that belies its closeness to the city. The route follows the shore of Pollaphuca Reservoir, past Ballyknockan – famous for its granite quarries – and through Valleymount (46km), with its curious Mexican-style church. The section from here to Donard is the prettiest of the day, with the mature woodland and pasture around the lake contrasting with the brown summits of the surrounding hills. The V-like gorge of Hollywood Glen leads towards Donard – one of the most peaceful villages in Ireland.

Hollywood Glen was carved by glacial meltwaters escaping from a lake impounded by ice against the western flanks of the Wicklows.

On the Road

Some road improvements were ongoing just west of Tallaght in 2008 (from 13.6km), so the directions may change slightly. There are plenty of opportunities to shop and go to the bank on the way out of Dublin. The first place for a break is Tallaght (12km), which has some benches in the middle of town that are away from the traffic. There are a couple of small shops around Pollaphuca Reservoir and also a shop in Donard.

Accommodation

Moat Farm Caravan and Camping Park at Donard (045 404727) is a spacious site with excellent facilities. It is a hundred metres or so from the centre of the village – look for the sign on the road in the opposite corner of the village square to the shop. Also near the village is an An Óige franchised hostel at Ballinclea – Mountain Ventures (045 404657, www.mountainventures.ie), 4km along Stage 2.

Options

A short-cut across Blessington bridge (32.5km) followed by a turn south on the N81 will save 12.5km to Donard.

STAGE 2
DONARD TO KILKENNY
90.7km Hilly

Quiet roads, traditional villages, rolling hills and plenty of historical interest – this stage is inland Ireland at its best. The early part of the stage involves a climb through the Wicklow foothills to the Dwyer–McAllister Cottage (9km), which is interesting as a fine example of a traditional thatched cottage, as well as for its associations with the 1798 rebellion. After the suppression of the rebellion, Michael Dwyer and other remnant forces of the United Irishmen took to the Wicklow Mountains, where they tied up thousands of British troops in a prolonged guerilla campaign. In December of 1799 troops surrounded three cottages in Derrynamuck where Dwyer and his associates were sheltering. In the firefight that followed, the cottage where Dwyer was sheltering caught ablaze. One of his wounded comrades, Sam McAllister, stood in the doorway to draw the fire, allowing Dwyer to escape over the snowy slopes of the Wicklows, where he remained a thorn in the side of the British for another four years.

Turning west to cross the Slaney river, the mountain scenery is soon replaced by broad rolling fields, first of green pasture, then of cereal crops. Duckett's Grove (42km) is Ireland's finest ruined house. This castellated Gothic fantasy is the result of the conversion in 1830 of an earlier castle, by Thomas A Cobden for JD Duckett.

The River Barrow is crossed at Leighlinbridge (63km) on a bridge that dates from the 14th century – making it one of the oldest in Ireland still in use. The river crossing is guarded by the remains of a 14th-century tower-house. On the climb out of the Barrow valley to the west is Old Leighlin (66km). St Gobban founded a monastery here early in the seventh century. It grew to be one of the foremost monasteries in Leinster, with more

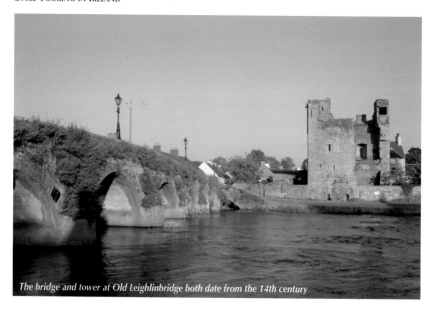

The bridge and tower at Old Leighlinbridge both date from the 14th century

than 1500 monks. The rollercoaster run along the hilltops of the Castlecomber plateau into Kilkenny has views over the Barrow valley, but this is a tiring end to the day, and it is a relief when the city comes into view.

At a synod in AD630 at Leighlin Cathedral (the Synod of Mag Léne) the Irish church adopted the Roman system (rather than the Celtic system) for calculating the date of Easter.

Expect a lively though good-natured time in Kilkenny – this is a popular party city. Medieval Kilkenny Castle (056 7704100 www.kilkennycastle.ie) can be visited by guided tour, although the surrounding park is free. This was the seat of power of the Butler family, the Marquesses and Dukes of Ormonde.

On the Road
There are no shops until Tinryland (52km), so stock up at Donard before leaving. The top lunch spot is at Duckett's Grove (42km), where there are picnic tables, and as the site has been bought by the county council, new facilities might be on the way.

From Rathdangan (15km) to Leighlinbridge (63km) there are many unsigned road junctions, so take care with the directions. The same applies from Old Leighlin to Kilkenny. Kilkenny has the handy Map Shop (056 7756516) on Upper John Street, which is an OSI agent (89.9km).

Accommodation
Kilkenny Tourist Hostel (056 7763541, www.kilkennyhostel.ie) is in the centre of things on Parliament Street – after crossing the bridge turn right into High Street which soon turns into Parliament Street. For camping, Tree Grove (056 7770302, www.treegrovecamping.com) is less than 2km from the city centre – just follow the road out past the castle and it's on the right past the first roundabout.

Options
This is a long stage with more than its fair share of hills, and unfortunately there are no obvious places to split the route. Carlow (turn at 47.4km) is about halfway, and while it is a nice enough town, it does not have a hostel or camping nearby. Scooting straight along the N9 then the N10 from Leighlinbridge to Kilkenny (turn at 64km) saves a lot of climbing, but is about 4km further and the road can be busy.

STAGE 3
KILKENNY TO WATERFORD

53.6km Gentle climbs

After the rigours of the previous day, Stage 3 is a relatively relaxing spin into Waterford. The highlight of the day comes quite early, with the fabulous Cistercian abbey of Jerpoint, which dates from the second half of the 12th century (19km, 056 7724623, www.heritageireland. ie). The sculptured cloister arcade here is one of the finest in Ireland. The abbey opens from 10am daily, and guided tours, which take about an hour, are available but not essential. Other architectural interest on the route includes a slightly bizarre, turreted Gothic Revival Royal Irish Constabulary barracks at Bennettsbridge (8km).

Waterford itself has barely spread onto the north side of the River Suir, making the approach from this side quiet, although it is a bit of a shock to suddenly arrive on the waterfront of a large port.

On the Road

At the time of writing the new M9 motorway was being built, with some major construction works in the Blackwater Valley around Lukeswell (33km). This stage tries to steer clear of any problems, but roads might be re-routed in the area, so be careful with the directions. It is also possible that, when the motorway opens, the old N9 valley route will be a useful direct route for cyclists from Kilkenny to Waterford. There are a number of shops on the way. Mullinavat (36km) is as good a place as any to take a break.

Accommodation

Waterford has no hostels or camping nearby. The closest camping in the right direction is at Fethard (turn at 20.4km) – see Stage 4. The alternative for both hostelling and camping is Tramore (15km) to the south – see Route 10, Stage 4 for details. The tourist office office on the quay (051 875823 www.discoverireland. com) is closed on Sundays.

Options

From the Thomastown area (16km) consider heading northeast via the R700 to New Ross (a further 25km). There is a hostel here (MacMurrough Farm Hostel, 051 421383 www.macmurrough.com) and it is a fine town.

Jerpoint Abbey's cloister arcade is one of Ireland's best

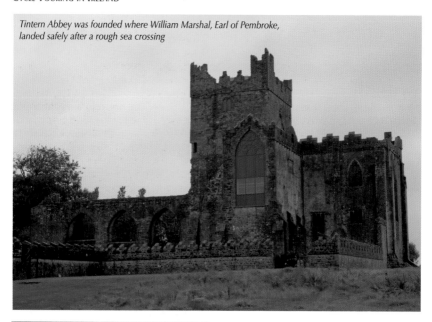

Tintern Abbey was founded where William Marshal, Earl of Pembroke, landed safely after a rough sea crossing

STAGE 4
WATERFORD TO ROSSLARE

64.7km Low coastal hills

The coast between Waterford and Ireland's southeastern tip at Carnsore Point is an intriguing mixture of long sweeping sand bars and rocky headlands. The exit from Waterford is remarkably similar to that from Cork, ending with a ferry ride across, in this case, the estuary of the River Suir.

The long limestone promontory of Hook Head, guarding the east side of Waterford Harbour, is home to the oldest lighthouse in Europe, dating from 1172. It is a long way out there though (turn at 14.9km and the round trip is about 32km). Closer to this stage is Cistercian Tintern Abbey (22km, open mid-June to late September, 10am–6pm and to 5pm in October, 051 562650, www.heritage ireland.ie) at the head of Bannow Bay. The abbey is most interesting for its later life as a family home after the dissolution of the monasteries. Tintern and its lands were granted to Anthony Colclough, an officer in Henry VIII's army in 1536, and remained in the same family until the 1960s – the complete cycle of the rise and fall of Protestant power in Ireland.

Irish nationalist Thomas Meagher fought in the US Civil War and rose to the rank of General in the Union Army. He also created the tricolour Irish flag. His statue stands by the quay in Waterford.

It was through this corner of the island that the Normans streamed into country, first landing in Bannow Bay in 1169. Bannow itself was one of the country's first corporation towns, before it was buried by drifting sands. A big-skied, open coastline of long sandbars and low dunes follows, but the through-route to Rosslare Harbour is away from the coast, along some quiet inland roads.

On the Road

The Waterford harbour ferry runs continuously from 7am (9.30am on Sundays) to 10pm in summer and 8pm in winter (051 382480). There is ample opportunity to pick up a few supplies on the way out of Waterford, the most convenient being the local shops and supermarket just after the roundabout at 2.8km. Tintern Abbey (22km) or Cullenstown Strand (35km) are good spots for lunch. The former has a small café.

Accommodation

Rosslare does not have a hostel. There is an excellent campsite about 9km from the harbour near Lady's Island. To get to Saint Margaret's Beach Caravan and Camping Park (053 9131169) take the turn at Tagoat (60.4km) and follow the signs. Other than that, the nearest hostel is Kirwan House (053 9121208, www. wexfordhostel.com), 19km away in Wexford. Early in the day you might try Ocean Island camping (051 397148) at Fethard (20.4km to turn).

Options

If you are not actually catching a ferry there is probably no reason to go all the way to Rosslare Harbour. If you continue straight on at the turn at 50.7km, it is about 14km from here to Wexford. You can pick up the directions at the R730 roundabout approaching the town (15km on Stage 4).

STAGE 5
ROSSLARE TO COURTOWN
66km Flat

Wexford is Ireland's sunniest and driest county, and all that sun isn't wasted – it falls on some superb beaches. Wexford town (19km) has the historic feel you would expect of a town established by the Vikings around AD800. The layout of the streets is that of a medieval walled town, and although there are few buildings of that age, there are nevertheless some solid Georgian houses and public buildings.

Sections of the town walls still stand, including Westgate Tower, and nearby are the ruins of Selskar Abbey (29.8km). To visit the ruins, continue straight on at the Ferrybank bridge turn (19.8km), and after 200m follow the R730 around to the left at the station. Turning left into Selskar Street, after about another 100m you reach the pedestrianised

> Henry II of England reputedly spent Lent at Selskar Abbey in 1172 as penance for his role in the murder of Thomas a Beckett, Archbishop of Canterbury.

town centre, while continuing straight on leads to Selskar Abbey and Westgate Tower, on the left after another 150m or so.

The first chance to see the beach comes at the Ravenswood Nature Reserve. North from here a small road leads along the back of the dunes, before rejoining the R742 coast road at Ballinesker. The beach landing scenes from the 1998 Steven Spielberg film *Saving Private Ryan* were shot near here (33km). From any of the beach access points the dune-backed strand sweeps as far as the eye can see, with scarcely a person or building in sight. All the beaches along here are good, but Morriscastle (turn at 48.9km) is the pick of the bunch because of the view from the high dunes.

At the end of this stage Courtown is a picturesque harbour and beach village. The harbour was built in the 1830s by the Courtown family, on their estate, and soon became a thriving fishing port.

> Tourists started to arrive in earnest at Courtown in the 1860s when the railway from Dublin reached nearby Gorey.

On the Road

There is a supermarket on the right about 700m from the ferry port, and also an ATM here. The cheapest place to stock up for the road is the discount supermarket on the way into Wexford, and the town is worth a look around – the tourist office is on Crescent Quay if you need a map (19km). This is the town in which to pick up any bike or camping supplies. Map and Compass (086 2335927, www. outdoorshopwexford.com) is in Corn Market, in the old town, and the Bike Shop is nearby on Selskar Street (053 9122514).

Accommodation

There are no hostels at all between Rosslare and the Wicklows, and Courtown itself is a bit of a washout for budget accommodation too. For alternatives, Morriscastle Strand Caravan Park (053 9130124, www.morriscastlestrand. com) near Kilmuckridge (turn at 48.9km) is a good choice, backing right onto the beach, although there are limited numbers of tent

Morriscastle beach is part of a 27km long, continuous strand north of Wexford

pitches. Ferrybank Caravan and Camping (053 9166921, www.wexfordcorp.ie) overlooks Wexford Harbour (20km), but closes from mid-September.

Options
None.

STAGE 6
COURTOWN TO RATHDRUM

43.5km Surprisingly flat

Stage 6 is a day of transition. After a couple of days of long sandy beaches, dunes and a coastline sculpted from glacial deposits, it's hard to believe that the next morning you will be waking up surrounded by granite mountains. Although the mountains are coming, this is for the most part a gentle stage through pillow-shaped dark-green hills scattered with black and white cows, where narrow wooded valleys snake up from a silver-blue sea.

Arklow (23km) is the first town of any note on this stage. It is an historic town of Viking foundation that seems to be suffering growing pains from traffic at the moment.

Avoca sprang to fame in the BBC television series *Ballykissangel* (1996–2001) and tourists still want their photos taken outside Fitzgerald's Bar.

The route into the Wicklow Mountains from this direction is through the Vale of Avoca. Copper mining here may well date back to the Bronze Age, and the mines only closed in 1982. Gold has also been found in the area, provoking sporadic rushes. Avoca (33km) itself is an attractive village in a well-wooded gorge-like section of the valley.

Next stop is the Meeting of the Waters (37km). The natural beauty that inspired Thomas Moore to pen the song of that name has been a little diminished by the landscaping work needed to cope with visitors.

On the approach to Rathdrum is Avondale House (41km, open Tuesday to Sunday, mid-March to October, and seven days a week May to August, 0404 46111, www. coillte.ie), the birthplace and home of one of Ireland's great political leaders, Charles Stewart Parnell (1846–91). Parnell was one of the foremost politicians of the 19th century in Britain or Ireland. He was first elected to

Courtown harbour

the Westminster parliament in 1875, and in a 16 year political career brought Irish Home Rule from the periphery to the centre stage of British politics.

Rathdrum is a quaint hilltop village with many 19th-century terraced buildings. It manages to maintain a rather appealing down-at-heel appearance while still being clean and tidy.

On the Road

There are no logistical problems here, with plenty of shops and ATMs along the route. All of the beaches are good, although there is usually a walk to the strand. The supermarkets approaching Arklow (23km) are the cheapest places for a few supplies.

Rathdrum, at the end of the day, has a good shop, as well as pubs and takeaways.

Accommodation

The Old Presbytery Hostel (0404 46930) is on the Fairgreen – turn left at the central square. For camping, continue through the village, take the right fork after 250m, and the well laid-out Hidden Valley Caravan and Camping Park (0404 46080 www.irelandholidaypark. com) is on the left a hundred metres or so after rejoining the main road.

Options

Push on to the hostel at Glendalough (13km into Stage 7) and take a chunk out of the next day.

STAGE 7
RATHDRUM TO DUBLIN

81km Big climbs

The Wicklow Mountains back almost right onto Dublin, and fortunately there are fast cycleways almost right into the centre of the city from this side, allowing plenty of time to be devoted to exploring the granite massif of the Wicklows.

On a day with one 350m climb, throwing in an extra 250m one might seem a little cruel – but the extra ride up to the Shay Elliott

> Shay Elliott was the first Irish cyclist to make his mark on the Continent. He won stages in all the Grand Tours, and in 1963 was the first Irishman to wear the Yellow Jersey in the Tour de France.

Glendalough is one of Ireland's holiest places

Powerscourt House

Memorial combines fine scenery with a chance to pay tribute to a trailblazing Irish cyclist (turn at 10km). The first stop actually on the route is Glendalough (13km), with its sixth-century monastery founded by St Kevin. This is one of Ireland's holiest sites, and although sometimes a little swamped by visitors, natural beauty and tranquillity prevail. The directions here take you to the Lower Lake, from where it is a short walk to the monastery.

The way into Dublin from here is via Ireland's highest road pass, Sally Gap (510m or 1 670ft). The road over the top is a section of the military road built between 1800 and 1809 in the wake of the 1798 rebellion, and the switchbacks and clever use of topography are a 19th-century engineering masterpiece. The gradient is gentle and constant, making the climb about selecting a steady gear and spinning to the summit (35km).

On the way up the route passes the rocky cascade of the Glenmacnass Waterfall (23km), where the river tumbles off the rounded granite uplands into a deep glacial trough. From Sally Gap the road hovers above the 500m mark for a while, passing the headwaters of Dublin's River Liffey on the way. A turn down Glencree leads to Powerscourt Waterfall – Ireland's highest at 130m (turn at 51.3km).

Nearby, Powerscourt House and Gardens (open daily 9.30am to 5.30pm, 01 2046000, www.powerscourt.ie) is the grandest of Ireland's grand houses. This is Ireland's Versailles, with the house presiding over a terraced Italianate garden that took 100 men 12 years to complete. On the top terrace are statues of Apollo, Belvedere, Diana, and Fame and Victory, while two magnificent winged horses guard the fountained lake below.

The final scenic highlight of the route is the narrow rocky defile of the Scalp, with its heaped granite boulders and Scots pines clinging to the cliffs (60km). Suburban Dublin starts after the pass, but there is only about 5km on the roads before it is almost continuous cycleway to St Stephen's Green.

On the Road

Fitting in everything is going to be an issue on this stage. Fortunately the run from Powerscourt into Dublin is quite quick (25km), especially on the N11 cycleway – it is possible to do this stretch in two hours without pushing hard. Stock up with food for the day at Rathdrum or Laragh (11km).

Depending on where you are staying in Dublin, you might want to find your own way from St Stephen's Green, although directions through to the Customs House are included for completeness. Once past St Stephen's Green the traffic is usually hectic and the one-way system tortuous. Sometimes it is just easier to walk.

Accommodation

There is no camping anywhere near Dublin. The Dublin International (01 8301766, www.anoige.ie) An Óige hostel in the city is 1km north of the river on Mountjoy Street (follow O'Connell Street, which becomes Parnell Square, then Frederick Street, then Blessington Street, then look for Mountjoy on the left). This is not the smartest area of town, but the hostel takes security seriously, and there is a bike shelter in the secured car park. Otherwise there are many independent hostels in town.

Early in the day there is another An Óige hostel at Glendalough (13km) – Glendaloch International (0404 45342 www.anoige.ie).

Options

Consider basing yourself at Glendalough or Rathdrum and taking a few day rides around the mountains.

ROUTE 11 DUBLIN TO WATERFORD

Stage 1 Dublin to Donard		
0.0		Dublin, George's Quay, across river from Customs House, outside Ulster Bank, join cycleway at pedestrian crossing
0.2	↑	Tara Street crosses
0.5	↑	O'Connell Street bridge to right, pass Heineken building
0.8	☆	Pass the Ha'penny Bridge (footbridge)
1.1	↑	Cross Parliament Street, narrow section – no bus lane – follows
1.4	↑	Cross Winetavern Street, note Four Courts across the river
1.6	▲	Pass Four Courts Hostel
1.7	←	'N81', at lights
1.8	↑	'N81', at lights
1.9	↑	'N81', at lights
1.9	☆	Painted cycleway starts
2.0	☆	St Audoen's Church – 12th century, oldest church in Dublin
2.1	→	'N81', at lights, have to cross traffic but OK, cycleway starts after junction
2.3	♦	P&K Cycles
2.5	☆	St Patrick's Church
2.6	↑♦	'N81', at lights, small shop here
2.9	↑	At lights
3.0	↑	At lights
3.4	↑	At lights, Cross South Circular Road
3.7	☆	Cross Grand Canal on Emmet Bridge, named after nationalist leader Robert Emmet
4.1	↖	'N81Blessington' (at Harold's Cross)
4.5	♦ ATM	Shop
5.0	↑	At lights
6.0	↗	'N81', at lights, in Terenure – James Joyce was born in Terenure
6.2	↑	At lights, very slight swing to left
6.6	←	Turn onto cycleway
	O→	Along Rathdown Crescent
7.1	↑	Enter Bushy Park

Stage 1 Dublin to Donard		
7.4	↑	Rejoin road at lights
7.7	↑	Use cycleway to left and lights to cross junction
7.9	◆	Hollingsworth Cycles
8.0	↑ATM	Use cycleway, local shops and ATM at Templeogue
8.5	↑	At lights, short section without cycleway
8.9	↑	Cycleway ends, join road – dual carriageway, but wide shoulders
9.3	O↑	'N81', roundabout OK, can join bus lane afterwards
9.8	◆	Spar Express shop in service station
9.9	←	Look for cycleway on left under roundabout
10.2	←	At T-junction in cycleway
10.4	↑	Emerge from cycleway tunnel on to suburban street
10.8	O↑	'Tallaght'
12.0	◆ ATM	Shops and ATM on left
12.1	↑	At crossroads, lights
12.4	←	At lights, centre of Tallaght, seats behind wall on left
12.5	↑	At lights, more shops to left
12.6	→	At lights, join off-road cycleway on far side of N81 (unless on a tandem then stay on road)
12.9	☆	Gate impossible for tandem
13.6	↑	Cross road in front of leisure centre – building in progress – junction may change
14.2	↗	Cycleway moves on-road – take care crossing side roads
14.3	↑	Lights, cycleway under construction
14.5	↑	Lights, cycleway under construction
15.1	↑	At lights
15.2	☆	Cycleway ends – join road – take care, busy and narrow
15.3	↑	At lights
15.7	↑	At lights
16.0	←	First turn after lights, takes you past golf club
19.0	△(340)	7–8% climb
21.6	→	At crossroads
21.7	←	'N81 Tullow', at T-junction
22.3	←	Pass golf club

Stage 1 Dublin to Donard		
25.5	↗	Road veers right
25.7	→	At T-junction
25.9	←	At T-junction
26.3	◆	Shop at Kilbride
26.9	↖	Take left fork
28.9	☆	Start to see Pollaphuca Reservoir on right
32.4	☆	Access to lake
32.5	⇨	Alternate route to Donard, 21km
37.7	◆	Shop at Lackan
	↗	'Valleymount' – take right fork
42.3	☆	Picnic area, at Ballyknockan – granite village
45.5	→	'Blessington'
46.8	☆	St Joseph's Church; Valleymount – Mexican-style church
47.7	☆	Picnic area
48.3	☆	Picnic area by water
	←	First turn after bridge
50.1	←	Unsigned, road has woodland on right, pasture on left
54.6	→	'Hollywood', at T-junction
55.3	←	'L8342'
56.4	→	'St Kevin's Way' – road is muddy, wet, potholed
58.6	←	At T-junction
59.7	☆	Entering Hollywood Glen
60.8	↖	Take left fork
65.9	←	Turn past O'Keefe's Country Store
66.0		Arrive Donard central green area

Stage 2 Donard to Kilkenny		
0.0		Donard, in front of Mary statue, head towards post office/shop
0.1	→	At O'Keefe's Store
	→	'Knockanarrigan', note 19th-century gate lodge and carriage gates to Donard House
1.4	△(270)	Steady climb
4.0	▲	Mountain Ventures Hostel
4.5	→	Road swings right
6.6	↑	At crossroads in Knockanarrigan

Stage 2 Donard to Kilkenny

7.3	→	'Dwyer – McAllister Cottage'
9.0	☆⇨	To Dwyer – McAllister Cottage 300m, leave bike in car park on left
10.5	→	'Rathdangan'
11.8	△(360)	Steep climb to here – 10%
15.2	→	At crossroads in Rathdangan
19.1	↑	'Baltinglass', at crossroad
20.5	☆	Gate lodge for Humewood Castle
22.2	←	'Baltinglass'
24.4	←	'R747 Hacketstown'
25.5	→	'L7277'
26.1	☆	Victorian gate lodge to Fortgranite House
26.8	↑	At crossroads, signed 'R. Slaney'
27.2	☆	Cross River Slaney
28.7	↑	Cross N81
32.2	→	At T-junction
32.5	←	Unsigned, after 300m
32.8	☆	Disused handball court
33.8	→	Unsigned
35.2	→	At T-junction
35.9	←	At T-junction
36.0	←	'Butler Road'
39.1	←	At Knocknacree crossroads
39.4	△(140)	Summit has views over Co Carlow
41.1	→	'Duckett's Grove'
42.0	☆	'Duckett's Grove'
43.8	↗	Through gatehouse, bear right (not hard right)
44.7	☆	Cross new bypass – not on some maps
47.4	↑	'Recycling centre' (turn right here for Carlow, 4km)
48.9	→	'Carlow R725'
49.3	←	'Rathtoe'
49.7	☆	Early 18th-century house on left – Bennekerry House
50.1	→	Unsigned
50.3	←	Road swings left
51.5	↑	'Tinryland', crossroads slightly staggered to right, crossing N80
52.1	←	'Tinryland'
52.8	♦	Decent-sized shop at Tinryland

Stage 2 Donard to Kilkenny

54.9	↑	'Nurney', at crossroads
56.9	△(120)	High above the Barrow valley to right
58.1	→	'Leighlinbridge', at crossroads in Nurney
60.1	→	At T-junction
	←	'Leighlinbridge'
63.1	←	At T-junction
	→	Immediate right
63.3	♦	Shop just before bridge over River Barrow at Leighlinbridge
63.4	↗	'Old Leighlin', complicated junction over bridge – head uphill
64.0	→	'N9 Dublin' – turn left for flatter route to Kilkenny (30km)
	←	'Old Leighlin'
66.6	←♦	'Monemore', before you reach cathedral. Shops before turn
66.7	←	'Monemore', road swings left
66.8	→	Unsigned
69.6	↑	At Milebush crossroads
69.6	☆	1798 memorial
70.4	△(260)	5–6% climb from Old Leighlin
70.9	→	Unsigned, descent then climb up to Castle Hill, stream at hill foot is Co Kilkenny border
72.9	→	At T-junction
73.0	←	Unsigned, after 80m
74.4	↑	'Castlewarren'
75.3	←	T-junction at Castlewarren
78.7	→	Unsigned, comes as sharp descent starts to flatten out
79.4	↑	At crossroads
82.3	←	'Kilkenny', at T-junction
82.4	→	'Kilkenny'
88.2	O↑	'City centre', at Hebden Road roundabout – fringe of Kilkenny
88.7	↑	At lights
89.1	O↑	'City centre'
89.6	↑	At lights
89.7	↖O	Still following the same road into city
89.8	↑	At lights, need to be in right-hand lane for straight on
89.9	♦	The Map Shop
90.3	☆	Cross bridge
90.4	☆	Tourist office on right

Stage 2 Donard to Kilkenny		
	ATM	
	←	'The Parade', towards castle
90.6		Castle entrance
90.7		Entrance to Castle Park, bike racks through iron gates

Stage 3 Kilkenny to Waterford		
0.0		Kilkenny, Castle Park, by the gates, head away from town
1.3	♦	Service station and shop
1.6	O↑	'New Ross'
1.9	▲	Tree Grove camping and caravan park
8.1	▲⇨	Nore Valley Park about 3km
8.3	ATM ♦→	'New Ross', road swings right, shop and ATM straight on in Bennettsbridge
8.6	☆	Gothic Revival RIC barracks from about 1850
8.9	♦	Service station and shop
16.5	←O♦	'New Ross', shop in Thomastown, in front
16.6	O→	'New Ross'
17.1	→	'Jerpoint Abbey'
17.2	←	'Jerpoint Abbey', Thomastown is on the right
17.4	→	At end of bridge, road swings right
17.6	↑	'Jerpoint Abbey N9'
19.4	☆	'Jerpoint Abbey'
20.2	←	At Ave Maria shrine
21.4	△()	Gentle climb to plateau
23.3	↑	At crossroads
27.8	☆	Tower-house ruin on right
33.2	←	At T-junction, then cross Lukeswell bridge
33.3	←	'South Leinster Way' – easy-to-miss road goes between buildings just past pub
35.8	→	Swing right under railway
35.9	←	At T-junction
36.7	♦	Shop at Mullinavat
37.8	←	Under railway
37.9	→	Unsigned
40.1	←	Cross new M9 bridge – see notes in text
41.0	→	At T-junction
44.7	←	At T-junction
46.1	→	'Waterford'

Stage 3 Kilkenny to Waterford		
48.1	♦	Shop
50.4	O↑	All routes
52.0	→	'Waterford', at lights
52.8	←O	'City centre'
53.0	←	At end of bridge
53.3	☆	Tourist office
53.6		Arrive Waterford Quay clocktower

Stage 4 Waterford to Rosslare		
0.0		Waterford, the Quay, by clocktower, head along quay, river on left
0.5	←	Reginald's Tower and Thomas Meagher statue on right
0.6	→	Just past hotel
0.7	←	At T-junction
0.9	☆WC	Park on right has benches
1.1	←♦	Shop and service station
2.1	←O	'Passage'
2.6	♦	Shop in service station
2.9	O ↑♦	'R683 Passage East', local shops and supermarket here
3.2	O↑	'R683 Passage East'
4.0	☆	300m section of cycleway
4.3	O↑	
	♦ ATM	Shopping centre after roundabout has ATM and supermarket
4.5	☆	500m section of cycleway
6.1	←	'R683 Passage East'
12.1	←	'Ferry'
12.2	←	'Ferry'
	→	'Ferry', board ferry at Passage East
12.4	♦→	'Wexford', after leaving ferry at Arthurstown, small shop here
13.7	↑	'R733 Wexford', at crossroads
14.2	☆	Dunbrody House Cookery School
14.9	⇨	'Ring of Hook' – approx 16km one-way to Hook Head light
15.9	♦ ATM	Shop has ATM
16.1	↑	'Wexford'
20.4	↑⇨	Fethard on right, 7km
22.0	⇨	Side-trip to Tintern Abbey, 4km return
28.8	→	'R736 Duncormick'

Stage 4 Waterford to Rosslare		
30.7	☆	Bannow Bay to right
31.8	⇐⇨	At crossroads, right here will take you towards Bannow Island, approx 6km
33.2	↑	At crossroads in Carrick, unsigned, Breens Inn is across road
35.1	⇨	To Cullenstown strand
35.9	⇨	To Cullenstown strand
36.0	↗	Road swings right
39.4	→	'Rosslare', at Duncormick
39.9	♦	Small shop in service station
42.6	☆	Unusual spired church at Rathangan
45.0	↑	'Rosslare', at crossroads
47.3	→	'Rosslare', at T-junction
47.4	☆	Bridgetown railway station
47.4	←	'Rosslare'
50.6	←	'Wexford'
50.7	→	'Rosslare', straight on is to Wexford via R739, 14km
53.9	↖	Road swings left
55.9	↑	At crossroads
58.1	→	'Rosslare', at T-junction
58.2	←	'Rosslare'
60.0	♦ →	'Rosslare Harbour N25', small shop on right at Tagoat
60.4	▲⇨	Turn to St Margaret's Camping
62.3	☆	Cycleway starts
62.9	♦ ATM	Medium shop
64.0	♦ ATM	Supermarket
64.3	☆	Cycleway ends
64.7	O	Roundabout at entry to Rosslare ferry terminal

Stage 5 Rosslare to Courtown		
0.0	O↗	Rosslare Harbour, at roundabout, exit to ferry port, take N25 Cork, Waterford
0.7	♦ ATM	ATM and supermarket – cycleway starts, turn left just past here for town
1.0	☆	Cycleway ends
1.6	☆	County Wexford tourist office
1.9	♦ ATM	Shop
4.4	⇦▲	Turn to St Margaret's Camping
4.7	⇨	To Rosslare town 4km

Stage 5 Rosslare to Courtown		
	♦	Small shop in Tagoat
9.7	♦ ATM	Shop
11.5	☆	Rest area
14.8	♦	Small shop in service station – short, narrow section of road
15.1	O↑	'R730 Wexford' – busy roundabout
15.3	☆	Cycleway starts
17.8	☆	Wexford Creamery
17.9	♦ ATM	Shop in service station, cycleway ends
18.2	↗	Road swings right
18.9	☆	Supermarket – Aldi
19.1	↑	'R730 town centre'
19.3	☆	Tourist office on right, but don't cross road here – dangerous
19.5	⇨	To get to tourist office cross tracks here and head back across bridge
19.7	ATM	Bank of Ireland
19.8	→ ⇧ ☆♦	'Ferrybank', cross bridge For town centre, abbey and tower
20.4	▲	Ferrybank Caravan Park on right
22.2	♦	Shop in service station
23.0	♦	Shop in service station
23.4	→	'R742 Blackwater'
28.9	♦ →	'White Gap R743', supermarket on corner
29.8	→	'Ravenswood Nature Reserve'
31.0	←	Turn onto road through dunes, straight on to nature reserve car park
31.1	↑	Unsigned
31.8	WC	Large car park at White Gap
31.9	→	After car park
33.3	☆	Ballinesker Beach – Saving Private Ryan filmed here
33.8	→	'R742 Courtown'
39.3	♦	Decent shop at Blackwater
39.4	↑ ♦	'R742 Kilmuckridge', shop on right
39.6	⇨	Ballyconnigar Strand, 2km
44.4	⇨	Ballynamona Beach, 1km
45.1	☆	Sand extraction here – note red sand
45.7	⇨	Beach, 2km

Stage 5 Rosslare to Courtown		
48.5	◆ ATM	At Kilmuckridge
48.9	▲⇨	Morriscastle Beach 2km and campsite
52.4	☆	Wind farm on right
57.2	◆	Shop
57.3	⇨	Turn to Cahore Point 2km
57.6	☆	1798 memorial
64.6	◆ ATM	Decent shop
65.0	→	'R742 Courtown' – easy to miss turn, look for 'Jimmy Z' salmon-coloured pub on left
65.5	↗	At fork, pass to right side of 'Courtown Harbour' sign
65.8	WC	
65.9	←	At T-junction
66.0		Arrive Courtown quayside car park, shops nearby

Stage 6 Courtown to Rathdrum		
0.0		Courtown, in car park next to quay, in middle of village
	→	Turn right out of car park
	←◆ ATM	Up main street, shop on right
0.2	◆	Supermarket in service station
1.3	→	'Ballymoney', through fringe of fine estate woodland
5.9	◆ ATM	At Ballymoney
6.0	→	'Inch', at crossroads
7.2	△(60) →	At T-junction
9.3	↗	'Arklow'
11.1	⇨	Turn to beach 1.5km
11.9	↑	'Clones'
12.0	⇨	Turn to Clones Strand
14.3	⇨	Kilmichael Strand
17.8	⇨	Clogga Strand, 2.5km return
18.4	←	Road turns left, quarry straight ahead
19.1	↗	Road swings right
20.3	→	'R772 Arklow'
21.8	O↑	'Arklow'
22.2	◆	Service station and large shop
22.3	☆	Cycleway starts
22.4	O↑	Unsigned
22.6	☆	Cycleway ends
22.8	◆	Supermarket
23.0	◆	Supermarket

Stage 6 Courtown to Rathdrum		
23.1	◆	Supermarket
23.3	O↑ ⇨	'Avoca'; right takes you to Arklow centre, tourist office 400m
25.8	☆	Glenart Castle
29.0	☆	Gothic gate lodge to Kilcarra House
29.7	◆	Service station has small shop
29.8	↗	'Avoca', Woodenbridge Hotel – claims to be oldest in Ireland
33.3	⇨	Across bridge is Avoca – 'Ballykissangel'
36.8	WC	Hidden on right at Meeting of the Waters
37.0	☆	Meeting of the Waters
40.5	→	'Avondale House', at crossroads
41.1	←	'Avondale House'
41.8	☆	Access to Avondale House
43.2	↑	Town centre, at crossroads
43.4	☆	Pass park
43.5		Arrive town centre, Main Street, Rathdrum

Stage 7 Rathdrum to Dublin		
0.0		Rathdrum central square opposite post office, turn left (away from church)
0.3	↖	'R755 Roundwood'
1.7	☆	Ballygannon Wood
9.2	☆	Picnic area
10.0	⇦	Shay Elliot memorial 8.5km return, 250m climb
11.4	←	'Glendalough R756', at Laragh
11.5	◆	Shop in service station
13.0	↖⇧	'Glendalough', straight on to Wicklow Gap
13.4	↑↓	Heritage centre car park, turn around at bike racks
	→	Turn right out of car park, left to upper lake (1.2km) and hostel (600m)
15.3	↑	'R755 Roundwood', back at Glendalough turn
15.4	←(150)	'R115 Sally Gap'
23.1	△(350)	At Glenmacnass Waterfall car park
35.0	△(500)	Sally Gap sign
35.3	↑	'Dublin', at crossroads

Stage 7 Rathdrum to Dublin		
38.5	☆	Bridge crosses source of River Liffey
42.9	→	'Powerscourt waterfall'
49.4	☆	Crone Woods
51.3	☆	Cross River Dargle
	⇨	Powerscourt waterfall, 3km return, charge
52.4	↑	'Enniskerry', at crossroads
53.2	←	'Enniskerry', at T-junction
56.0	⇦	Powerscourt entrance, house 1.5km
56.6	ATM ♦→	At centre of Enniskerry, shops and ATM in village
	←	'Dublin', cross bridge
58.0	♦→	On to R117, shop in service station
60.1	♦	Small shop in the Scalp
61.9	↑	At lights
62.0	↑ATM ♦	At lights, service station on right has ATM and shop
64.5	↑	At lights
64.7	☆	Cycleway – painted
65.2	O↑	On-off cycleway follows
66.0	↑	At lights
66.2	↑	Cycle lane stops
66.3	→♦	'No Heavy Vehicles' at crossroads, Gala shop on left just before turn
66.9	↑	Cycleway starts
67.0	↑	At lights, then join cycleway on right of road, when safe
67.7	←O	Cycleway still on right side of road
67.9	O↗	Cycleway still on right side of road
68.2	↑	At lights, Bewleys Hotel on right
68.6	O↗	'Leopardstown Road', TAKE CARE – busy. Look for third exit, dismount, follow pavement around right of roundabout and cross Leopardstown Road to join cycleway on left side of road

Stage 7 Rathdrum to Dublin		
68.7	☆	Pass Leopardstown race course
69.9	←	'N11 Dublin' – cycleway on and off road until St Stephen's Green
72.3	♦	Shop in service station
74.8	↑	At crossroads, RTE mast on right
75.8	☆	Cross River Dodder
76.3	ATM	
77.8	☆	Cross Grand Canal
78.4	→	Lights at St Stephen's Green, turn right
78.9	→	'N11 Dawson Street', about halfway down second side of square
79.1	↑	At lights
79.3	→	At lights, end of Dawson Street, turn left to tourist office 250m on left
79.7	←	'N1, N2', at lights
79.9	←	One-way, into Westland Row
80.1	←	At lights, just past Pearse Station, still following one-way system
80.5	→	Just past Trinity Capital Hotel, with distinctive redbrick tower – use lights if you don't fancy crossing four lanes of traffic
80.8	↑	At lights, cross bridge – need to get in right-hand lane for next turn
80.9	→	'Dublin Port', at lights
81.0		Arrive Dublin Customs House

ROUTE 12

DUBLIN TO BELFAST – A TRAIL OF TWO CITIES

Stage		Terrain	Distance (km)	Summit (distance from start/height)
1	Dublin to Navan	Fast and flat	56.9	40km/170m
2	Navan to Carlingford	Flat	92.7	38km/120m
3	Carlingford to Newcastle	Some climbing	63.4	40km/220m
4	Newcastle to Strangford	Gentle coastal hills	46.9	25km/40m
5	Strangford to Belfast	A few drumlins	80.0	66km/150m
		Total	339.9	

Few tours pack in as much to see as this one. Head north from Dublin through fabulous Phoenix Park to the cradle of Irish civilisation in the Boyne Valley, cross the border at Newry, then the Mountains of Mourne to Newcastle, before pushing up to Belfast along one of Ireland's most beautiful coastlines – these are five memorable days in the saddle.

Options
The Dublin–Belfast railway line can either be an alternative to riding, or provide a return route.

Getting to the Start
For information on Dublin, see Route 7. The start of this route is easy to find – it is outside the Ulster Bank on George's Quay, across the river from the Customs House.

When to Go
Any time, spring to autumn. The Ulster coast is going to be busiest from mid-July to mid-August.

Accommodation
Budget accommodation is a little sparse, and the route makes best use of what is available at the cost of some rather uneven stage distances. The only accommodation 'hole' is the Strangford area, where if not camping, a bed and breakfast will be required. There is no camping in the Navan area, but there is a hostel.

Maps
For 1:250 000 coverage, the OSI Ireland North and Ireland East sheets are needed. Coverage at 1:50 000 requires the following sheets from the OSI Discovery series: 50 Dublin Kildare Meath Wicklow, 43 Dublin Louth Meath, 42 Meath Westmeath, 36 Armagh Down Louth Meath Monagan, and the following from the OSNI Discoverer series: 29 The Mournes, 21 Strangford Lough and 15 Belfast. The OSI 1:20 000 Dublin street map is handy around the city, but not absolutely necessary.

Onwards
Connects with Route 1 at Belfast.

STAGE 1
DUBLIN TO NAVAN

56.9km Fast and flat

The central lowlands north of Dublin are the true heart of Ireland. When the ice sheets retreated, it was through the river valleys between present-day Dublin and Dundalk that Stone Age man made some of his first incursions into the virgin landscape. The impressive archaeological legacy of this area survives into modern times, and the Boyne Valley in

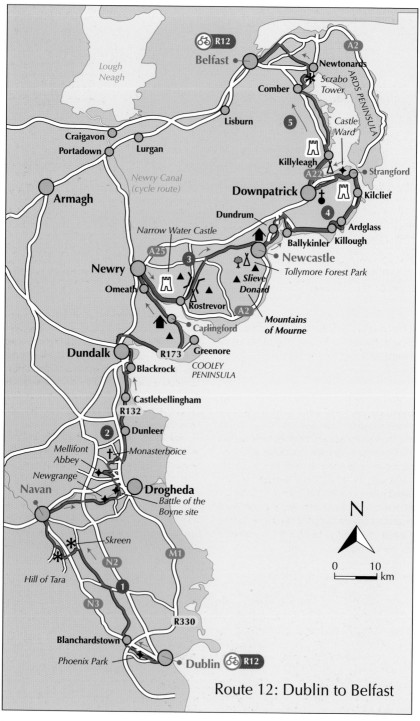

Route 12: Dublin to Belfast

Phoenix Park

Phoenix Park's name is nothing to do with the mythical bird. It is a corruption of the Irish phrase for 'clear water'.

particular retains an important role in Irish identity through the Hill of Tara – once the seat of the High Kings of Ireland.

The panoramic view from Tara (45km) is a fine way to end this stage, but before that there is plenty to see on the run out of Dublin, which begins with a road/cycleway through Europe's largest park – Phoenix Park. Some well-heeled attractive suburbs follow, then a high-tech industrial corridor along the N3 before, within 20km of the heart of Dublin, the wheatfields and pasture begin.

The Hill of Tara is one of the hills of the Galtrim morraine – actually a belt of deltas formed by glacial meltwaters streaming into lakes along the ice front. High ground here has assumed both spiritual and strategic importance, and this is best seen at Skreen Hill (39km), where a 14th-century church, on the site of a ninth-century monastery, commands views over most of Meath.

The Hill of Tara covers a huge site, and it is well worth a wander around just to take in the view and the atmosphere. There are pre-Celtic, neolithic structures here, including the Mound of the Nine Hostages. Also on the hill are an Iron Age hilltop enclosure surrounded by a ditch and bank, known as Ráith na Ríogh (the Fort of the Kings or Royal Enclosure). Within the enclosure are two circular earthworks and

The Mound of the Hostages is a Bronze Age passage tomb on the Hill of Tara

a standing stone, which is believed to be the Lia Fáil (Stone of Destiny) at which the High Kings were crowned.

Onwards are just a handful of small settlements before the county town of Navan, centred on a classic defensive hilltop location overlooking the Boyne river.

On the Road

Supplies are no problem early in the day. You can leave central Dublin with empty pockets and an empty stomach and rely on a choice of suburban shops and ATMs at Castlenock (8km), Blanchardstown (10km) and Hollystown (19km). This is one of the fastest stages in the book, so don't be afraid to linger in Phoenix Park. At the time of writing the new M3 motorway was being put through the valley between Skreen and Tara (close to the old N3). This may affect the directions slightly.

Accommodation

Navan has a hostel, Millrace Lodge (046 9028222, www.navanaccommodationcentre. ie), which is more like a motel (at hostel prices) than a hostel. It is a bit tricky to find – head out on the R153 towards Duleek/Kenstown, then 1.2km after the river bridge in Navan take the left fork by a service station, and the hostel is a few hundred metres on the left.

Options

None.

STAGE 2
NAVAN TO CARLINGFORD

92.7km Flat

The route starts with a spin along the valley of the Boyne and two sites of prehistoric and historic interest respectively. Newgrange is a megalithic passage tomb and a designated World Heritage List site, while the Battle of the Boyne is the most symbolically important battle in Irish history.

Newgrange passage tomb was built around 3200bc. At dawn on the winter solstice the sun illuminates the inner chamber via a roof box over the entrance passage. There is a lottery to be one of the lucky few to see this sight. For the rest of the year an electric light provides a simulation for visitors who brave the 20m long inner passage.

Newgrange is open year round, except over Christmas, and access is only through the new Brú na Buinne Visitor Centre (17.9km), which is also the access point for Knowth (open Easter to October). Newgrange is very popular and you might have to queue for a tour (041 9880300, www.heritageireland.ie). The visitor centre opens from 9am, May to mid-September, 9.30am at other times.

Not far from Newgrange is the site of one of Ireland's most important battles. Victory at the Battle of the Boyne for William of Orange's (William III) Protestant forces here, and a year later at Aughrim, effectively secured a Protestant monarchy in England and the Protestant Ascendancy in Ireland. The Williamite forces were on the north side of the river, while the armies of the deposed Catholic King James II (the Jacobites) held the south side of the Boyne valley. A visitor centre was opened in 2008 (24km, open daily from 10am to 6pm May to September, slightly shorter hours at other times, 041 9809950, www.battleoftheboyne.ie). Just over the river from the centre, the gully down to the river is called King William's Glen.

Even if the above two sites don't interest you, the valley, with its fertile pastures and woodlands, is pretty enough. It is also possible to continue down the valley to Drogheda if supplies are needed.

North of the valley the country becomes more undulating. Tucked away in the hills is Mellifont Abbey (29km). This 12th-century Cistercian abbey has a partially intact lavabo that once housed a fountain for washing hands. Another ecclesiastic site nearby is fabulous Monasterboice (36km). This fifth-century foundation was an important Christian centre until Mellifont came on the scene. Muiredach's High Cross, with its carvings of scenes from the Old and New Testaments, is the finest in

---

Mellifont Abbey is where the treaty ending the Nine Years War (between the Gaelic lords of Ulster and the English) was signed in 1603.

Ireland. There are also two other high crosses and a round tower on the site.

After all the sightseeing, a few kilometres need to be covered. Fortunately the fast and quiet coastal road leads all the way to Dundalk via the delightful seaside village of Blackrock (60km). Dundalk is a tidy place with a wealth of buildings from the late Georgian and Victorian eras. The approach to the cathedral area along Seatown Place and Jocelyn Street is one of the best-preserved period boulevards in Ireland – it even has a windmill (not working) (67km).

From here onwards the rocks are of volcanic origin, and leaving Dundalk a gap in the mountains to the northwest becomes obvious – this is the strategically important Moyry Pass, traditional route of entry into Ulster. The route described here, however, heads east. Keep an eye out for the Corinthian facade of the Franciscan Convent at 73km. This was once the home of Sir John MacNeill (1793–1880), who worked on many rail projects in Ireland, including the Dublin to Drogheda railway.

Rounding the Cooley Peninsula, the granite massif of the Mountains of Mourne comes into view. The day finishes at the medieval town of Carlingford.

The Cooley Peninsula between Dundalk Bay and Carlingford Lough is the site of 'The Cattle Raid of Cooley', from the Ulster Cycle – see Route 1, Stage 6, on Emain Macha.

On the Road

This stage covers plenty of kilometres, but is relatively fast, with just a few hills north of the Boyne Valley. It's best to take a few provisions from Navan, as unless a detour into Drogheda is made, the first shop is at Dunleer (44km). Dundalk (69km) has a choice of food shops, as well as Bicycle Doctor on Bridge Street (042 9327033). If going to Newgrange, arrive early before the queues build up.

Accommodation

The Foy Centre (042 9383624, www.carlingford beds.com) on the way into Carlingford village offers hostel-style accommodation. If you want to camp, the only site on the route

is at the 83km mark, but Gyles Quay Caravan Park (042 9376262) closes at the beginning of September. Drogheda (turn at 24km) has an An Óige franchise hostel – Green Door (041 9834422, www.greendoorireland.com) is on Dublin Road.

Options

None.

> ### STAGE 3
> ### CARLINGFORD TO NEWCASTLE
>
> 63.3km One long climb

Waking up in Carlingford, with any luck there will be a view across to the Mountains of Mourne over the quiet waters of the sea lough. But before the Mournes there is an international frontier to cross – as usual in Ireland, it is only noticeable from traffic signs. Far older than the nearby border is the Newry Canal, which opened in 1742. The ship canal section allowing sea-going vessels right into Newry starts at Victoria Lock (12km). This was opened in 1769, and made Newry the most important port in Ulster.

The long tail of Carlingford Lough means riding another 15km or so of shoreline barely a stone's throw away from where you were riding a couple of hours before. Guarding the tightest section of the channel is the aptly named Narrow Water Castle (26km). This exceptionally fine 16th-century tower-house castle is in a stunning location (open July and August, 10am–1pm on Tuesdays and Saturdays, 2pm–6pm Wednesday and Thursdays). There is a 19th-century Elizabethan revival house, also called Narrow Water Castle, behind the trees – but it is private.

The loughside route continues to Rostrevor (33km), which is delightfully situated, hemmed

The obelisk memorial approaching Rostrevor is to Major General Robert Ross-of-Bladensburg (1766–1814), a British army officer. He is most famous for burning Washington during the War of 1812, between the US and the British Empire.

Narrow Water Castle is a 16th-century tower-house

Newcastle is, as the song goes, 'Where the Mountains of Mourne sweep down to the sea', and there is a statue to the song's writer, Percy French (1854–1920), on the seafront.

in by mountains on three sides. The way across the Mournes from here is via a steady climb up the valley of the Kilbroney river. This is a peaceful little glen, with only the sound of water rushing over grey granite boulders breaking the silence. There are some aromatic pine woods towards the valley head before open hillsides, then a descent down the Shankys river valley. Keep an eye out for the reindeer – Santa Claus's official residence in Ireland is along this road (028 417 72052, www.santascottage.co.uk). Another gentle climb crosses the Mourne foothills eastwards towards the coast, passing scenic Tollymore Forest Park (59km) on the descent.

The coastal town of Newcastle sits on a sweeping bay backed by the highest mountain in Ulster, Slieve Donard (849m). Recent improvements have made the town worthy of its fine location.

On the Road
There are no logistical problems along this route. The last chances to spend any euro coins are at Carlingford and Omeath, although food

is generally far cheaper in Northern Ireland (shops in Newry will generally take euro notes). The route here avoids the busy centre of Newry, but still passes a few shops and ATMs. The centre of Rostrevor (33km) has benches, and is a good place to stop for lunch before the climbing starts.

Accommodation
Newcastle has an official youth hostel (028 4372 2428, www.hini.org.uk). It is open all though the cycling season, but check if you are travelling in winter. The hostel also closes during the day from 11am to 5pm. It is easy to find, on Downs Street – see the start of Stage 4. Tollymore Forest Park (59km, 028 43778664, www.forestserviceni.gov.uk) has excellent camping on the former estate of Lord Roden. Rostrevor also has a campsite – Kilbroney Park (028 4173813) – turn at 32.9km.

Options
An alternative route to Belfast is to take the Newry Canal towpath to Knock Bridge and pick up Route 1, Stage 7 at 25.9km, along the Lagan Valley cycle route into the city. To get to the canal towpath, continue straight on at the junction at 18.6km and it is a further 600m to the start of the cycleway. The approximate distances are: Carlingford to Newry 19km, Newry to Knock Bridge 27km,

Knock Bridge to Belfast, 55km – or 101km in total. As the towpath and the Lagan Valley are easy going, Belfast is easily reachable in a day. The Newry Canal Towpath leaflet (available as part of the Sustrans Northern Ireland pack) will help.

Dundrum Bay is where Isambard Kingdom Brunel's great steamship the SS *Great Britain* came aground in 1846 – it took nine months and Brunel's intervention to refloat her.

STAGE 4
NEWCASTLE TO STRANGFORD

46.8km Gentle coastal hills

When it comes to beautiful coastline, Ireland sets a very high standard, and the next couple of days include some of the very best. The good stuff starts early on, with Murlough Nature Reserve and its sand dune system (4.3km). On a clear morning the view back to the Mournes is breathtaking, and a regular feature of tourist posters and calendars.

North of here the coast is rockier, but two of the safe anchorages, at Killough and Ardglass, are attractive small ports. Killough village (27km) was an 18th-century creation of Michael Ward, of Castle Ward, and at one time the busiest port in Ulster. The harbour was re-modelled in the 19th century to the design of Alexander Nimmo – he also designed Knight's Town on Valentia Island (Route 8, Stage 6).

After Ballyhornan (38km) and Killard Point, the narrow strait dividing the Ards Peninsula from the mainland becomes apparent. This deep channel is about 8km long, but only 500m in width at its narrow point. The white light-tower on Angus Rock, the blue waters of the channel and the low rocky coastline of the peninsula, make this a picturesque section.

Kilclief Castle, a 15th-century tower-house, is one of the many fortifications along this coast (42km). The castle is in state care and opens in July and August from Tuesday to Friday, 10am to 6pm, and 2pm to 6pm at weekends. This stage finishes at the quay of the quiet village of Strangford, where there is another tower-house of a similar age. A regular ferry service runs to Portaferry on the Ards Peninsula.

On the Road
Dundrum (7km), Ballykinler (15km), Killough (27km) and Ardglass (31km) all have shops, and the last two in particular are good places

Newcastle is where the Mountains of Mourne come down to the sea

to stop. There is the occasional stretch on the A2, but it is generally quiet. For a swim try Tyrella (19km), which is patrolled in summer.

Accommodation
This area is hopeless for hostels. For bed and breakfast try www.go2strangford.com for an up-to-date list. For campers the National Trust has a campsite at Castle Ward (2.4km, 028 4488 1204 www.nationaltrust.org.uk) just at the start of Stage 5 (reception is at the main office at the house), or there is Delamont Country Park 20.8km along Stage 5.

Options
Roads radiate from Downpatrick to this coast, so there are many potential short-cuts.

STAGE 5
STRANGFORD TO BELFAST

80km A few drumlins

Strangford Lough is a place of rare natural beauty. This 150km2 or so of water, with a sea entrance less than a kilometre wide, is Mediterranean in miniature. On a fine day the blue water and shimmering sunlight transform humble Ulster into a Levantine paradise.

Strangford is also an important wildlife habitat, and no comparable area in Europe has such a range of luxuriant habitats. There are populations of seals and porpoises, and birds flock here in thousands.

The area is also of great cultural importance, as it was on the lough shore that St Patrick first set foot in Ireland. Saul Church (10km) is on the site where he is believed to have given his first sermons, some time in the fifth century. Nearby Downpatrick has the traditional graves of St Patrick, St Bridget and St Colmcille, by hilltop Down Cathedral.

> St Patrick's mission to Ireland began in ad432 when his boat was swept into Strangford Lough by strong tidal currents.

Before Downpatrick, however, there is the National Trust property at Castle Ward to visit. One facade of the house is Gothic, the other classical, because a wife and husband had different tastes. The house is open 1pm to 5pm daily in July and August and Easter week, otherwise weekends only from late February to October. The gardens are open from 10am all year, closing at 8pm in summer, otherwise 4pm (028 4488 1204, www.nationaltrust.org.uk).

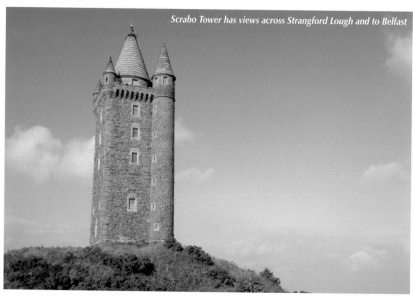

Scrabo Tower has views across Strangford Lough and to Belfast

Belfast Waterfront Hall from Lanyon Quay – the start and end of the book

Scrabo Tower sits on a dolerite sill overlying softer sandstones.

Killyleagh (25km) is the first of the pretty coastal villages on this stage. High Street, with its many Georgian buildings, the castle at one end and the lough in the distance at the other, is one of the best-presented streetscapes in Ireland. Killyleagh Castle is one of the oldest inhabited castles in Ireland. Next door to the castle is Shrigley, which during the 19th century was the site of one of Ireland's leading textile mills. A Gothic clocktower and drinking fountain were erected outside the factory gates in recognition of the mill's founder, John Martin. The industrial village around it has now been swept away.

The lough-shore scenery continues through tranquil Ballymorran Bay (34km) and Whiterock. Approaching Comber, Scrabo Tower (56km) comes into view, perched on a lone rocky hill. Suburban Belfast is close, so the ride up to the car park and climb of 122 steps is worth the effort for a final view of Strangford Lough (open Saturday to Thursday 10.30am to 6pm, from end of March until late September, 028 91811491, www.ni-environment.gov.uk).

The final pull into Northern Ireland's capital is over Belfast's Hollywood Hills, then via cycleway (albeit alongside a busy dual carriageway) almost all the way into the city centre.

On the Road
Roadworks along the A2 cycleway between Hollywood (after 73.1km) and Belfast may have affected the distances slightly. Picking up something to eat is no problem on this stage. Killyleagh (24km) has the best shop. The foreshore at Ballymorran Bay (34km) is the most beautiful picnic spot on the stage.

Accommodation
The Belfast International Youth Hostel (028 9031 5435, www.hini.org.uk) has a cycle parking area (albeit in the open) inside the secured car parking area. All Belfast hostels are busy, especially at weekends, and do book out. For directions to the hostel, see Route 1, Stage 7. Delamont Country Park (20km) has an excellent campsite (024 7669 4995, www.delamontcountrypark.com).

Options
The route skirts Downpatrick – to go into the town, turn left at 13.4km and follow the signs to the St Patrick Centre. From there, steps lead up to Down Cathedral and St Patrick's Grave.

ROUTE 12 DUBLIN TO BELFAST

Stage 1 Dublin to Navan		
0.0		Dublin, George's Quay, across river from Customs House, outside Ulster Bank, join cycleway at pedestrian crossing
0.2	↑	Tara Street crosses
0.5	↑	O'Connell Street bridge to right, pass Heineken building
0.8	☆	Pass the Ha'penny Bridge (footbridge)
1.1	↑	Cross Parliament Street, narrow section – no bus lane – follows
1.4	↑	Cross Winetavern Street, note Four Courts across the river
1.6	▲	Pass Four Courts Hostel
1.7	↑	'N4, N7', at lights
2.0	↑	'N4, N7', at lights
2.1	↑	'N4, N7', at lights
2.3	↑	'N4, N7', at lights
2.6	☆	Guinness Brewery
2.7	→	'N2, N3' at lights
2.8	←	After bridge
	↑	Cross Luas tracks at lights
3.1	↑	'N4, N7', at lights
3.2	→	At lights, through Phoenix Park gates
3.3	↑	Cycleway starts
3.5	☆	Wellington Testimonial obelisk on left
3.7	O↑	
3.9	☆	Tearoom on right
5.6	O↑	US ambassador's residence on left, president's residence on right, Phoenix on plinth at centre of roundabout
6.9	O↑	
7.5	↑	At lights through park gates
8.2	↑	At lights
8.5	ATM ♦	Local shops on right at Castlenock
8.6	↑	At lights
8.8	↑	At lights
9.2	O↑	'Goss, N3'
9.6	↑	At lights
9.7	☆	Cross railway and Royal Canal
10.1	←	'National Aquatic Centre', at lights

Stage 1 Dublin to Navan		
10.2	↑	At lights, now in Blanchardstown
10.3	↑	At lights
10.6	♦	Shopping centre
10.9	↑	At lights
11.1	↑	At lights, just after Topaz service station
11.3	☆	Pass eBay building
11.4	O→	Unsigned
12.2	O↑	'Mulhuddart'
12.9	→	'Hollystown' at lights
13.3	O↑	Unsigned
14.3	O↑	'Tyrrelstown, Hollystown', cycleway soon after
14.7	O↑	Unsigned
15.1	O↑	Cycleway ends after roundabout
16.5	←O	'Hollystown', look for iron statue in centre
16.8	♦	Service station with decent shop at Hollystown
19.0	☆	Now in open country
19.7	ATM ♦	Service station with decent shop and ATM
20.2	←	At fork, pass to left of church (at Priest Town)
26.8	←	'Ratoath', at T-junction
27.1	O↑	Don't bother with cycleway – soon disappears
27.8	ATM ♦	Supermarket ATM and bank at Ratoath
28.0	☆	Benches in town, but quite heavy traffic
28.1	←	Road swings left after church
28.3	→	At crossroads
28.5	←	At crossroads
38.3	↑	'Navan', at crossroads
38.7	←	'Skreen'
39.7	↑	At crossroads
39.8	←☆	At Skreen Church – great view
40.0	→	Unsigned
40.1	☆	Skryne Castle on left (private) – interesting mix of medieval tower-house, 18th and 19th century extensions
41.5	☆	New M3 construction
42.1	↑	'Rath Maeve', at crossroads over old N3

Stage 1 Dublin to Navan		
44.0	→	At T-junction, Rath Maeve fort in field straight in front
45.9	☆	Hill of Tara car park etc on left; route continues straight on, don't take right fork back to valley
47.5	←	'Kilmessan', at crossroads
48.2	→	'Navan', at T-junction
49.4	↑	'Navan', at crossroads
50.1	☆	Bridge over the River Boyne
51.0	☆	M3 bridge construction
53.6	←	At crossroads, join N3
54.8	↑	At lights
55.5	ATM ♦	At Maxol service station
56.0	←	'Town centre', at lights
56.4	O→	'Town centre', tourist office on left
56.5	ATM	
56.6	→	'Town centre', at lights
56.9		Arrive central diamond, Navan

Stage 2 Navan to Carlingford		
0.0		Navan Market Square, outside main Bank of Ireland, opposite Meath Chronicle Printing Works, head downhill
0.2	→	At lights, bottom of the hill
0.3	←	'R153 Kentstown', cross fine stone bridge
0.7	←	'Beauparc, Newgrange'
6.5	♦	Medium shop in supermarket
11.0	→	'N2 Dublin'
	←	'L1600 Newgrange'; note Hill of Slane is across river to north
17.9	☆	Entrance to Newgrange car park and visitor centre
20.2	←	At T-junction in Donore
20.7	←	'Oldbridge, Battle of the Boyne'
23.7	☆	Battle of the Boyne site
24.0	←	At T-junction, Drogheda is 4km to right
24.5	→☆	Turn over bridge, Oldbridge Battle of the Boyne centre is on left
25.0	↑	Battle of the Boyne viewing point, at N51 crossroads
26.4	↑	At crossroads, top of King William's Glen
26.5	←	First turn after crossroads

Stage 2 Navan to Carlingford		
29.4	→⇦☆	At crossroads, turn right Side-trip on left to Mellifont Abbey; 600m return (picnic area)
31.0	←	'Monasterboice', at T-junction
32.7	→	'Monasterboice'
34.4	←	'Monasterboice'
36.1	☆	Monasterboice
36.8	→	At T-junction
37.3	O↑	'Dunleer'
37.5	←	'R132 Dunleer'
38.3	△(120)	Views of Carlingford Mountain and Mournes beyond
44.0	♦ ATM	In Dunleer
44.3	↗	'R132 Castlebellingham'
	♦	Shop
47.0	→	'R132 Castlebellingham', at crossroads
49.0	♦	Small shop
51.1	♦	Small shop
52.1	☆	Gothic Revival gate lodge to Castlebellingham estate
52.3	♦	Shop and pharmacy in Castlebellingham
52.4	↗	'R132 Dundalk'
52.5	♦	Shop in service station, bench nearby
59.1	→	'R172 Blackrock'
60.6	☆	Blackrock promenade – benches etc
60.8	♦	Shop
60.9	♦ ATM	Small shopping centre has fruit and veg shop and ATM
64.6	O↑	'Red Burn's Road', cycleway starts after roundabout
65.2	O↑	Unsigned
66.0	☆	Cycleway ends
66.1	←	At T-junction
67.3	♦ ATM	Decent-sized shop
67.4	← ♦	Road swings left, shop on corner
67.5	→	Then right
	↑	At lights, down fine Victorian boulevard in Dundalk
67.7	↑	At crossroads – note windmill on right
68.3	☆	Tourist office on left
	→	'Chapel Street'
68.4	←O	Unsigned

Stage 2 Navan to Carlingford

68.7	→	At T-junction in Dundalk, join Church Street
69.1	↑	'Bridge Street'
69.2	◆	Bicycle Doctor
69.5	↑	'R132 Newry'
69.7	◆ ATM	Shop in service station
69.8	↑	At lights, need to be in right-hand lane
70.1	◆	Supermarket
71.7	→	'All routes', cycleway continues – views of Moyry Pass to left
72.1	←○	'N52 Belfast'
72.7	○→	'R173 Carlingford' – easiest to cross before roundabout – cycleway ends but road OK
73.5	◆	Shop in service station
73.8	☆	Franciscan convent once home of railway engineer Sir John MacNeill
77.8	◆	Shop in service station on right
83.6	▲⇨	Gyles Quay Camping 1km
86.9	←	At Bush village
	→	Garage in front
87.1	←	Road swings left
91.8	▲⇨	Foy Centre on right
91.9	☆	Carlingford Abbey
92.0	→	One-way system
92.2	▲→	With one-way system, Carlingford Centre straight on through arch
92.4	←	At T-junction
92.5	←	At tourist office (old railway station)
92.6	←	At T-junction, Londis shop opposite
92.7		Arrive Carlingford town centre

Stage 3 Carlingford to Newcastle

0.0		Carlingford at tourist office near waterfront – head towards castle
0.2	☆	King John's Castle
0.5	☆	Picnic area by road
5.0	☆	Greer's Quay – good view of lough
7.3	◆	Omeath has several shops – last before border
11.2	☆	Cross Northern Ireland border

Stage 3 Carlingford to Newcastle

12.7	☆	Victoria Lock on Newry canal
17.1	↗	Take right fork after concrete works
18.1	☆	Fine brick mill building and entrance to shops
18.6	→	At lights, cross canal – continue straight on for Newry Canal towpath
18.8	→	'Warrenpoint A2', at lights. Join here, Kilmorey Street, from Route 1 Stage 7.
19.5	ATM ◆	Shop/service station on right has ATM for Sterling
19.7	○↑	'A2 Warrenpoint', cycleway starts after roundabout
26.7	☆	Narrow Water Castle
27.3	○↑	'Warrenpoint', cycleway ends for short distance
29.0	○↑ WC	'A2 Newcastle', WC on the right in centre of Warrenpoint
29.3	☆	Clonallon Park – picnic spot
29.4	←	At T-junction, along shore
32.2	☆	Obelisk memorial to Major General Robert Ross-of-Bladensburg
32.5	◆	Shop in service station
32.9	○ ↑▲	'B25 Hilltown', right to Kilbroney Caravan Park
33.0	◆ WC	Centre of Rostrevor – shop over road, benches, nice spot
33.1	◆	Shop
33.7	→	'Newtown Road' (after phone box)
33.8	◆	Shop
38.2	☆	Picnic area
39.9	△(220)	Gentle Climb
40.7	☆	Santa's Cottage
42.0	☆	Picnic area
42.2	↗	'Newcastle'
44.4	☆	Rockyriver Bridge picnic area
45.8	↑	'Newcastle', at crossroads
46.2	→	'Newcastle B180'
58.0	☆	Gates to Tollymore Forest Park, but exit only here
58.2	◆	Shop in Bryansford – does not open late
58.9	→	'Newcastle'
59.6	▲	Entrance to Tollymore Forest Park

Stage 3 Carlingford to Newcastle		
61.5	↖O	
62.1	←	At lights, one-way
62.3	♦	Wiki Wheels cycle shop on right
62.4	→	Road swings around circulation
62.6	↖	'Town centre', at fork
62.7	→	'Tourist information centre', down Main Street, parallel to shore
63.2	☆	Cross Tollymore river
63.4		Arrive Newcastle tourist information centre

Stage 4 Newcastle to Strangford		
0.0		Newcastle, on promenade at rear of carpark next to tourist information centre, route starts where railings start on left.
0.2	→	After bridge, continue along shore – take care with pedestrians
0.5	☆WC	Percy French memorial, toilets nearby
	←	At end of prom, turn through car park
0.7	▲→	Out of car park, HI Hostel on left
0.8	O→	'Golf Links Drive'
1.0	←	'Golf Links Crescent' (at entrance to golf club)
1.1	→	'Merrion Avenue', T-junction
1.4	→	At T-junction with A2 – join cycleway
1.5	♦	Supermarket, cycleway ends
3.9	⇨	Murlough Beach
4.3	→	'Murlough Nature Reserve' – down gravel track opposite bridge – can go through gate here to shore, 2.4km return
4.7	↖	Track swings left
5.8	←	Turn onto road and cross bridge
6.4	→	On to A2
7.0	♦	Shops in Dundrum
8.5	←	'Belfast Road', gets you off main road
9.2	←	On to A2
9.3	→	'Dundrum Road'
9.5	→	'Ardilea Road'
11.4	→	'Tyrella A2'

Stage 4 Newcastle to Strangford		
12.2	⇦	Turn to Downpatrick
12.9	→	'Ballykinler'
15.8	♦ ATM	Service station on corner has shop and ATM, now in Ballykinler
17.1	→	'A2 Ardglass'
19.4	☆WC	Tyrella Beach, patrolled in summer
23.4	☆	Road passes close to beach
27.1	←	At crossroads in Killough
27.3	♦ ATM	Fine sycamore-lined avenue through village
27.9	O↑	'Ardglass A2'
30.6	→	View back towards Killough on climb
31.6	→	'Killough A2'
31.6	←	Road swings left, turn right for Ardglass harbour, shop and WC
31.7	☆	Jordan's Castle on left
31.8	♦	Small shop
32.2	→	'Strangford A2'
37.7	→	'Ballyhornan'
38.5	☆	Nice picnic area at Ballyhornan
40.9	☆	Beach and views across mouth of Strangford Lough
42.4	→	'Strangford A2'
42.5	☆	Kilclief Castle
	☆	Beach and picnic area
46.7	♦ →	At T-junction in Strangford, shop on corner
46.9	♦	Arrive Strangford Quay

Stage 5 Strangford to Belfast		
0.0		Strangford, from apex of triangular grassed area furthest from quay, head into village
0.1	♦	Shop on corner
0.2	♦	Shop
1.2	▲	Castle Ward Caravan Park – need to go to main entrance to check in
2.4	☆⇨	Entrance to Castle Ward, house about 1km
5.2	☆⇨	Road to Audley's Castle, 4km
6.1	←	'Raholp'
8.1	△(55)	St Patrick monument on Slieve Patrick to left

Stage 5 Strangford to Belfast

10.2	←	'Saul Church'
10.3	☆	Saul Church – reputedly site of St Patrick's first sermon in Ireland
10.5	→	'Saul Road', at T-junction
11.1	O↑	Unsigned
11.2	◆	Shop
12.6	↖O	Unsigned
13.2	→	'Scotch Street'
13.3	↗	Road swings right, pedestrian area in front
13.5	◆ →	At lights, bottom of hill, service station/shop on left; for Downpatrick, turn left
13.8	◆	Shop in service station
13.9	O↑	'Killyleagh (A22)'
20.1	☆	Gate lodge to Delamont
20.8	▲	Entrance to Delamont Country Park; can use cycleway on other side of road
21.4	→	Signed 'Ulster Way'
22.7	☆	Alongside Strangford Lough
24.4	←	At harbour
24.6	→	Into Killyleagh
24.8	◆	Supermarket
24.8	←	'Car park'
25.1	ATM WC →	At castle, WC on left; High Street on left is lovely and has Ulster Bank ATM
26.2	→	At Gothic monument – the Martin Memorial
27.3	↑	At crossroads
27.9	△(40)	Views of drumlins in lough
28.2	←	At T-junction on A22
28.5	→	'Ulster Way'
29.8	←	At crossroads after golf club
31.2	→	Road swings right
32.3	→	'Ulster Way'
34.1	→	'Ballymorran Road', at T-junction
34.7	☆	Ballymorran Bay
35.9	→	At T-junction
38.1	WC	Picnic area at Whiterock
40.3	→	'Comber', at T-junction
40.5	→	'Comber', at T-junction
44.2	→	'Comber', at T-junction
45.7	☆	Castle Espie Wetland Centre

Stage 5 Strangford to Belfast

47.3	☆	Views of Scrabo Tower over Comber Estuary
49.4	→	'Comber, A22'
49.7	◆	Shop in service station
49.8	O↑	'Town centre'
50.2	ATM	
50.3	◆ →	'A21 Newtonards', at lights in centre of Comber
51.4	←O	'Newtonards A21', mixture of cycleway and hard shoulder
52.1	←	'Scrabo Garden Centre'
54.7	→	'Scrabo Road'
55.1	→	'Newtonards', at T-junction
55.5	☆	Killynether Wood – walking tracks
55.9	←	'Scrabo Golf Club'
56.5	↑↓ ☆	Turn around, Scrabo Tower car park
57.2	←	Back at golf club turn
59.1	→	At T-junction
59.3	←	'Belfast A2'
59.6	O↑	Unsigned
59.9	◆	Ards shopping centre on right
60.2	←	'Craigantlet'
60.7	☆	Lake with views to tower
63.0	→	'Hollywood'
65.5	↑	'Hollywood', at crossroads
65.8	↑	'Hollywood', continue straight on
67.0	←	'Creighton's Green Road'
68.9	△(150)	Views over Belfast Lough
70.1	→	'Croft Road', at T-junction
71.1	←	'Bangor Road', at T-junction
71.7	↑	At lights in Hollywood
73.0	◆	Shop at service station
73.1	↑	Cycleway starts – alongside 100mph road
76.1	⇨	Turn at these lights for Belfast City Airport
78.8	↑	Cycleway ends
79.0	O↑	'City centre'
79.8	←	At lights, end Queen Street Bridge, join NCN9
80.0		Arrive Lanyon Quay

APPENDIX 1
ROUTE SUMMARY TABLE

View east from Malin Head

Route	Start/Finish	Stages	Total distance (km)	Average stage (km)	Longest stage (km)	Highest point (m)	Page
1	Belfast/Derry	8	476	59.4	80.9	390	44
2	Derry/Donegal Town	9	541	60.1	79.4	280	66
3	Donegal Town/Sligo	7	493	70.4	84.7	330	84
4	Sligo/Achill Island	6	467	77.8	100.1	210	100
5	Galway	9	408	45.3	68.1	110	112
6	Galway/Tarbert	8	441	55.1	130.6	190	128
7	Dublin/Limerick	4	252	62.9	71.6	190	145
8	Tarbert/Tralee	9	468	52.0	69.7	410	160
9	Kenmare/Cork	6	359	59.9	94.5	160	180
10	Cork/Killarney	4	239	84.1	104.7	230	195
11	Dublin	7	466	66.5	90.7	520	208
12	Dublin/Belfast	5	340	68.0	92.7	220	227

APPENDIX 2
GRAND TOURS

The routes in this guidebook have been designed to link together into longer tours. Below are four suggested longer routes – there are, of course, many more possibilities.

TOUR OF THE ISLAND OF IRELAND: BELFAST TO BELFAST
59 stages, 3634km, 62km/day

This is the big one. It can, of course, be started from anywhere and don't forget to allow some extra days for rest and sightseeing!

Highlights: wild Donegal, the Fermanagh lakelands, the Aran Islands, Inishbofin, the peninsulas of the southwest, County Wexford's coast, the Wicklow Mountains and Strangford Lough, and many more.

Stage	From	To	Route and stage	Distance (km)
1	Belfast	Carnlough	1, 1	62.4
2	Carnlough	Ballycastle	1, 2	70.7
3	Rathlin Island		1, 3	25.8
4	Ballycastle	Portrush	1, 4	36.5
5	Portrush	Derry	1, 5	79.8
6	Derry	Culdaff	2, 1	77.5
7	Culdaff	Clonmany	2, 2	55.1
8	Clonmany	Letterkenny	2, 3	79.4
9	Letterkenny	Portsalon	2, 4	47.9
10	Portsalon	Downies	2, 5	55.8
11	Downies	Bunbeg	2, 6	67.5
12	Bunbeg	Portnoo	2, 7	52.6
13	Portnoo	Carrick	2, 8	59.9
14	Carrick	Donegal Town	2, 9	45.6
15	Donegal Town	Castle Archdale	3, 1	76.6
16	Castle Archdale	Garrison	3, 2	64.5
17	Garrison	Crom Estate	3, 3	62.1
18	Crom Estate	Ballyconnell	3, 4	57.9
19	Ballyconnell	Carrick-on-Shannon	3, 5	62.5
20	Carrick-on-Shannon	Sligo	3, 6	84.7
21	Sligo	Ballina	4, 1	88.4
22	Ballina	Belmullet	4, 2	100.1
23	Belmullet	Achill	4, 3	64.9

Stage	From	To	Route and stage	Distance (km)
24	Achill Tour		4, 4	75.1
25	Achill	Westport	5a	45.7
26	Westport	Tully	5, 3 and 4	77.0
27	Tully	Clifden	5, 6	49.7
28	Inishbofin tour		5, 7	15.7
29	Clifden	Kilkieran	5, 8	45.0
30	Kilkieran	Rossaveal (Aran Ferry)		33.4
31	Tour of Inishmore		6, 2	37.6
32	Tour of Inisheer	(Doolin via Ferry)	6, 3	10.4
33	Tour of Burren		6, 4	63.7
34	Doolin	Kilrush	6, 5	130.6
35	Kilrush	Ennis	6, 6	60.1
36	Ennis	Limerick	6, 7	39.8
37	Limerick	Tarbert	6, 8	59.4
38	Tarbert	Tralee	8, 1	69.7
39	Dingle	Killorglin	8, 4	54.9
40	Killorglin	Portmagee	8, 5	65.8
41	Portmagee	Caherdaniel	8, 6	45.5
42	Caherdaniel	Kenmare	8, 7	48.2
43	Kenmare	Allihies	9, 1	76.1
44	Allihies	Glengarriff	9, 2	57.6
45	Glengarriff	Schull	9, 3	94.5
46	Schull	Clonakilty	9, 4	61.1
47	Clonakilty	Kinsale	9, 5	44.8
48	Kinsale	Cork	9, 6	25.2
49	Cork	Youghal	10, 1	68.9
50	Youghal	Waterford	10, 4	96.8
51	Waterford	Rosslare	11, 4	64.7
52	Rosslare	Courtown	11, 5	66.0
53	Courtown	Rathdrum	11, 6	43.5
54	Rathdrum	Dublin	11, 7	81.0
55	Dublin	Navan	12, 1	56.9
56	Navan	Carlingford	12, 2	92.7
57	Carlingford	Newcastle	12, 3	63.4
58	Newcastle	Strangford	12, 4	46.9
59	Strangford	Belfast	12, 5	80.0
			Total (Average	**3641.8 62km/day)**

TOUR OF THE SOUTH: DUBLIN TO DUBLIN

24 stages, 1489km, 62km/day

For a fabulous month's riding full of variety, try a circular route from Dublin via Limerick and the southwest peninsulas. After Mizen Head, Ireland's most southwesterly point, the prevailing wind should be behind you all the way home.

Highlights: Grand Canal, the Shannon valley, Dingle Peninsula, the Ring of Kerry, Beara Peninsula, Mizen Head, Kinsale, County Wexford beaches, Wicklow Mountains, Powerscourt House.

Author riding along south side of Mizen Peninsula

Stage	From	To	Route and stage	Distance (km)
1	Dublin	Edenderry	7, 1	68.6
2	Edenderry	Shannon Harbour	7, 2	71.6
3	Shannon Harbour	Mountshannon	7, 3	62.4
4	Mountshannon	Limerick	7, 4	49
5	Limerick	Tarbert	6, 8	59.4
6	Tarbert	Tralee	8, 1	69.7
7	Tralee	Dingle	8, 2	48.5
8	Dingle	Dingle	8, 3	57.1
9	Dingle	Killorglin	8, 4	54.9
10	Killorglin	Portmagee	8, 5	65.8
11	Portmagee	Caherdaniel	8, 6	45.5
12	Caherdaniel	Kenmare	8, 7	48.2
13	Kenmare	Allihies	9, 1	76.1
14	Allihies	Glengarriff	9, 2	57.6
15	Glengarriff	Schull	9, 3	94.5
16	Schull	Clonakilty	9, 4	61.1
17	Clonakilty	Kinsale	9, 5	44.8
18	Kinsale	Cork	9, 6	25.2
19	Cork	Youghal	10, 1	68.9
20	Youghal	Waterford	10, 4	96.8
21	Waterford	Rosslare	11, 4	64.7
22	Rosslare	Courtown	11, 5	66
23	Courtown	Rathdrum	11, 6	43.5
24	Rathdrum	Dublin	11, 7	81.0
			Total (Average	**1497.1** 62km/day)

TOUR OF THE NORTH: BELFAST TO SLIGO

21 stages, 1309km, 62km/day

Entrance to Mulroy Bay from Rosguill Peninsula

If the wild, the wonderful and staying off the beaten track appeal, the Tour of the North is for you. Added to that, with 10 of the 21 stages at least partly in Northern Ireland, this tour is easy on the pocket as well as the eye.

Highlights: wild Donegal, the Fermanagh lakelands, Sligo's mountain scenery.

Stage	From	To	Route and stage	Distance (km)
1	Belfast	Carnlough	1, 1	62.4
2	Carnlough	Ballycastle	1, 2	70.7
3	Rathlin Island		1, 3	25.8
4	Ballycastle	Portrush	1, 4	36.5
5	Portrush	Derry	1, 5	79.8
6	Derry	Culdaff	2, 1	77.5
7	Culdaff	Clonmany	2, 2	55.1
8	Clonmany	Letterkenny	2, 3	79.4
9	Letterkenny	Portsalon	2, 4	47.9
10	Portsalon	Downies	2, 5	55.8
11	Downies	Bunbeg	2, 6	67.5
12	Bunbeg	Portnoo	2, 7	52.6
13	Portnoo	Carrick	2, 8	59.9
14	Carrick	Donegal Town	2, 9	45.6
15	Donegal Town	Castle Archdale	3, 1	76.6
16	Castle Archdale	Garrison	3, 2	64.5
17	Garrison	Crom Estate	3, 3	62.1
18	Crom Estate	Ballyconnell	3, 4	57.9
19	Ballyconnell	Carrick-on-Shannon	3, 5	62.5
21	Tour of Sligo		3, 7	84.3
			Total (Average	**1309.1 62km/day)**

TOUR OF THE SOUTHWEST: CORK TO CORK

16 stages, 966km, 60km/day

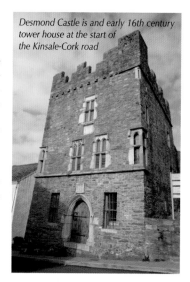

Desmond Castle is and early 16th century tower house at the start of the Kinsale-Cork road

Cork is one of the most convenient places to arrive in Ireland, having excellent ferry and air connections. It is also close to much of Ireland's best scenery. However, following the usual route west from Cork, along the south coast and into the prevailing winds, can be tiring, so try this less-travelled way of getting to the glories of the southwestern peninsulas via Youghal and the Blackwater valley.

Highlights: historic Youghal, the Blackwater valley (the 'Irish Rhine'), Killarney, the Dingle Peninsula, the Ring of Kerry, Beara Peninsula, Mizen Head, Kinsale.

Stage	From	To	Route and stage	Distance (km)
1	Cork	Youghal	10, 1	68.9
2	Youghal	Fermoy	10, 2	66.0
3	Fermoy	Killarney	10, 3	104.7
4	Killarney	Tralee	8, 9	30.4
5	Tralee	Dingle	8, 2	48.5
6	Tour of Dingle		8, 3	57.1
7	Dingle	Killorglin	8, 4	54.9
8	Killorglin	Portmagee	8, 5	65.8
9	Portmagee	Caherdaniel	8, 6	45.5
10	Caherdaniel	Kenmare	8, 7	48.2
11	Kenmare	Allihies	9, 1	76.1
12	Allihies	Glengarriff	9, 2	57.6
13	Glengarriff	Schull	9, 3	94.5
14	Schull	Clonakilty	9, 4	61.1
15	Clonakilty	Kinsale	9, 5	44.8
16	Kinsale	Cork	9, 6	25.2
			Total (Average	**965.5 60km/day)**

BEST OF THE WEST: GALWAY TO LIMERICK

13 stages, 563km, 43km/day

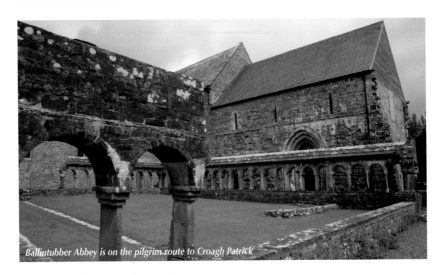

Ballintubber Abbey is on the pilgrim route to Croagh Patrick

This is an easy tour to get to and from, with Galway and Limerick both having airports close by. Routes 5 and 6 combine into a memorable fortnight's trip, including the Aran Islands and Connemara.

Highlights: Lough Corrib, Croagh Patrick, Inishbofin, Connemara, Aran Islands, the Burren.

Stage	From	To	Route and stage	Distance (km)
1	Galway	Cong	5, 1	63.6
2	Cong	Westport	5, 2	53.0
3	Westport	Tully	5, 3 and 4	77.0
4	Tully	Clifden	5, 6	49.7
5	Inishbofin tour		5, 7	15.7
6	Clifden	Kilkieran	5, 8	45.0
7	Kilkieran	Rossaveal (Aran Ferry)	5, 9 (part)	33.4
8	Tour of Inishmore		6, 2	37.6
9	Tour of Inisheer	(Doolin via Ferry)	6, 3	10.4
10	Tour of Burren		6, 4	63.7
11	Doolin	Kilrush	6, 5	130.6
12	Kilrush	Ennis	6, 6	60.1
13	Ennis	Limerick	6, 7	39.8
			Total (Average	**563.0 43km/day)**

APPENDIX 3
USEFUL CONTACTS

TRAVEL

Ferry

Very cheap combined rail and ferry tickets are available from the ferry companies, and also from www.sailrail.co.uk (0845 0755755).

Brittany Ferries
www.brittany-ferries.com
UK 0871 2440744,
Ireland 021 427 7801,
France 0825 828828

Celtic Link Ferries
www.celticlinkferries.com
0844 5768834

Irish Ferries
www.irishferries.com
UK 0870 5171717,
Ireland 0818 300 400,
France 01 70720326

LD Lines
www.ldlines.co.uk
0844 5768836,
UK 0825 304304

Norfolkline
www.norfolkline.com
UK 0844 4990007,
Ireland 01 819 2999

P&O Irish Sea
www.poirishsea.com
UK 0871 6644999,
Ireland 01 407 3434

Stena Link
www.stenaline.co.uk
UK 0870 5707070,
Ireland 01 204 7777

Swansea–Cork service
www.bringbacktheswanseacorkferry.com

Rail

Irish Rail
www.irishrail.ie

Translink
www.translink.co.uk
028 9066 6630
or for cross-border tickets, 028 9089 9409

Buses

Translink (Northern Ireland)
www.translink.co.uk
028 9066 6630

Bus Eireann
www.buseireann.ie –
contact local bus station

Visas

Northern Ireland Visa Information
www.ukvisas.gov.uk

Republic of Ireland Visa Information
www.dfa.ie
(follow 'services to the public' link)

ACCOMMODATION

Hostels

IHH
www.hostels-ireland.com

IHO
www.independenthostelsireland.com

An Óige
www.anoige.ie
01 830 4555

Hostelling International Northern Ireland
www.hini.org.uk

Camping

Irish Caravan and Camping Council
www.campingireland.ie

Forest Service (Northern Ireland)
www.forestserviceni.gov.uk
(look under activities) 028 9052 4480

Coillte (forests in the RoI)
www.coillte.ie

Lower Lough Erne at Crom Estate

Bed and Breakfast

Town and Country Homes Association
www.townandcountry.ie
071 98 22222 (Republic of Ireland)

EMERGENCIES

Crime

Emergency numbers for police, fire and ambulance are 999 or 112 (all of Ireland)

The police in the Republic of Ireland are the Gardai – but if you ask for the police, people will usually know what you mean. For non-emergency police matters, contact the nearest Garda station, or in Northern Ireland, police station. The Police Service Northern Ireland (PSNI) also has a non-emergency contact number – 0845 600 8000 – or see www.psni.police.uk. In the Republic, the nationwide free Irish Tourist Assistance Service aims help with the practical and emotional aftermath (www.itas.ie, 01 6610562).

Healthcare

To access free care in the Republic, it is important to see a GP contracted under the Primary Care Reimbursement Services (PCRS) scheme. If you can't find one, the local Health Service Office (www.hse.ie) will have numbers. In Northern Ireland there are fewer doctors working privately, but in all cases it is worthwhile mentioning you want to be treated under the EHIC arrangements.

APPENDIX 4
FURTHER READING

Geology

Geology and Scenery in Ireland, JB Whittow, Pelican Books, Harmondsworth, 1974. Out of print and, in parts, out of date, but a comprehensive tour of Ireland's geology and landscape for the layman.

Classic Geology in Europe 5: The North of Ireland, Paul Lyle, Terra Publishing, Harpenden, 2003. More technical than the above, and just covering Ulster, but still comprehensible to the average reader and well illustrated.

Wildlife and Flowers

Ireland: A Smithsonian Natural History, Michael Viney, Blackstaff Press, Belfast, 2003. A loving account of the Irish landscape that is not overly scientific.

History

Teach Yourself the History of Ireland, FJM Madden, Hodder Education, London. Get the latest edition – it is regularly updated; a comprehensive and easy-to-digest history that is kept bang up to date.

The Concise History of Ireland, Sean Duffy, Gill and Macmillan, Dublin, 2005. Well-illustrated history, particularly good on the 14th century onwards.

Culture

Irish Writing: An Anthology of Irish Literature in English 1789–1939, ed Stephen Regan, Oxford University Press, 2004. Bit heavy in places (like the Connor Pass), but includes some key political writings, travelogues and poetry (including WB Yeats) as well as fiction. Also includes JM Synge's *Riders to the Sea* and an excerpt from *The Aran Islands* (1907) – which may leave you wanting more.

Opened Ground: Poems 1966–1996, Seamus Heaney, Faber and Faber, London, 2007. Bit big to carry, but peerless poetry, especially when reflecting on an Ulster childhood.

Creatures of the Earth, John McGahern, Faber and Faber, London, 2007. Short stories intimately engaged with the Irish landscape – particularly County Leitrim.

A Border Station, Shane Connaughton, Penguin, London, 1994. A dark yet affectionate look at a 1950s childhood in the border country of Cavan and Fermanagh (even includes some cycling!).

The Butcher Boy, Patrick McCabe, Picador, London, 1992. Disturbing account of descent into madness in 1960s Ireland – based on Clones, County Monaghan.

Miscellaneous

Round Ireland in Low Gear, Eric Newby, Picador, London, 1988. Required reading for anyone mad enough to think of touring Ireland in winter.

Towpath Tours: A Guide to Cycling Ireland's Waterways, John Dunne, Collins, 2005. A valuable companion on Route 7.

Author on Inishmor (photograph: Charlotte White)

LISTING OF CICERONE GUIDES